DATE DUE

DEMCO 38-296

Competing in the Third Wave

Competing in the Third Wave

*The Ten Key
Management Issues
of the
Information Age*

Jeremy Hope
Tony Hope

HARVARD BUSINESS SCHOOL PRESS
Boston, Massachusetts

Library of Congress Cataloging-in-Publication Data

Hope, Jeremy
    Competing in the third wave: the ten key management issues of the
information age / Jeremy Hope and Tony Hope
        p. cm
Includes bibliographical references.
ISBN 0-87584-807-9 (alk. paper)
1. Industrial management—Communication systems. 2. Information
technology. 3. Social history—1945– 4. Social change. 5. Civilization,
Modern—1950– I. Hope, Tony, 1945– .
II. Title.
HD30.335.H67 1997   97-5197
303.48'33—dc21   CIP

The paper used in this publication meets the requirements of the American
National Standard of Permanence for Printed Library Materials Z39.49-1984.

Contents

Preface

We have written this book in response to those managers who need to see more clearly what it takes to compete effectively in the information age. We have chosen ten discussion topics ranging from strategy and business organization to management accounting and transformation. They can be read independently, but greater value lies in the whole. Our choice is inevitably selective but represents, in our view, the crucial issues that will make a difference to the third wave manager.

Our review of key management issues meant covering a broad range of current thinking in areas such as strategy, organizational structures, and human resources, where we do not profess to be experts. Here we have relied heavily on other management writers, past and present, including Levitt, Drucker, Hamel and Prahalad, Bartlett and Ghoshal, Simons, Pfeffer, and Reichheld. To all of these, and many others, we offer our sincere thanks. We hope we have added value to their ideas by providing a series of threads and insights that connect one managerial perspective with another, particularly as they are affected by information technology and the arrival of the knowledge-based organization.

Apart from the books and articles of those writers we have mentioned, our primary sources include other business books and journals (especially the *Harvard Business Review*) and the plethora of articles and papers that are now published—in some cases by the authors themselves—on the World Wide Web. In all cases we have given as much reference detail as we can find. We have also gained much from our international clients around the world. Special thanks are also due to the team at the Harvard Business School Press, especially Kirsten Sandberg and Barbara Roth, whose professional skills have added much-needed polish to our words and illustrations.

We hope this book will benefit all those business executives, managers, and students who are interested in updating their knowledge of good business practice within the setting of the third wave (knowledge-based) organization. One thing is certain as we enter the third wave: good management practices will be needed more than ever. This book will remind you what they are and help you to apply them in a modern context.

Jeremy Hope   Tony Hope
Bradford, England April 1997

The Challenge

Managing in the Third Wave

Every few hundred years in Western history there occurs a sharp transformation.... Within a few short decades, society rearranges itself—its world view; its basic values; its social and political structure; its arts; its key institutions. Fifty years later there is a new world. And the people born then cannot even imagine the world in which their grandparents lived and into which their own parents were born.[1]

Peter F. Drucker

TWO HUNDRED YEARS AFTER THE INDUSTRIAL revolution dramatically changed the established world order, we are once again in the midst of a sharp transformation, the likely effects of which will be a period of dislocation followed by a period of prosperity. How long either will last is uncertain. Variously heralded as the digital revolution, the information age, and the knowledge economy, there is little doubt that the present transformation elicits in today's industrial and service workers the same fears and uncertainties that were felt by eighteenth-century agricultural workers as they migrated from the fields to the factories. Job security seems but a memory as one large organization after another downsizes and reengineers. The prospects for growth, jobs, education and social stability are less predictable today than at any time since the 1930s.

Peter Drucker, for one, believes we are now entering a post-capitalist society in which capitalists and proletarians will be replaced by knowledge workers and service workers.[2] He first used the term "knowledge worker" as far back as 1960

1

FIGURE 1

The Three Waves of Economic Change

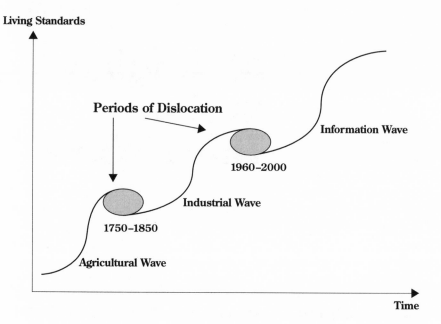

and has recently asserted that "the economic challenge of the post-capitalist society will be the productivity of knowledge work and knowledge worker."[3]

In his best-selling book *The Third Wave*, published in 1980, American futurist Alvin Toffler[4] describes three periods of economic evolution: the *agricultural wave*, which lasted from 8000 B.C. to the mid-eighteenth century; the *industrial wave*, which lasted until the late twentieth century; and finally the *information wave*, which began in the 1960s and will last for many decades to come. These dates are of course approximate and overlapping. The first wave was driven by physical labor, the second wave by machines and blue-collar workers, and the third by information technology and knowledge workers. From here on we will refer to the coming information or digital age as the *third wave economy* to distinguish it from the industrial age (or the second wave economy) we are now leaving behind.

The transitional periods between these three great waves of change have been anything but smooth. In Figure 1 each wave is represented by an "S" curve that shows an early period of dislocation, followed by a long spell of maturity, and then its eventual demise as new technologies take over. Old jobs become obsolete, vast retraining programs are needed, and education formats have to adapt as new wave businesses demand more appropriate skills and relevant knowledge.

The business organization as we know it today has evolved during the second wave, but many of the accepted management principles and practices that brought success throughout that period are now out of kilter with the competitive environment of the information age. This book is concerned with the key management issues that will determine success or failure in the third wave. We believe that unless managers face up to them now they will be ill-prepared to meet the challenges ahead.

The Third Wave Economy

The third wave economy is dominated by service organizations, which now provide the vast majority of added value and jobs in all industrialized countries (in the U.S.A. the figures are 77 percent of added value and 74 percent of jobs).[5] In fact, the line between manufacturing and services is now so blurred as to be almost meaningless. Even in manufacturing companies the percentage of production activities is declining and service activities such as design, marketing, and customer support now provide most of the value. Indeed, many manufacturers, including the giant GE Corporation, increasingly see their future profitability to come from services and (at least some of) their products as loss-leaders. In most service companies the *intellect* of the people is now the primary resource (46 percent are the so-called knowledge workers such as managers and professional staff).[6] But how will this resource be accumulated and deployed in the battle for competitive advantage? Few managers understand the question let alone the answer.

Accepting these new realities and their implications is not easy for economists and politicians brought up to believe that only the manufacturing sector can provide large numbers of jobs and increasing levels of prosperity. The notion that services are intangible, ephemeral, not capital intensive, produce only low-paid jobs, and generally play a minor role in national economic activity and wealth creation is hard to shake off. What can be said with some certainty, however, is that the service sector now accounts for most of the new jobs, the bulk of capital investment (largely in the form of information technology), and its economic contribution in terms of value-added per job is comparable to that of the manufacturing sector.[7] Figure 2 shows the extent to which the third wave economy (using the service sector as a proxy) now dominates economic activity.

Even these figures fail to tell the full story. The real engine of the third wave economy is the high-tech sector, which is now accelerating at a rapid rate. A recent report noted that while this sector accounted for

FIGURE 2

U.S.A.: Real Value-Added by Sector, 1950–1990

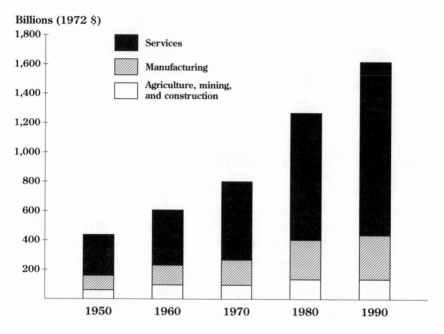

SOURCE: Bureau of Economic Analysis, "The National Income and Product Accounts of the United States," series in the Survey of Current Business.

only 5½ percent of American GDP, it produced almost 40 percent of GDP growth over the past two years. Moreover, it has been growing at an annual rate of 25 percent while prices have been *falling* at the rate of 10 percent. By contrast, the remainder of the economy has been expanding at a sluggish 1½ percent. When recent economic activity is viewed in this light, it is hardly surprising that inflationary pressures have not been a major concern.[8]

The balance of power in industrial relationships has also shifted dramatically in favor of service providers. Retailers such as Wal-Mart, Toys "R" Us, Marks & Spencer, and many large supermarket chains now dictate terms to their manufacturing suppliers. The same goes for direct mail, distribution, computer, communications, and airline companies. Moreover, many so-called manufacturers no longer consider production to be an essential core competence. Firms such as Nike and Apple outsource production to low-cost manufacturers elsewhere.

The competitive landscape of the third wave is changing rapidly. We can see a number of seismic changes that bring in their wake powerful and unpredictable consequences for countries, businesses, and individuals. We will examine the effects of these changes under the following headings:

- The impact of technology
- The global market
- Government-driven changes (such as deregulation)
- The changing face of competition
- The changing pattern of employment
- The rise of knowledge as the key economic resource

The Impact of Technology

The rapid pace of technological change is creating a wide array of new business opportunities. The development of the Internet, for example, with its global reach and tens of millions of users, is opening up possibilities for electronic banking, education on demand, digital photography, virtual shopping, and virtual factories; ultimately it has the potential to change almost every aspect of business life. The battle for the "digital living room" is currently being fought among a number of the world's giant companies and their networks of partners. Global telephony and satellite communications are leading us toward personal telephone numbers and video links no matter where we happen to be on the planet. The winners of these technology wars will reap a huge harvest of new products and services and create large numbers of jobs.

Technology is also changing economic and trading relationships and creating new forms of organization. Managers have always compared the costs of making their own products and providing their own services with the costs of buying these in the marketplace. Such was the cost advantage in pursuing the former approach that most second wave managers built their businesses on the basis of extended ownership. The result was a proliferation of mergers and takeovers, an extension of vertical and horizontal integration, and the creation of vast multidivisional enterprises. But information-based networks have changed the economic equation. Transaction costs between independent firms have plummeted as they integrate their information systems. There is no longer any significant cost advantage in owning supply and marketing chains when transactions between independent partners are conducted within one large computerized network with, more often than not, little human intervention. This realization has resulted in an explosion of outsourcing, the breakup of conglomerates, and the development of alliances and economic webs. Its ultimate expression is being found in the virtual corporation, which uses these technology links to coordinate its supply and marketing activities without owning any of them.

One outcome of these developments is a dramatic reduction in inventory levels. Indeed, inventory is no longer seen as an asset that enables companies to take advantage of market opportunities. Its very presence (beyond the level held to meet specific customer orders) is now more a sign of weakness than strength—a liability rather than an asset. Consequently, buffer stocks that absorbed the ebbs and flows of production volumes and customer demand are largely disappearing. And such techniques are spreading beyond the manufacturing arena. In the same way that just-in-time inventory systems have helped to reduce manufacturing inventories, so retailers are evolving new delivery systems that preclude the need for on-site inventory. The technology now exists for retailers to offer greetings cards, books, CDs, and videos by printing or copying them on demand. Some retailers have developed virtual warehouses whereby stocks appear to be available behind the counter but in reality exist in some remote physical location still under the ownership of the supplier. Such retail goods (for example, washing machines and fridges) are then delivered directly to the customer.

Existing industries are being transformed. The pace of technological change is shortening product life cycles and creating new opportunities for mass customization. Companies such as USAA in insurance, MBNA in financial services, and Levi-Strauss in jeans are all using technology to find and satisfy the exact needs of their customers.

The Global Market

The flow of money and information is now global. Corporations of every nationality are buying, selling, and investing in each growth region of the world, but unlike earlier times, this doesn't mean relocating armies of professionals for years on end. These same professionals can now control and respond to events and deploy their expertise from central computer hubs located where they live. Consumer buying patterns are also changing. Nintendo kids have more in common with other Nintendo kids around the world than with their parents or their own cultural backgrounds. Regions are defined as much by their satellite footprints as by their places in the atlas.

Global marketing is leading to more homogenous buying patterns. Taking the greatest gamble in its history, Ford Motor is coordinating its global operations to produce a series of so-called world cars. McDonald's can place its famous golden arches in any part of the globe and be immediately recognized—and successful! Global shopping via the Internet is creating huge marketing opportunities for any enterprising organization that can display its wares on the World Wide Web and deliver products directly to the consumer. Amazon's on-line bookshop now has the largest stock of books in the world (over two and a half million titles) but such stock is only virtual—the company buys in to match customer orders. Dell is now selling computers over the Internet at the rate of $1 million per day and over 80 percent of buyers are new to the company. According to CEO Michael Dell, "It's like zero–variable–cost transactions. The only thing better would be mental telepathy."[9]

The third wave is spawning new regions of economic prosperity, primarily in East Asia. In 1960, East Asia accounted for just 4 percent of world economic output, but today its share has risen to 25 percent. Such spectacular changes were unthinkable barely 20 years ago. This growth is not due simply to a transfer of second wave industries such as textiles or cars. Malaysia, for example, is now the world's foremost producer of semiconductors. National economies can no longer be protected. What matters in the third wave is where global corporations invest, not where they are headquartered or where they pay taxes. Knowledge can be deployed from anywhere at any time by any person or organization. Moreover, knowledge has no respect for place, history, or tradition.

As many skills become computer based and more easily transferable, corporate loyalty to a particular place or region will decline. Routine processing work, for example, can be done as easily in Bombay or Bangkok as in Chicago or Cardiff. In the intensely competitive environment of the third wave, global organizations will seek out the lowest costs and the highest productivity—wherever these can be achieved. By investing in developing countries, for example, firms can now have new technology, high quality, high productivity, and *low wages*. The average cost for a worker in the Volkswagen Skoda plant in the Czech Republic, for example, is approximately one-tenth of that for a worker in the company's German plants, but productivity in the Czech plant is 60 percent that of its German-based counterparts and increasing rapidly.[10]

Government-Driven Changes

In the past ten years or so, much of the established world order has crumbled. We have witnessed, for example, the collapse of communism in Eastern Europe; the explosion of China as an economic power; the emergence of East Asia as the most dynamic trading bloc in the world; the privatization of state-owned industries; and deregulation in airlines, telecommunications, and utilities. The combined force of these changes has been twofold: to unleash a wave of competition onto the world economy the like of which has never been seen before, and to open up huge new markets in East Asia, India, and Eastern Europe, where billions of new consumers are eager for products and services.

Many companies that were previously protected by government monopoly now have to learn new skills. Monopoly practices breed high costs and poor service, and companies such as British Telecom (BT) and AT&T are now realizing how far they have to go to meet customer expectations. Just consider that prior to privatization the British Gas Corporation did not feel obliged to list its hundreds of retail outlets in the telephone directory, even though it had a U.K.-wide monopoly on the sale of gas appliances![11]

To some companies, the release from state control has offered new opportunities to establish a strong international position, as British Airways has demonstrated to great effect. For others, however, deregulation has come as a profound shock, as they see just how quickly dissatisfied customers can defect without fanfare from firms that have serviced their needs in some cases for decades.

The Changing Face of Competition

Traditional industrial boundaries are becoming increasingly blurred. For example, to which industrial category does Microsoft belong? Computing? Software? Communications? Consumer electronics? Information? Many companies now span multiple industrial categories and join forces with partners with equally wide spheres of activity. Indeed, some firms simultaneously compete and cooperate with each other. Through these new forms of alliances, variously known as ecosystems or economic webs, firms are feeling their way into third wave competition. A recent alliance between AT&T, America Online, Microsoft, and Netscape (most of which market competing software products) is just one example of this emerging trend. Others include the proposed mergers and alliances between BT and MCI, and British Airways and American Airlines. All seek to establish their own global webs that can then be used to attract other partners and thus strengthen their competitive positions.

According to American economist Brian Arthur, the emergence of knowledge-based businesses has turned much of traditional economic thinking on its head. Many high-tech companies no longer "go it alone" the way IBM, DEC, and other computer companies did in the 1960s and 1970s. They are now more likely to be involved in some form of economic web that will have one or two leaders (e.g., Microsoft and Intel) and a large number of followers who find niche ways to add value. The difference is that once formed, these webs can break the laws of diminishing returns. In fact, they are subject to *increasing returns* as their web leads the market, attracts more supporters, and locks out other possible competitors. Arthur sees a clear divide between the second wave economic model espoused by British economist Alfred Marshall at the end of the nineteenth century and the emerging third wave model. This is Arthur's view:

> At the beginning of this century, industrial economies were based largely on bulk processing of resources. At the close of this century, they are based on the processing of resources *and* on the processing of knowledge. Economies have bifurcated into two worlds—intertwined, overlapping, and different. These two worlds operate under different economic principles. Marshall's world is characterized by planning, control, hierarchy. It is a world of materials, of processing, of optimization. The increasing-returns world is characterized by observation, positioning, flattened organizations, missions, teams, and cunning. It is a world of psychology, of cognition, of adaptation.[12]

The second wave economic model that underpins traditional managerial thinking and provides the framework for most accounting systems is fast becoming irrelevant as third wave managers contemplate competitive actions. Its makers never envisioned a world of alliances and webs where companies such as Microsoft or Netscape would compete for the minds and wallets of software developers and advertisers by offering *end users* free products (such as web browsers); nor did the early economists imagine that competitive advantage would be based on speed, innovation, service, and customization as well as volume, scale, and low cost. But above all, such mechanistic models can find no mathematical formulae that can simulate the effects of trust, loyalty, and the strength of relationships—the critical factors that will determine third wave success. Finding the right employees, suppliers, customers, and partners, fostering trust between them, and designing the right systems of measures and rewards will have a far greater impact on third wave performance than models based on cost-volume-profit analysis.

The Changing Pattern of Employment

In Toffler's language, the second wave formed an entirely new concept—that of "massification," in which we find mass production, mass markets, mass consumption, mass media, mass political parties, mass religion, and weapons of mass destruction. At the apex of their power in the late 1950s and early 1960s, five hundred giant American corporations produced half the nation's industrial output and employed more than 12 percent of the workforce. General Motors, the world's biggest corporation, had earnings in 1955 equivalent to 3 percent of the GDP of the country.[13] By the 1970s, up to 90 percent of the working population worked for "organizations,"[14] and for many people (particularly in Japan) their working career was lifetime employment within one corporation. In Toffler's view, the

third wave will witness the reverse trend—that is, toward demassifica-
tion, where factories, cities, and even nations will recede, and smaller
minority interests will come to the fore. One only has to note the recent
period of downsizing, the proliferation of niche-market television channels around the world, and the explosive growth of the Internet to confirm that this is now happening.

We are currently in the dislocation phase between the second and
third wave economies, and the early impact on business and jobs is largely
negative. Indeed, many writers suggest that we are entering a downward
spiral of fewer jobs, unsustainable welfare states, bankrupt companies, and
ultimately social unrest. The primary driving force is the reengineering of
work and the displacement by technology of routine jobs. Andersen
Consulting estimates that in just one service industry, commercial banking
and thrift institutions, reengineering will mean a loss of 30 to 40 percent of
jobs over the next seven years.[15] Reengineering the American economy,
according to Michael Hammer, could result in an unofficial unemployment
figure of as much as 20 percent by the time the current (reengineering)
phenomenon runs its course.[16] Rifkin uses the analogy of the bank teller to
contrast the productivity of technology with that of people:

> A human teller can handle up to 200 transactions a day, works 30
> hours a week, gets a salary anywhere from $8,000 to $20,000 a year plus
> fringe benefits, gets coffee breaks, a vacation, and sick time…. In con-
> trast, an automated teller can handle 2,000 transactions a day, works 168
> hours per week, costs about $22,000 a year to run, and doesn't take cof-
> fee breaks or vacation…. Between 1983 and 1993, banks [in the United
> States] eliminated 179,000 human tellers, or 37 percent of their work-
> force…. By the year 2000, upwards of 90 percent of banking customers
> will use automated teller machines.[17]

But the previously accepted productivity dividends arising from such
restructuring are now being questioned. Indeed, the eminent American
economist Stephen Roach has suggested that the result of this restructuring "is increasingly hollow companies that may be unable to maintain—let alone expand—market share in the rapidly growing global economy. If that's all there is to the productivity-led recovery, the nation could
well be on a path toward industrial extinction."[18]

Not only are jobs disappearing but the way the remaining work is performed is also changing. The traditional world of career-based jobs, with contracts of employment, holiday and pension entitlements, and clearly defined
promotion structures, is giving way to part-time work, contract work, project
teams, self-employment, and many other types of independent work-group
activity—often separated from the apron strings of the organization itself.
Charles Handy graphically illustrates the likely pattern of new employment:

Driving this trend is heightened competition in the global market-place. Price wars and quality wars are forcing companies to slim down their employment rolls to a hard core of operatives whose only function is to serve the needs of customers and to tight little nuclei of managers whose only function is to find and hold on to customers. The result is a mighty extrusion of personnel. Employees who are not connected to the core tasks of the business—all those cooks and lawyers, accountants and PR people, art directors and security guards, bank economists and ATM maintenance crews—will soon find themselves in a new relationship, if any, to their former employers. They will become more or less independent actors on the business's contractual support network—jobbers, pieceworkers, consultants, accommodators, 'temps' of all sorts and degree, all plying their different trades and skills.[19]

So where will the new (third wave) jobs come from? At this stage there are no clear answers. Some believe that because new technology will make workers far more productive, there will be a declining need for large numbers of them. Others have more faith that the capitalist system can renew itself and, through increased productivity, create enough wealth to continue the rise in living standards and spending power sufficient to trigger a new cycle of growth in both investment and jobs. Indeed, these new jobs are to some extent already happening in health-care, entertainment, community services, software, and education.

However, one thing is certain as individuals contemplate their futures in the third wave job market. They must learn to become more independent and take charge of their own career development. This will mean ensuring that their *knowledge is current and useful*. Consequently, continuous learning must become an essential part of their self-development program. How much value they can add to a firm will become more important than the certificates they hold or the positions they have achieved. Résumés will track contribution and results rather than position and salary. Faced with this new reality, more people will try their hand at self-employment. A more fractured world made up of relatively few large corporations supported by networks of small independent businesses that share and exchange knowledge with their corporate elders will likely become the pattern for the third wave.

The Rise of Knowledge as the Key Economic Resource

Whereas the second wave organization was built around the availability and use of land, labor, and money, the third wave company will be firmly based on the deployment of knowledge and the imaginative use of technology. If you have any doubts, consider that in most large American manufacturing companies the intangible assets are now worth *twice* the tangible assets—a reversal of the position only ten years ago. In service and high-tech companies this multiple is five- to fifteen-fold. These intangible or *intellectual* assets are based primarily on the skills and capabilities of their so-called knowledge workers, who will within a few short years outnumber blue-collar workers at their highest historical level of employment.

These changes have challenged the product costing and pricing techniques of many firms. In pharmaceutical, software, and entertainment companies, for example, products such as pills, accounting systems, and movies are simply the packaging of knowledge. The primary cost components are R&D, design and marketing; but we would be hard-pressed to find such notions of cost in standard accounting textbooks, which still preach the age-old standard costing techniques of controlling labor and materials.

There has been much talk recently of the "knowledge-based business" and the "learning organization"; but what do we mean by "knowledge," and how will it become the new source of competitive advantage? Clever and creative people have always used their knowledge to design innovative products and services, but knowledge will take on a different and much broader meaning in the third wave. Instead of knowledge being vested in one or two clever people it will become embedded in systems and databases and made available to all. To achieve maximum effectiveness, knowledge must be systematically accumulated, shared, and purposefully deployed in building the core competencies of the firm. It will mean, for example, providing frontline workers with instant access to important information about customers so that their needs can be satisfied and their problems quickly solved; it will mean improving business processes through understanding not just the results of management actions but *how* and *why* those results came about; and it will mean applying knowledge to how work is done.

Continuously improving the stock of knowledge will be critical to success. But simply creating knowledge-sharing networks and feeding them with information will not necessarily generate the desired results. New insights are emerging into how people learn and where such learning takes place. In the third wave economy, work is as much a social as an economic activity, and learning is at its sharpest if conducted informally, outside working hours or at natural breaks during the day. Moreover, learning can be more tightly focused if conducted on a one-to-one, mentor-to-apprentice type basis. While the economics of such relationships were prohibitive in the second wave, computer networks are now being adapted to facilitate this type of interaction.

New performance measures must also be found to support the knowledge-based organization. Neither the use of return-on-capital and sales per employee, nor the comparison of accounting results with preset budgets will measure success in the third wave. Nor is there any reliable relationship between knowledge investment and financial results. Any comparison of spending on R&D, training, or IT demonstrates that it is the productivity of such investment that matters and that this is determined by managerial competence. New measures must be developed that link actions to strategies, monitor changes in intellectual capital, and encourage value-creating work. Traditional second wave accounting numbers will not only be wide of the mark, they may well undermine the future of the company. Nor do accountants seem to have much clue how to measure productivity in a third wave organization. Output per hour as a productivity measure has little relevance when it is innovation, service quality, and customer loyalty that need to be encouraged.

Succeeding in the Third Wave

Economic success is driven by improvements in private sector productivity. *Crucial to this success is world-class managerial performance.* This has, in fact, always been the case. A backward glance at the fluctuating fortunes of the second wave reveals why. The early running was made by British companies who, with their high levels of innovation and their domination of international trade, achieved global success in the nineteenth century. This was followed by American mastery of mass production and industrial productivity, which created the world's richest economy in the first half of the twentieth century. And finally we have seen the innovative products and practices of Japanese manufacturers capture many world markets as we approach the millennium. Each of these three periods of economic leadership was also based on management leadership. But who will lead in the third wave, and what factors will determine such leadership? Peter Drucker provides us with some clues when he notes that "the only thing that increasingly will matter in national as well as international economics is management's performance in making knowledge productive."[20]

Here we can see parallels with the second wave. Despite huge investments in factories and capital equipment throughout the second half of the nineteenth century, it was only when Frederick Taylor started to organize work flows around new machinery and take advantage of the available electric power that the productivity revolution finally took off. Just substitute "computer" for "electric" and you begin to see what has perplexed economists for the past twenty years, as huge investments in information technology have failed to bring significant productivity growth. You may also see a similar solution, but with a crucial difference.

Once people could see the benefits of reorganizing work around the new technology, productivity benefits started to flow; but whereas productivity in the second wave flowed through people into machines, productivity in the third wave flows through computers into people. This switch in the balance of power has far-reaching implications for third wave management. Alan Webber notes how dramatically the tables have turned when he suggests that it is now "the job of the organization to market itself to the knowledge worker. Managers, therefore, have to attract and motivate the best people; reward, recognize, and retain them; train, educate, and improve them—and, in the most remarkable reversal of all, serve and satisfy them."[21]

With sophisticated customers in charge of the marketplace and technology at their fingertips, firms must choose their strategies carefully. Whether they select technical leadership, opt for low cost and convenience buying, or pursue specialized niche markets and customization, complexity is likely to be the order of the day. But learning how to handle this complexity will not come easily, particularly when the second wave structure of management education remains largely intact. Functional managers must learn to tie their actions to strategic needs and to *support one another*. To assume that functional specialists live (and are measured) in a world of their own will lead to disaster in the third wave.

Management at the Crossroads

Second wave managers have reached a fork in the road. One turn leads to a slow decline, the other to a prospect of long-term success. But the road signs are unclear, and the weary manager cannot turn to well-documented maps and guides, for these are only now being written. This book will act as a preliminary guide, but it is more of a geological survey than a detailed road map. To continue the metaphor, we already know some key features of the third wave terrain. For example, the bedrock will be knowledge, the river valleys will be digital, and customers will be reached along horizontal pathways.

As customers learn to use the new digital pathways, suppliers can expect a rough ride. Once customers begin to choose products and services that *exactly* suit their needs at the lowest price, suppliers will need to build capabilities that are flexible and adaptable. Moreover, entry to the global market will be both fast and inexpensive, and those who continue to rely on protective barriers will become highly vulnerable. The quality of management will matter more than ever.

As we pass through the transitional period, such pronouncements can sound overhyped and unconvincing. But such an interpretation would be a big mistake. To those managers who remain skeptical—who believe that their markets are stable, that value chains with their spread of costs and margins will remain intact, and that new low-cost, high-speed competitors will not appear on the horizon—the message is clear: Examine the evidence. Indeed, look no further than those two most conservative and stable industries, banking and insurance. Who would have thought that within the last few years First Direct in banking and Direct Line in insurance would have revolutionized their industries in the United Kingdom. Also consider that most car manufacturers and large retailers now offer their own credit cards, and some supermarket chains offer savings and loans. Where did Wal-Mart and CNN come from to become the the world's most successful retailer and newsgatherer? And who predicted that British Airways would become the world's favorite—and as it turns out, one of its most profitable—airlines?

Of course descriptions like "second wave" and "third wave" don't matter. They are only labels to help the reader envision a clear fault line between two quite different economic worlds. At the moment these fault lines are blurred; only future historians will see them with clarity. What does matter, however, is that existing firms match their competencies to their customers and, by strengthening this link, continue to improve the value they offer. Third wave ideas are no longer the preserve of top managers. They are diffused throughout the organization, but they must be harnessed and nurtured. This requires a new relationship between managers and workers, one based more on trust and partnership than on control and compliance.

The Ten Key Management Issues of the Third Wave

Many challenges confront managers as they prepare for the third wave. The remainder of this book has been divided into ten key issues rather than ten traditional chapters (see Figure 3). Each issue concerns a critical management area that must be reconsidered in the perspective of the third wave. Taken as a whole, the ten issues comprise an action plan for third wave success. Let's take a brief look at what the ten key management issues are about.

Issue 1 Strategy: Pursue Renewal, Not Retrenchment

Study after study shows that the vast majority of downsizers fail to revive their ailing companies. While short-term cost cutting may bring quick relief, it invariably leaves the remaining workforce demoralized, fearful,

FIGURE 3

The Ten Key Management Issues of the Third Wave

Issue 1
Strategy: Pursue Renewal, Not Retrenchment

Learn to think "outside the box."

Trust people to think and act strategically.

Build core competencies and avoid core rigidities.

Leverage value through strategic alliances and economic webs.

Issue 2
Customer Value: Match Competencies to Customers

Choose the right value proposition and build the right operating model.

Evolve the model continually.

Issue 3
Knowledge Management: Leverage Knowledge for Competitive Advantage

Learn how to define and acquire knowledge.

Learn how to learn.

Leverage knowledge for competitive advantage.

Issue 4
Business Organization: Organize around Networks and Processes

Move from hierarchies to networks and emphasize processes and teams.

Recognize the organization as a social structure.

Issue 5
**Market Focus: Find and Keep Strategic, Profitable, and
Loyal Customers**

Build the value of customer capital.

Find out which customers are worthwhile and keep the right customers.

Issue 6
Management Accounting: Manage the Business, Not the Numbers

Know how to analyze product and service profitability.

Use accounting to help improve processes.

Move toward more relevant accounting systems.

and shouldering an increasing workload. It also damages customer confidence. Companies can cut only so much fat before they start cutting muscle. The trouble is that their information systems can't tell the difference. The best people—often the key knowledge workers—are usually the first to leave, moving on to stronger competitors. Long-term success

FIGURE 3

(continued)

Issue 7
Measurement and Control: Strike a New Balance between Control and Empowerment

Beware of the behavioral implications of budgets.

Strike a new balance between control and empowerment.

Implement a strategic measurement system.

Issue 8
Shareholder Value: Measure the New Source of Wealth Creation—Intellectual Assets

Understand the changing shape of share values.

Note the uses of accounting information and the problems of valuing intellectual assets.

Note the changes needed in capital expenditure appraisal.

Issue 9
Productivity: Encourage and Reward Value-Creating Work

Beware of the second wave model—in pursuit of the lowest unit cost.

Adopt the third wave model—in pursuit of value-adding work.

Look for new measurement systems.

Issue 10
Transformation: Adopt the Third Wave Model

Question the effect of the second wave model.

Migrate to the third wave model.

Question the value of management education.

---

does not come from squeezing assets and stretching people to their limits, but from investing in knowledge-based competencies to satisfy customer needs profitably. Restructuring and retrenchment are no substitutes for innovation and investment.

Third wave managers must look over the horizon to global markets, employ technology wisely, and anticipate the next wave of business opportunities. The emphasis in the third wave will be on building competence-based platforms that transcend organizational boundaries. Issue 1 looks at many examples of how companies are using core competencies to spawn new products and services across a number of markets and how different organizations are making new economic arrangements through strategic alliances and economic webs.

Issue 2   Customer Value: Match Competencies to Customers

Second wave companies tend to be product or service based, leaving the task of achieving revenue targets to the sales and marketing departments. Targets and incentives are rippled down through the sales divisions and teams, and local plans are devised to achieve the objectives. There is little to distinguish one customer from another, and in most cases individual salespersons do not really care, as incentive packages are usually tied to revenue or gross margin. This product-based approach has rarely been the key link between the chosen core competence and the customer, and thus for each new product or advertising campaign the same sales effort is needed all over again.

New information technology is enabling third wave companies to understand better the needs of their customers. Issue 2 looks at how these companies can match highly focused customer segments with their chosen core competencies, thereby strengthening long-term customer relationships.

Issue 3   Knowledge Management: Leverage Knowledge for Competitive Advantage

Second wave companies are built on the familiar bedrock of buildings, plant, and inventories. Competitive advantage is viewed in terms of scale and volume stemming from high-capacity use of machine-based factories. Service firms have similarly looked to large branch networks to display their power. Such an approach fails to recognize the importance of the switch from tangible to intangible assets and how the leverage of knowledge is becoming key to long-term success.

Third wave organizations recognize that power now resides in the minds of their best people, who are diffused throughout the business. Utilization of this knowledge, which is embedded in systems, databases, and core competencies, is the new source of competitive advantage. Issue 3 examines the rise of the knowledge worker and shows how knowledge can be systematically accumulated and used to build long-term capabilities. We also question the accepted methods of defining and disseminating knowledge and consider whether accounting systems can play a useful role.

Issue 4   Business Organization: Organize around Networks and Processes

The hierarchical model that typifies the second wave organization deals largely with internal issues of management control and financial performance. In fact, this structure was built on certain basic premises: workers have little interest in doing anything other than their particular jobs; managers make major decisions; and accountants and supervisors check that the correct work has been performed and that costs are in line with expectations. But with knowledge as the key resource, managers are finding that their old hierarchical structures are proving to be a major competitive handicap. They need to review their management structures and styles and study how they can best be adapted to support their chosen value propositions.

Many leading-edge companies have now reorganized around group-wide networks focusing particularly on how (and how well) work is performed. This is essentially a horizontal model with business processes at its heart, teams as its implementers, and a clear focus on a highly skilled, creative workforce that consistently delivers profitable products and services to profitable customers. Perceptions of status and work are also changed—team members now work for customers, not for superiors, and their authority derives from what they know rather than who they are. Issue 4 examines these new process-based structures and how groups of companies are reforming themselves into networks and virtual organizations.

Issue 5   Market Focus: Find and Keep Strategic, Profitable, and Loyal Customers

Second wave managers have an unbending faith that by increasing scale and market share, fixed costs will be recovered and each additional dollar of contribution will flow through to the bottom line. This accepted principle has become seriously flawed as costs are seen to be increasingly driven by factors other than volume. Driving volumes at maximum capacity and speed without concern for customer demand and process quality leads only to *higher costs and loss of competitiveness*. Evidence shows that companies who aggressively pursue market share during boom periods of the business cycle tend to suffer the consequences on the downswing, which finds them in poor shape to face competitors who have adopted alternative policies. Market share, contrary to popular belief, does not correlate easily with *net* profitability. The route to long-term success is to find loyal profitable customers, not the sort likely to be attracted by special offers.

Whereas building market share has been one of the primary driving forces of the second wave company, third wave managers will be more concerned with attracting the *right customers*: customers that represent a close strategic fit with the company or have the potential to grow, but—most importantly—are also likely to be *profitable*. Recent research at Bain & Co. has found that a cause-and-effect relationship exists between loyal employees and loyal customers and that the best employees prefer to work for companies that deliver the kind of superior value that builds customer loyalty.[22] Issue 5 includes some ideas that will help managers find and keep desirable customers.

Issue 6   Management Accounting: Manage the Business, Not the Numbers

Managers now realize that costs do not simply correlate with the functions on the organization chart. They are caused by the work people do and how well it is done. By failing to understand these causes, second wave accountants have also failed to learn how to develop new insights into the performance of key business processes. Moreover, traditional accounting statements show only results. They seldom tell readers *how* the results were achieved. Nor do they reveal how performance compared with the competition. A 10 percent increase in profits can hardly be termed successful if key competitors have increased profits by 20 percent. More important, accounting statements are a poor guide to future performance because they give few clues to the changes in key processes and capabilities that determine the business's strength.

Second wave cost management has focused on cost-volume-profit analysis, which is rooted in the belief that only by ramping up scale and speed can companies compete on cost. However, third wave managers will recognize that the route to lower costs is via stable, balanced processes that run to customer demand and perform the right work correctly first time around. Issue 6 also looks at the usefulness of such techniques as activity-based costing, and at some new ideas for defining and implementing processes, activities, products and services.

Issue 7   Measurement and Control: Strike a New Balance between Control and Empowerment

It is well documented that measures drive performance, particularly if those measures are reinforced by reward systems. Many second wave managers have tried to introduce well-intentioned changes in direction, only to be thwarted by the control system. Strategic targets and mission statements point in one direction but budgetary control systems often point in another. Moreover, unless accounting systems are realigned with the current move toward horizontal processes, managers must not be surprised when their structures are snapped back into the old shape by the overpowering force of departmental budgets and reward systems.

Issue 7 examines one of the great managerial dilemmas of the third wave. While second wave companies emphasize control and short-term targets rather than long-term improvement, third wave companies seek a different balance. The problem is how to achieve this new balance without totally forfeiting the virtues of management control. We believe that there is a way forward whereby longer-term targets (both financial and strategic) are agreed, and milestones are monitored along the way. However, the way that managerial performance is monitored is crucial, particularly when incentives are also involved.

Issue 8   Shareholder Value: Measure the New Source of Wealth Creation—Intellectual Assets

In most cases, share values are based on the ability of managers to generate growing streams of profits and dividends. The resources available were clearly identified on the second wave organization's balance sheet. And return on capital employed (or one of its many variants) was the tried and true yardstick for measuring performance.

However, the mix of resources is rapidly changing as intangible assets (such as brands, intellect, and the strength of information systems) assume far greater importance and value. These changes set new and difficult challenges for investors, managers, and accountants. Issue 8 examines some of these concepts and explores some new ideas for measuring intangible assets.

Issue 9   Productivity: Encourage and Reward Value-Creating Work

Restructuring and reengineering have been the primary tools of second wave managers in their efforts to improve productivity. Such a "denominator" approach to improving long-term success has indeed boosted short-term results but has left a trail of undesirable side effects such as low morale, declining quality, and indifferent customer service.

Economic success is driven by productivity. This is as true for a business as it is for an economy. But the way productivity is improved and measured will be very different in the third wave. Instead of using the traditional approach of minimizing unit costs by cutting jobs and introducing labor saving technology, third wave measurers will look at how much value is added by companies, processes, and people. However, value-added will be more than just a financial measure. It will also embody measures of quality and service. Issue 9 looks at how managers can encourage, reward and measure the *right work*.

Issue 10   Transformation: Adopt the Third Wave Model

The second wave organization was built on the premise that the maximization of shareholder wealth ought to be the overriding objective against which every managerial action is tested. This ideology is now being seriously questioned.

Issue 10 suggests that the traditional economic model is unconvincing as an explanation of third wave activity and examines the problems confronting managers as they attempt to migrate from the second to the third wave model. It also takes a long, hard look at management education and its relevance for third wave organizations.

Common Threads

In their frantic efforts to compete, many companies have overextended their product ranges, distribution channels, research projects, supply lines, and customer lists, thus creating a tangled web of managerial complexity and exposing the inadequacies of accounting systems that are unable to distinguish profitable from unprofitable work. Successful third wave managers must be able to see through this fog of complexity and eliminate those processes, activities, products, services, and customers that absorb all the time and all the costs, yet contribute little but red ink to the bottom line. Unless precious resources support today's winners and tomorrow's opportunities, then the life of the third wave company will be short.

Are there any companies we can already describe as "third wave"? The few contenders that spring to mind include Hewlett-Packard, British Airways, and Toyota. But there are two outstanding candidates: General Electric (GE) and Asea Brown Boveri (ABB).

Under the leadership of Jack Welch, GE has changed from a fading industrial behemoth to an information-driven world-class managerial icon with the largest market capitalization in the world and the highest profits in corporate America. Welch has scrapped top-down strategy and concentrated on core competencies and flattened hierarchies; he has introduced team working. The result: improved quality, the eradication of huge amounts of non-value-adding costs, new measures that link directly to strategic targets, and partnerships (based on trust) with employees, suppliers, customers, and other business partners. The final period of transformation is now under way with a new emphasis on adding service value to its product-based customers. In some cases this simply means helping them to improve their business management by adopting GE's own managerial principles. GE has embraced most of the principles of success necessary to become a truly third wave organization and the results are stunning.

Following Europe's largest ever cross-border merger in 1988, newly promoted CEO Percy Barnevik has implemented most of the ingredients of third wave success at ABB. Like Welch, his first task was to flatten multiple management layers, slim down the head office and change its role, and foster trust and a new set of common values throughout the company. But it is his emphasis on a federation of independent small businesses that must (and do) share resources and knowledge that has made Barnevik one of the real pioneers of the third wave organization. With profits in 1995 up by 73 percent over the previous year, his approach is proving to be an outstanding success.

The success of companies such as GE and ABB has been based on the evolution of a managerial structure, style, and culture that is suited to the competitive imperatives of the third wave. In particular, they have understood the subtle interplay between strategy, measures, controls, and behavior. And they have fostered horizontal cooperation (particularly the sharing of knowledge and resources) across and between business units and partners. These attributes require levels of trust and loyalty that are alien to most second wave companies. Trust and loyalty are two sides of the same coin. They are not responsive to management decree. They can only be earned through mutual respect, particularly within communities of knowledge workers who will ultimately determine organizational success. These communities cannot be driven: they can only be managed. Good management practices will remain the key to success in the third wave. The remainder of this book will tell you what they are.

Issue 1

Strategy
Pursue Renewal, Not Retrenchment

STRATEGIC PLANNING IS MAKING A COMEBACK. Now that the tidal wave of downsizing and reengineering seems to be subsiding, executives are once again asking questions of growth and renewal. But for many, the mentality of downsizing and cost saving has become so deeply ingrained that real strategic thinking either is impossible or has become confused with operational effectiveness. How do companies learn how to grow again and recapture the essence of strategic thinking? Certainly not by returning to the sterile strategic planning departments of the past. Head-office functionaries handing down the tablets of stone are not part of the new agenda. Real strategy in the third wave is about anticipating the future rather than extrapolating from the present. Moreover, it is a continuous process, not a once-a-year brainstorming exercise.

Every business, to some degree or another, needs to reinvent itself for success in the third wave. Previous formulas are unlikely to be successful. Assumptions about strategy, values, missions, core competencies, products, services, markets, competitors, management structures and styles, and how knowledge can be accumulated and used productively must all be questioned. Relationships with customers, suppliers, partners, and employees need to be reconsidered. Notions of shareholder and customer value and how this value should be measured and reported are also in the melting pot. These questions go the heart of the matter: What businesses are we in? Which markets do we serve? How will these markets look in five or ten years' time? What changes need to be made to achieve our growth objectives? Issue 1 looks at how strategic thinking is developing as we enter the third wave.

Know What Strategy Is and Isn't

According to strategy guru Michael Porter, strategic competition can be thought of as the process of perceiving new positions that woo customers from established positions or draw new customers into the market. He notes that strategic positionings are often not obvious, and finding them requires creativity and insight. For example, new entrants often discover unique positions that have been available but overlooked by established competitors. But most new positions open up because of change. New customer groups arise; new needs emerge as societies evolve; new distribution channels appear; new technologies are developed; and new information systems become available. These changes create opportunities for new entrants unencumbered by a long history in the industry (and not bound by its accepted rules and practices), thus creating the potential for new ways of competing.[1]

Porter also notes that many executives fail to distinguish between operational effectiveness and strategy. Operational effectiveness means performing similar activities *better* than rivals, whereas strategic positioning entails performing activities *different* from those of rivals, or performing similar activities in different ways. He believes companies that compete on the basis of operational effectiveness alone typically engage in mutually destructive wars of attrition leading to a spiral of lower costs, lower prices, and ultimately lower profits. He notes that this is why many Japanese manufacturers—arch exponents of operational effectiveness-based competition—have achieved consistently low profits. He cites Southwest Airlines and IKEA as examples of companies that clearly offer a service that sets them apart from the competition. Southwest's low-cost, no-frills service clearly appeals to a particular group of air travelers, while IKEA's large furniture stores with integral creches cater to the needs of young families. The activity of each of these companies is geared

FIGURE 1.1
The Quest for Competitiveness

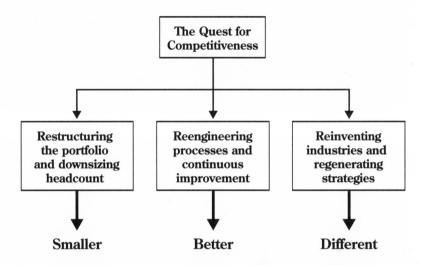

SOURCE: Gary Hamel and C.K. Prahalad, *Competing for the Future* (Boston: Harvard Business School Press, 1994), 15. Reprinted by permission of Harvard Business School Press.

entirely to the special needs of its customers. These strategic positions support Porter's view that competitive strategy means deliberately choosing a different set of activities to *deliver a unique mix of value.*[2]

In recent years, Gary Hamel and C.K. Prahalad have taken corporate strategy into new dimensions. Instead of the business school case studies that typically deal with *known* competitive factors (e.g., Coca-Cola versus Pepsi-Cola), they have stressed that building future prosperity—both for companies and for countries—is about imagining *unknown* business opportunities. It is about shaping the structure of future industries; it recognizes that competition for core competence leadership precedes competition for product leadership; and it recognizes that competition often takes place within and between coalitions of companies, and not only between individual businesses. They stress that getting *better* is not enough. Getting *different* is what matters. Figure 1.1 shows the three approaches to the quest for competitiveness.

In support of their views, Hamel and Prahalad cite the example of Xerox, which received many plaudits for its efforts at quality, team-based management, and benchmarking, but failed miserably in the acid-test of creating new businesses. Although Xerox pioneered icon-based computing, laser printing, and the laptop computer, Hamel and Prahalad suggest that "Xerox has probably left more money on the table, in the form of underexploited innovation, than any other company in history."[3]

But they are not suggesting that corporate executives spend their time dreaming about the future or that firms create think tanks or skunk works where small groups of scientists tinker about with "tomorrow's world" type products. The future will no longer be shaped by small garage-based products such as the original Apple computer. It will be the result of well-crafted and coordinated efforts to foresee what might happen and *prepare for it* through intellectual leadership, structured thinking, influencing industry standards, and eventually battling for market share. In particular Hamel and Prahalad suggest that executives must use their foresight to see where future opportunities lie and build a range of *core competencies* that will act as a springboard for new products and services. This is a painstaking process. It doesn't happen overnight. For example, it took JVC 20 years to finally win the battle of the VCR market with its VHS technology, but the result was billions of dollars of profits for the company and its suppliers.

In every market some companies are able to think differently and take the industry in a new direction. Compaq in personal computers, Hewlett-Packard in printers, Direct Line in insurance, Wal-Mart in retailing, Swatch in low-price watches, Federal Express in parcel delivery, and British Airways in customer service are a few examples. They all looked at the marketplace and set new standards of competition based on their use of chosen core competencies. This was not the result of traditional market research: rather, they anticipated the needs of their customers and built products and services to satisfy them.

This brings us to the essence of successful strategy. Is it the outcome of deliberate and painstaking analysis and planning? Or is it the result of entrepreneurial necessity, where the only option is to outwit the incumbent players? What part does experimentation play? And how can large organizations create the behavioral context that allows real entrepreneurial activity to thrive? MacMillan and McGrath believe that the entrepreneurial route is fundamental to discovering distinctiveness, or outperforming competitors by doing things differently. They note that two of Porter's exemplars, Southwest Airlines and IKEA, were started by mavericks—resourceful, adaptive entrepreneurial thinkers who forged strategic opportunities that incumbents overlooked. The same goes for Swatch, Direct Line, Dell, and The Body Shop. They make another perceptive point. It is one thing to admire a company's strategic positioning with hindsight. It is another to recognize it as one of a range of strategic opportunities that could have been taken. While Southwest Airlines has been successful, what happened to companies that tried similar approaches, such as Laker Airways, People's Express, and Kiwi International Airlines?

According to MacMillan and McGrath the lessons are clear: defensible strategies seldom emerge from analysis alone. The critical process is continuous experimentation within a strategic framework. Undisciplined experimentation is worse than none at all. They believe that strategy is first about analyzing and then experimenting, trying, learning, and experimenting some more. Today's strategy has to do with the fundamentally entrepreneurial process of driving toward destinies as yet unknown.[4]

Despite the pontifications of many strategic thinkers, strategy defies narrow definition. In its broadest sense it is the identification of the needs of a particular set of customers and the design of activities that fulfill those needs more profitably than the competition does. But this is a dynamic process and requires continuous adjustment and realignment as technology and market opportunities evolve. Where should this process take place? Should it be top-down or bottom-up? How is strategic thinking encouraged? How are those rare insights recognized and promoted? Is the development of core competencies an essential launching pad? What role do alliances and webs have to play? These are the issues we will now consider.

Two Contrasting Approaches— Visionary and Democratic

Great business leaders are either visionary or democratic. The visionary types see the future in a way that others can't. They anticipate how markets will evolve and gear their organization's capabilities accordingly. They are not looking for incremental improvement: they are looking to reinvent the industry. While market researchers are telling them that a wider range or new features are required, they are looking to develop products and services that customers have not yet even considered. Consider what happened at the dying Swiss watch company, SMH.

In 1985, due largely to intensive Japanese competition, SMH was losing money rapidly. The company's bankers suggested to Nicholas Hayek, SMH's adviser, that he buy a controlling stake. Now his stake is worth around $700 million, and the company's market value exceeds $3.5 billion. Hayek overturned conventional wisdom by proposing that the company *manufacture* a cheap watch in Switzerland (rather than subcontract the work to Taiwan or Singapore as most Western companies then did). His new Swatch watches have since sold millions around the world and at prices (around $40) that haven't changed for ten years. Hayek understood that with the right investment, the labor content in production would be minimal and therefore not a major factor in the competitive equation. He also knew that he had all the necessary experience and expertise on his doorstep and that imaginative designers were just over the Italian border. Initially his bankers were skeptical and some suppliers, on hearing his plan, were wary about selling parts, but his vision was a triumph of engineering and ideas over conventional advice.[5]

Democratic leaders, on the other hand, know that they have no monopoly on wisdom; they devolve strategic thinking to the front line and build organizations that encourage thoughtful inquiry and creative discussion. In this way they not only benefit from the knowledge of people who know what's happening in the industry, but also build commitment to success. They feed opportunities and starve problems; they back winners and discard losers; and they build alliances and partnerships to strengthen competitive positions.

In 1995, Finland's Nokia Group, which had being growing spectacularly at 70 percent per year, decided to involve 250 employees in a strategic review. Chris Jackson, head of strategic development, noted that "by engaging more people, the ability to implement strategy becomes more viable. We won a high degree of commitment by the process, and we ended up with lots of options we hadn't looked at in the past." Nokia has dispensed with the annual strategic exercise. The company's executive team now meets monthly and line managers have recently had training to enable them to make strategy a regular part of their jobs.[6] Third wave companies keep strategic options constantly under review.

Learning to Think "Outside the Box"

Gary Hamel[7] sees third wave strategy as nothing less than *revolution*. He suggests that if you look at any industry you will see three kinds of companies: the rule makers who built the industry (IBM, CBS, United Airlines, Merrill Lynch, Sears, Coca-Cola); the rule takers who follow the leaders (Fujitsu, ABC, U.S. Air, Smith Barney, J.C. Penny); and the revolutionaries who rewrite the rules (IKEA, The Body Shop, Charles Schwab, Dell Computer, Swatch, Southwest Airlines). In Hamel's view,

> Never has the world been more hospitable to revolutionaries and more hostile to industry incumbents. The fortifications that protected the industrial oligarchy are crumbling under the weight of deregulation, technological upheaval, globalization, and social change. But it's not just the forces of change that are overturning old industrial structures—it's the actions of companies that harness those forces for the cause of revolution.

Hamel poses and addresses the crucial question: "What if your company is more ruling class than revolutionary? You can either surrender the future to revolutionary challengers or revolutionize the way your company creates strategy. What is required is not a little tweak to the traditional planning process but a new philosophical foundation: strategy *is* revolution; everything else is tactics."

One such revolutionary company is Image Technology International,[8] an American firm that recently entered the photographic imaging market with a completely digital approach to the capture, organization, selection, manipulation, and distribution of photographic images. By using digital code rather than chemicals as its raw material, the company can offer its customers higher value (the costs of digitally produced photographs are lower than chemically based ones) and a much more versatile approach to how photographic images can be used. The company has, in effect, reinvented the industry by creating huge databases of photographs that can be tailored to meet the different requirements of newspapers, catalogs, magazines, printers, and so forth. By locking customers in to its "digital asset base," ITI has made it extremely difficult for any competitor to catch up.

Another revolutionary is Direct Line. When Peter Woods, founder of Direct Line, earned a £42 million bonus in 1992-1993 there were howls of protest. That a mere data processor who had risen from the shadows of the insurance business should be so lavishly remunerated seemed inexplicable. Only when he explained that he had saved every British motorist £100—or more than £2 billion for the whole country—did people begin to understand. Insurance, like most financial service organizations in the 1980s, was dominated by big groups with bloated overheads. But Direct Line changed all that. By offering telephone services and rock-bottom premiums together with a fast response, the company revolutionized the industry. Within a few years, direct banking, direct pensions, and direct investments have followed. By 1994–1995 Direct Line earned premiums of £664 million, had 2.2 million policyholders, and shortly after launching its direct mortgage service took £78 million in one month alone. But perhaps the most revolutionary finding was that Direct Line shattered the age-old belief that insurance (at least in Britain) was sold rather than bought. With simple sales techniques and low prices, the company proved once and for all that people will shop around for insurance in the same way they do for other services.[9]

Revolutionary companies do not accept the existing rules, practices, or traditions of an industry. Accor, the French budget hotels group is a prime example. Prior to 1985, when Accor launched Formule 1, its line of budget hotel, customers had two choices: stay in a no-star or one-star hotel (60-90 francs per night) with noisy rooms and poor beds, or pay over twice as much for a two-star hotel (200 francs per night) with better accommodations and service. Accor managers saw an opportunity to overcome the compromise that the industry had forced on the customer;

they decided to offer a good night's sleep for a low price. They looked at what customers valued, compared it with the industry standard, and realized they could strip out many of the nice but nonessential frills such as restaurants, lounges, writing desks, and permanent receptionists, and offer simple but clean rooms with good insulation at an extremely low price. Compared with the industry standard, Accor cut the costs of building rooms in half, incurred much lower staff costs, and gave two-star service for one-star price. The result is that the company now dominates the budget hotel market and has actually expanded it—for example, by attracting truck drivers who previously slept in their cabs. Instead of accepting industry norms and improving on them, Accor's breakthrough was to rethink customer value from scratch.[10]

Trusting People to Think and Act Strategically

Firms that fail to think "outside the box" are condemned to be followers, always playing catch-up football. They remain prisoners of their corporate culture as though a particular corporate gene were passed down through the management generations. The "IBM way" or the "Mercedes way" has proved successful in the past, so why not in the future? The reality is that in these highly regulated companies, managerial enterprise is stifled with strategic planning, budgets, performance-related pay, and extensive control systems. No one is thinking the unthinkable. No one is planning for markets that don't yet exist. There is no culture of belief or commitment to long-term developments that require years of patience and the building of cross-company skills and capabilities.

Many companies have changed their leaders in the belief that a new CEO can bring about the necessary changes. GM, IBM, American Express, Mercedes, Kodak, and many others have brought in new CEOs in the 1990s. In most cases the new chiefs were battle-hardened warriors of change programs who had driven through restructuring, downsizing, and reengineering projects; improved cycle times and customer satisfaction; and set more aggressive stretch targets. But as Porter has noted, such changes, important though they are in improving operating effectiveness, do not meet the tough criteria of strategic renewal. Third wave companies need a broader vision and, more important, a culture where difficult questions can be asked about the future. Such questions can be asked only if there is an atmosphere of trust and mutual support. They concern company values, culture, or even philosophy. They often involve a break with the past—a fundamental shift in the way that management is conducted and decisions are made.

Bartlett and Ghoshal[11] describe the strategic renewal process as establishing a new "behavioral context" or moving from a culture of compliance, control, constraint, and contract to one of discipline, support, trust, and stretch. Of these four they lay the emphasis on trust because it is essential for risk taking. They note its importance as follows: "On the organizational trapeze, trust provides the confidence necessary for someone to let go of the security of 'business as usual' and take an entrepreneurial leap, knowing that there will be supportive hands at the other end." In other words, trust means providing the support necessary to take acceptable risks and tolerate failure. These are deeply embedded management values that have been fostered by a number of companies over many years, but for those companies that need to move away from a different set of values—away from those, for example, that emphasize control and compliance—the challenge is a tough one indeed. Neither management exhortation about strategic renewal nor declarations of intent (including revised mission statements) get remotely to the point. Looking into a third wave crystal ball can be very uncomfortable and shake many existing assumptions about the business.

To say that renewal is tough is an understatement of huge proportions. As Jack Welch noted in 1985, following his first phase of restructuring at GE, "a company can boost productivity by restructuring, removing bureaucracy, and downsizing, but it cannot sustain high productivity without cultural change."[12] Nor can this be achieved without changes in top management *and* key managers who carry influence. Attitudes, beliefs, and behavior are parts of the human persona that are set in the formative years and they are not easily moved. People can be persuaded that black is white and vice-versa but whether it changes their fundamental beliefs is a different question. Ford is one company that has tried harder than most to do so.

Ford was the great classic second wave company. Its River Rouge plant was the forerunner of lean manufacturing. This extract from Henry Ford's 1926 book *Today and Tomorrow* describes the plant:

> Time waste differs from material waste in that there can be no salvage.... But having a stock of raw material or finished goods in excess of requirements is waste.... We do not own or use a warehouse.... Our production cycle is about eighty-one hours from the mine to the finished machine in the freight car, or three days and nine hours.[13]

By the 1960s the "three days and nine hours" had become five to six weeks through divisionalization, decoupling of processes, and the need to offer a wide variety of products. But more important, the culture had radically changed. Even though Henry Ford's management style was in tune with the times, he allowed his managers to run processes and had an acute sense of community welfare. By the dawn of the 1980s a "financial" culture had taken hold, fostered by Robert McNamara, Arjay Miller, Tex Thornton, and other so-called financial engineers. But Edwards Deming, the American quality guru, helped to change all that. From losses of $3 billion between 1980 and 1982, Ford recovered to profits of $5.3 billion in 1988; the return on equity reached 26.3 percent, and market share rose five points to 22 percent. Quality also rocketed and Ford shot up the J.D. Power charts.[14] Surveys and focus groups showed that employees recorded dramatic shifts in their perceptions of management, and morale and company loyalty were similarly changed. Ford had left behind its authority-based management culture and totally committed itself to quality, new products, and customer satisfaction. But how deep have these changes really gone? The jury is still out on whether Ford can achieve sustainable long-term results.

Motorola is another company that has changed its culture to permit strategic renewal to take place.[15] Earlier in its 65-year history, Motorola, like most second wave companies, was a collection of unruly fiefdoms run by fiercely independent engineers who believed that their products were unbeatable. But in the late 1970s CEO Robert Galvin saw the future differently. He saw the Japanese threat and recognized that the company was in no position to meet it. He dramatically changed the culture to one that stressed self-questioning, looking to the outside, and greater humility. Such changes have enabled the company to continuously anticipate and adapt to changes and achieve leadership positions in a number of emerging markets including semiconductors and cellular phones. Now Motorola imagines a future in which each individual can be reached through his or her personal telephone number anywhere on the planet. But despite its expertise in cellular phones, the company knows that to achieve this goal it will still need to combine a range of competencies from battery technology to data compression.

Another renaissance company is British Airways. When Sir Colin Marshall first declared that British Airways would be "the world's favorite airline," the notion was treated with disdain among employees and customers alike. But the cultural transformation from a typical nationalized industry to the number one in customer service within a short few years was brought about by dedication and attention to detail. Typical of this change has been the handling of customer complaints. When Charles Weiser arrived at BA in 1992, customer-service staff members were accustomed to a defensive approach. Callers were told to put complaints in writing. Letters could take weeks to be answered and replies were often delayed through exhaustive inquiries about what really happened and where the fault might lie. According to Weiser, "we used to spend more on lawyers' fees than we did on compensation to our executive club members. There were 13 steps to any inquiry, and it took until step 10 to reply to the customer." It took a year to change attitudes. "Now we ask, 'What can we do to keep this customer with us?' An apology, a refund, a bouquet or a bunch of flowers? It might even be a full refund. What people want is an apology, quickly, not in two or three months, and an assurance that it won't happen again."[16]

Other companies have been more fortunate than Ford, Motorola, and BA. They have always had a culture that encourages self-questioning and renewal. Often such beliefs stem from the founders and are maintained by their descendants. Hewlett-Packard and Wal-Mart are still influenced by the beliefs of their founders and have constantly renewed their businesses. Marks and Spencer, Britain's best-known retailer, has been a pioneer of most modern management techniques and is equally adept at anticipating market needs. In the 1930s the company defined its core competence as the ability to identify, design, and develop the merchandise it sold. It began to control its supply chain, employ target-costing methods, and use just-in-time delivery, long before such things became known as Japanese innovations. It then added another core competence: the ability to design and deliver prepackaged gourmet foods.

Building Core Competencies and Avoiding Core Rigidities

The first step in preparing for third wave competition is to choose the battlefield on which to fight. In the new vocabulary this means selecting one or a number of core competencies from which to project the firm's strengths into the marketplace.

Building Core Competencies

Core competencies comprise a set of skills and expertise that enable a company to deliver exceptional value to customers. They often involve an integrated system of capabilities that cannot easily be imitated by competitors. Issue 2 will examine how companies can match their competencies to customers by defining their *customer value proposition*. Although individual skill sets may not on their own be exceptional, it is how they blend together that creates a higher level of competence. Competencies are always evolving. They provide the platform from which future business opportunities are launched. Sony's early mastery of miniaturization led to a host of profitable opportunities including the Walkman, portable CD player, and pocket television. Federal Express's competence at parcel logistics provides fast on-time delivery for customers. Similarly at Wal-Mart, expertise in logistics and inventory management provides customers with "everyday low prices" and high stock availability. Motorola's expertise in wireless communications is opening up a wide range of new business opportunities in global telephony.

Success in building competencies is not a direct function of how much is spent on research and development. If it were, then GM would be years ahead of Honda, IBM well beyond Compaq, and Philips well ahead of Sony. What matters is not the level of R&D expenditure but the *productivity* and *leverage* of this combined knowledge. The development of core competencies as opposed to specific product lines is one of the key changes in management thinking that sets a company on the road to the third wave. A product line might provide a revenue stream sustainable over a short life cycle, but fail to open the way for the next product and the one after that. This contrasts with a core competence that defines a particular competitive strength such as technical leadership, operating excellence, or customer intimacy. Competence building enables a company to create a range of products and services that meet customer needs in rapidly changing markets. But it is important to note that successful companies focus on the performance of *competencies themselves*, not on the outputs. This focus is perhaps at its sharpest in measurement systems that look at quality, speed, and the value-adding work of the inner operations of these competencies: their processes, sub-processes, and activities.

Avoiding Core Rigidities

Core rigidities are yesterday's core competencies—the same sets of skills, knowledge, and systems that provided superior customer value in markets that have changed. They simply failed to evolve to meet these changing needs. If current industry leaders wish to remain in that position, they must constantly look to the future. Sears failed to see Wal-Mart as a threat until it was too late. A former senior executive at Sears recalled that inattention to outside events was compounded by the existence of a whole library of "bulletins" dictating responses to problems.[17] "God forbid there should be a problem that comes up for which there isn't a bulletin," he observed. "That means the problem's *new!*"

Competencies can become so sclerotic that it is incredibly difficult to get back into the competitive ring. Digital knows this better than most. Despite huge investments in its Alpha chip through the early 1990s as well as continuous restructuring and reengineering, the company is still facing an uphill struggle. This is CEO Robert Palmer's analysis of where the company got it wrong:

We got into trouble because we had the wrong strategies. In the 1980s, Digital was vertically integrated. We did everything ourselves, built the central processing unit, the operating system, the applications, the databases, all the networking protocols, everything. We even went to the extreme of bending the metal for the cabinets that we put our computers in. Then the business model changed. First was the emergence of personal computers, powered by single-chip microprocessors. Then came the emergence of open operating systems, and Digital failed to anticipate these changes. Then, once we saw the changes, we failed to adapt to them. Instead we gave our customers a lecture, told them what they said they wanted to buy wasn't appropriate.[18]

Digital found itself with core competencies that belonged in the mini-computer museum. The company had totally failed to see the future, and by the time its managers realized the depth of the problem it was too late. Hewlett-Packard saw the future differently. Lewis Platt,[19] Chairman and CEO of HP, put the issue of continuous renewal in the following way: "We have to be willing to cannibalize what we're doing today in order to ensure our leadership in the future. It's counter to human nature but you have to kill your business while it is still working."

Most companies are trapped within their own lines of second wave thinking. They see their organizational map as a series of strategic business units with product and service portfolios addressing specific market segments. Their strategic plans are geared to greater market share, better margins, newer versions of the same products, and improved quality and efficiency. They look at build, hold, or harvest strategies depending on the state of the market. They don't think in terms of building core competencies, nor is time spent imagining the markets of the future. Honda has used its core competencies in engines to create market positions in cars, lawn mowers, garden tractors, marine engines, and generators. Canon has used its expertise in optics, electronics, and chemicals to create openings in cameras, printers, and copiers. But neither company sees a portfolio of products. Instead they see a range of core competencies that they continue to improve and evolve.

Leveraging Value through Strategic Alliances and Economic Webs

Knowledge of products, local markets, and the need to combine different technologies such as computing and telecommunications, makes it difficult for any one organization, no matter how large, to possess all the experience necessary to carry out a complete (often long-term) strategic business opportunity. Alliances, partnerships, joint ventures, outsourcing, and the formation of economic webs (usually around a particular technology platform) have become the ways to harness a disparate range of expertise and economic resource. In some cases the size of the market potential and the cost of research and development are such that alliances are the only way to develop such opportunities.

The proposed alliance between News Corporation, MCI (its 20 percent partner in ASkyB), and Echostar Communications (the smallest but most entrepreneurial American satellite broadcaster) provides a good example. The explosive potential of digital broadcasting has been known for some time, but growth in the world's biggest market (the United States) has been slow as the competitive threat from satellite broadcasters has failed to appear—largely because they could not supply enough local programs to compete with the cable companies. And as cable supplies 70 million American homes, compared with only 5 million by satellite, there was little incentive for cable companies to rush ahead with the new technology. But the announcement in March 1997 of the new alliance, together with its innovative "spot-beam" technology, has turned the tables dramatically, causing an immediate fall of 6 percent in cable company shares. Spot-beam technology enables the new alliance to offer local programs with five hundred razor-sharp digital channels, video on demand, and home shopping, and it should be available to about 75 percent of American homes by 1999.[20] Could it be that the cable industry, currently entrenched in its comfortable niche, will go the way of the railroads?

The telecommunications industry is rife with alliances and most emerging countries make it a condition of entry that joint ventures are created with local companies. But alliances in all their forms are difficult to manage and are by no means always successful. The joint venture between Boots and WH Smith in the U.K. do-it-yourself market ended with heavy losses on both sides. Although both partners were good at retailing, neither joint venture partner had any proven expertise in the DIY market.

As with all cooperative ventures, success will be elusive unless there is strong leadership and clear objectives, mutual trust, respect, fairness, and dependency. These are hard values to build and the projected life of the venture, more often than not, does not provide time for sufficient courtship. Recent research suggests that around 60 percent of strategic alliances fail to achieve their objectives and that the problem comes down to leadership.[21] Many alliances bring in a leader from outside the organization, but the researchers found that strategic alliance managers need the knowledge, relationships, and credibility that only an insider can bring to the table.

Contrasting cultures among alliance partners is also a problem. Successful alliance managers are more akin to diplomats than to line managers. They foster cooperation and trust between partners and keep them focused on the big picture even when one partner feels to be disadvantaged.

The Emergence of Economic Webs

The rise of economic webs has been a phenomenon of the high-tech industry (although more recently they have also formed around customer and market segments). Technology webs are clusters of companies that collaborate around a particular technology platform. The best known web is probably the Microsoft/Intel (known as Wintel) web based around the personal computer. According to John Hagel III,[22] an economic web

> is a set of companies that use a common architecture to deliver independent elements of an overall value proposition that grows stronger as more companies join the set. Before a web can form, two conditions must be present: a technological standard and increasing returns. The standard reduces risk by allowing companies to make irreversible investment decisions in the face of technological uncertainty. The increasing returns create a mutual dependence that strengthens the web by drawing more and more customers and producers.

Each company is independent in a web. There are no formal ties such as joint ventures or alliances.

Companies in a web are either *shapers* who dictate events or *adapters* who endeavor to position themselves around the web to rapidly take advantage of any worthwhile opportunities. Netscape, which captured 70 percent of its market by handing out a free Internet browser,[23] has rapidly become a shaper in the field of commercializing the Internet and has lined up an impressive list of adapters (including Sun, Silicon Graphics, DEC, IBM, and Apple), who are implementing Netscape technology (see Figure 1.2).

The emergence of webs enables all participants to unbundle their business and focus only on those particular activities where they can offer unique value. Webs give participants the comfort of numbers—usually high-profile companies—which spreads the risk. This did not happen in the mainframe or minicomputer era when companies like IBM, DEC, Honeywell, and Burroughs each went their separate way with proprietary technology.

To pitch for the leadership of a web is a bold strategy and not without risk, but the rewards can be substantial. Consider the case of Novell. By the mid 1980s Novell's local area network (LAN) products were very successful. They had achieved a 40 percent share of the market and this

FIGURE 1.2

The Netscape Web

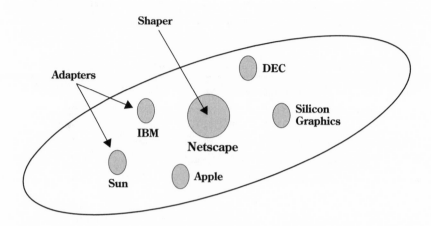

represented 70 percent of the company's revenue, but the company saw its future in software, not hardware products. To shape a new web around its Netware operating system, it decided to write off its networking products. This demonstrated its commitment to its chosen software strategy and paved the way for other web participants to cash in on the market opportunity for hardware and other products. Novell shares knowledge with its web participants and gives them access to proprietary technology, which enables them to add value to the core product (Netware). The result has been a stunning success. Between 1986 and 1994, Novell increased its market share in LAN operating software from 40 to 75 percent, and its revenues rose from $120 million to $2 billion.[24]

Webs encourage innovation as each player looks for added value niches. It is unlikely that software packages such as spreadsheets (Visicalc with the Apple II and Lotus 1-2-3 with the IBM PC) and desktop publishing packages (associated with the Macintosh) would have flowered so quickly without the web structure. The web shapers look to drive the web forward, allowing much of the peripheral value to be spread around the participants.

The well-known story of the IBM PC offers a salutary lesson for web shapers. IBM was always derided as the archetype monolithic corporation at the mercy of nimble fast-moving flexible competitors. But when the Apple PC was launched in the late 1970s, the giant astounded the corporate world by responding with great speed and agility to launch a rival PC within fifteen months. Indeed this rival established a whole set of standards that drove the industry for the next fifteen years. But to achieve these breakthroughs, the company formed a number of alliances with makers of peripherals, microprocessor companies, and software develop-ers. However, instead of retaining the core value of the web, it gave away the crown jewels to Intel and Microsoft and allowed them to take over the mantle of standard setters and profit makers. IBM's profits from the PC have been minimal (the cost of this mistake is reckoned to be $90 billion in lost market capitalization[25]). Successful web shapers have usually invested heavily in their own internal competencies. In fact they use their position at the center of the web to leverage their own knowledge-based capabilities. Microsoft, for example, captures only 4 percent of its web revenues, which are now estimated to be worth $66 billion.[26]

Web strategies present different performance perspectives to com-panies whether they be shapers or adapters. For example, web shapers might judge their performance not only from within their own corpo-rate boundaries, but also from the perspective of the web as a whole entity. Similarly, investment and marketing decisions take on a web role rather than a narrow business unit focus. Adapters must choose which web to join and hope that they choose wisely, as their decision could make or break the company (as many Apple web participants know to their cost).

Webs are also starting to form around customer segments. Readers Digest and a number of credit-card companies have recently created webs around their customer lists. Market-based webs are also forming around a particular customer transaction or relationship. Some mortgage providers, for example, are building webs around the buying and selling of residential mortgages.

The emergence of webs has not only shaken business strategy to its roots but upset traditional business economics, which to a large degree is predicated on the laws of diminishing returns. But, as we noted earlier, American economist Brian Arthur has discovered that webs can (and often do) lead to *increasing returns*.[27] Notes Arthur:

> Increasing returns are the tendency for that which is ahead to get fur-ther ahead, for that which loses advantage to lose further advantage.... Increasing returns generate not equilibrium but instability: If a product or a company or a technology—one of many competing in a market—gets ahead by chance or clever strategy, increasing returns can magnify this advantage, and the product or company or technology can go on to lock in the market. More than causing products to become standards, increasing returns cause businesses to work differently, and they stand many of our notions of how business operates on their head.

According to John Hagel III, "Webs may represent the opening salvo in the transition from industrial-age to information-age strategies."[28] Webs will be a growing feature of the third wave.

A Sprint or a Marathon?

Strategy is neither formulated in a vacuum nor produced as a result of some clever computer model that simulates all possible outcomes. It is rooted in experience and assumptions, usually forged in the first flush of sustained managerial success, and then laid down in procedures, systems, and working practices. These evolve into a behavioral context, or "the way we do things around here." But at some future point these accepted practices become out of kilter with the external environment. The story is familiar. Companies such as GM, IBM, and Sears develop a finely tuned synthesis between their competencies and their customers— a strong, watertight synthesis that survives for two or three generations (including a depression and a world war)—only to see it ruptured when fundamental assumptions about managerial philosophies, lines of authority, and measures and rewards are suddenly found wanting as new competitors and emerging technologies change the rules. Not only do competencies turn to rigidities, but the whole philosophy of business is unhinged as new realities place their very survival at risk. Fortunately, these particular organizations were strong enough to survive the shock and withstand the painful period of reconstruction, a process that can take a whole generation with no guarantee of final success. Alas, business history is littered with the bones of those companies that never made it.

Contrary to the impression given in many books, in which one company or another is seen (with hindsight) to have read the signposts to the future better than its rivals, strategy is not a once-and-for-all flash of genius. It is a constant battle for survival that must be judged over an extensive period. It is more a marathon than a sprint. How many "excellent" companies listed in Peters and Waterman's 1982 book *In Search of Excellence* remain at the top of the pile? Very few. Over what period should success be judged? Two, five, twenty, fifty, one hundred years? Can we reasonably compare the strategic record of young companies such as Dell, The Body Shop, Southwest Airlines, Microsoft, Intel, and Direct Line with that of more mature companies such as Ford, IBM, Motorola, HP, and Marks and Spencer? After all, the younger group has likely faced only one major strategic decision, whereas the older group has faced many. Moreover, wouldn't you expect the entrepreneurial flair and the level of strategic risk taking to be different in the first group compared with the second? And will the companies in the younger group continue to prosper once their founders have gone? Apple Computer without Jobs and Wozniak was soon derailed, despite the efforts of John Sculley, one of the best professional managers of his day. Making the transition from visionary founders to professional managers is incredibly hard and invariably changes the climate for strategy making. Owners are often willing to bet the business. Managers seldom are.

Strategy is also rooted in a business philosophy that defines a company's purpose. To put it simply: Do managers see their primary role as meeting the short-term demands of shareholders or ensuring the long-term survival of the company? Or put another way: Do they see the company as a profit-maximizing entity whose soul belongs to the market, or do they see a social organization whose soul is rooted in community values? Perhaps a more practical test question would be this: When the going gets tough, do managers eliminate people to save factories and equipment, or do they eliminate assets to save people? Long-term survivors know that assets can't learn and adapt, whereas people can. Surviving over many generations essentially means placing people rather than assets (and short-term profits) at the center of strategy. Judging by the average life span of most companies (fewer than twenty years), it appears that the profit-maximizing philosophy has been in the ascendancy. By 1983, one-third of the 1970 Fortune 500 companies had disappeared, having been acquired, merged, or broken up into smaller pieces. This is a telling indictment of corporate strategy in the latter phase of the second wave.

There are important lessons to be learned from those companies that have survived over many generations. Arie de Geus spent a lifetime at Royal/Dutch Shell, retiring in 1989 as group-planning controller. In 1983 he was part of a team that studied how older companies survive. The team found twenty-seven major companies worldwide that were more than one hundred years old and had well-documented histories, including DuPont, Kodak, Mitsui, Sumitomo, and Siemens. The team discovered four common characteristics that contributed to these companies' longevity: first, they adopted conservative financing policies; second, they constantly adapted to the changing competitive environment; third, their employees had a strong sense of belonging; and fourth, they tolerated new ideas, especially experiments and eccentricities that furthered their understanding. The most dramatic example is the Swedish company Stora, currently a major paper, pulp, and chemical manufacturer, which began as a copper mine more than 700 years ago. Over the intervening period, Stora survived the Middle Ages, the Reformation, the wars of the 1600s, the Industrial Revolution, and the two world wars of the twentieth century. Its business evolved from copper to forest exploitation, iron smelting, hydropower, and, eventually, paper, wood pulp, and chemicals.

Even more interesting were the managerial traits shared by the twenty-seven companies. The overarching purpose was to hand over a healthy company from one generation to the next. To achieve that, notes de Geus,

"A manager must let people grow within a community that is held together by clearly stated values. The manager, therefore, must place commitment to people before assets, respect for innovation before devotion to policy, the messiness of learning before orderly procedures, and the perpetuation of the community before all other concerns." Each company operated flexible systems of control that gave people the space and freedom to develop ideas without punishing failure. But perhaps their most important shared attribute is the ability to learn. As new technologies emerged, markets shifted, and customer needs changed, these companies were all able to alter marketing strategies, product ranges, organizational forms, and technology platforms.[29]

What does this tell us about strategy in the third wave? The first lesson is that behavioral context is all important. Strategy must incorporate a sense of organizational purpose. For a firm to survive from one generation to the next it must look beyond the narrow economic model that pervaded management thinking through the second wave. Those strategy makers who see their roles as agents of economic opportunity may well satisfy their shareholder masters in the short term, but they will do so at the expense of longer-term survival. However, those who see their companies as both social and economic entities with a sense of long-term destiny and community spirit will likely pass a different and more worthwhile strategic test. Employees who feel a strong sense of belonging and identify closely with a given set of values are more likely to respond positively to alliances and webs, where each firm remains independent, than to mergers or takeovers, where clashes of cultures and values are inevitable. That is why so few mergers and takeovers are successful.

The second lesson is that good strategy evolves continuously as the competitive environment changes. This lesson rings true particularly when major changes in technology reshape the environment. Otherwise today's success will turn into tomorrow's failure in the same way today's core competencies can turn into tomorrow's core rigidities. Theodore Levitt, writing forty years ago, had this warning for any organization who thinks that its destiny is preordained or that its industry will last into the foreseeable future. He was writing about the American railroads.

> Even after the advent of automobiles, trucks, and airplanes, the railroad tycoons remained unperturbably self-confident. If you had told them 60 years ago that in 30 years they would be flat on their backs, broke, and pleading for government subsidies, they would have thought you totally demented. Such a future was simply not considered possible. It was not even a discussible subject, or an askable question, or a matter which any sane person would consider worth speculating about. The very thought was insane. Yet a lot of insane notions now have matter-of-fact acceptance—for example, the idea of 100-ton tubes of metal moving

smoothly through the air 20,000 feet above the earth, loaded with 100 sane and solid citizens casually drinking martinis—and they have dealt a cruel blow to the railroads.[30]

The third lesson is that managers must keep learning by asking searching questions of the business— its products, markets, and operating models. Drucker's advice is to practice what he calls "abandonment." Every three years an organization should challenge every product, every service, every policy, every distribution channel with the question, If we were not in it already, would we be going into it now? This tests basic assumptions and forces managers to ask, Why didn't this work, even though it looked so promising when we went into it five years ago? Is it because we made a mistake? Is it because we did the wrong things? Or is it because the right things didn't work?[31]

The past fifty years of the second wave represent a period of relative economic stability. However, as the third wave gathers pace, change is accelerating, and managers need to be constantly on their guard as new opportunities arise and new threats appear. Even the best thought-out strategies can be successful only if well executed, and this depends on the commitment of a company's employees. To maximize their contribution, employees must share a common set of values and get due recognition and reward for their efforts. While many second wave companies paid lip service to these efforts, third wave companies will quickly recognize that their employees—people—are the only sustainable asset they possess. The preeminence of shareholders in the second wave economic model will be eclipsed by the preeminence of knowledge workers in the third wave model. The likely result will be longer lasting companies and more stable communities.

Issue 2

Customer Value

Match Competencies to Customers

MANY SECOND WAVE COMPANIES HAVE BECOME highly proficient at designing and delivering products and services with high quality and reasonable prices. They have learned to compete aggressively, offer their customers good value for money, become lean and efficient, but still they have failed to keep those customers. Over the past twenty-five years, customers have become more demanding. At one time they considered only price and quality; now they want products and services with fast delivery, wide variety, state-of-the-art technology, low cost, high quality, convenience of purchase, and excellent service. Firms have responded by instigating improvement initiatives in all these areas, but while second wave managers have been thinking about improving *products* and *services* to compete more aggressively in their markets, third wave managers have been thinking about *which* customers to serve and improving the value of the products and services they offer them.

Third wave managers, in other words, match customers to their *value proposition* and, with the power of strong competencies and processes

47

behind them, continue to distance themselves from the competition. Whereas strategy is about foresight and ideas leading to a set of competencies, the value proposition is about translating those ideas into a set of deliverable promises to the customer. Issue 2 considers how this can be achieved.

Choosing the Right Value Proposition

Third wave managers are able to think like their customers. They decide which market niche to attack, build a platform of competencies to undertake the assault, and with the backing of imaginative information systems, ensure that they deliver more value than the competition. Then they continue to distance themselves from competitors by increasing this value. They believe in three important principles: first, that different customers buy different kinds of value; second, as value standards rise, so do customer expectations, so they can stay ahead only by moving ahead; and third, that having an unrivaled level of a particular value requires a superior operating model dedicated to delivering it.[2] They understand that they cannot be all things to all people. Rather than trying to compete on all aspects of product and service delivery, they choose one of three propositions on which to compete: *product leadership, operational excellence,* or *customer intimacy.* The one chosen—the *value proposition*—defines the company in the eyes of the customer. This is not to say that the other propositions should be sacrificed. Companies must at least meet industry standards in these areas. But in their chosen specialty they must exceed customer expectations and build their operating model around this formula.

Customers fall broadly into three categories (see Figure 2.1). One set of customers is interested in the latest, state-of-the-art products. Their choices are usually driven by a taste for fashion or a desire for a particular technology. Thus companies pursuing this market segment compete primarily on *product leadership.* The launch of Windows 95, for example, was a must-have product for many personal computer users. Microsoft's relationship with its customers is defined by its technical leadership position in the market. Customers see the company as innovative, regularly bringing out new high-quality products, and they like to be associated with it. Nike shoes, Hewlett-Packard printers, and Sony Walkman products all fall into this category.

A second set of customers is more interested in buying products and services on the basis of low price and convenience. These customers still demand high quality but they are not prepared to pay premium prices or go out of their way to make a purchase. They typically buy on mail order,

FIGURE 2.1

The Value Proposition

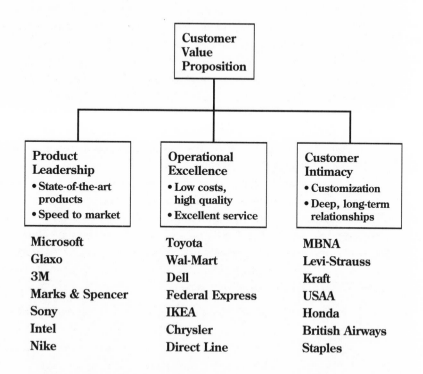

through membership warehouse clubs, and quality chain stores. They might buy their basics from Wal-Mart, their computers from Dell, and their insurance from Direct Line. Companies that define their customer value in this way compete on the basis of *operational excellence*. They must constantly increase speed and convenience and reduce costs in all their operations.

The third set of customers is interested in getting exactly what they want, even if they have to pay a higher price or wait a bit longer to get it. Such customers buy from suppliers that they can identify with their own special needs. Thus British Airways has dedicated its business to the needs of the executive traveler, and the Staples office supplies chain has identified itself with the small business customer. Customers see these companies as being responsive to their needs, and they repay this responsiveness with loyalty. Thus BA and Staples pursue a policy of *customer intimacy*—that is, they become specifically identified with the special needs of a particular niche market and satisfy it over a long period. In each case, once the value proposition has been chosen, managers must ensure that the whole company is dedicated to its pursuit and improvement and that the appropriate systems are put in place to support it.

A special word is required at this point about the management of *brands*. There is a case for looking at brand management as yet another value proposition and operating model. Indeed, for many years some companies have seen the brand itself as the reason why customers remain loyal, though they still need to pay close attention to operational excellence. They believe the primary feature of their operating model is the building of brand equity through excellent marketing, as Virgin and Swatch have done in recent years, and Coca-Cola and Marlboro have done for generations. In terms of the three value propositions, the closest fit here is with customer intimacy in that the ultimate objective of these companies is customer loyalty. We will look at brand management in more detail at the end of Issue 2.

There is nothing especially novel about defining a company's customer relationship in terms of delivering value. Marketing departments have been doing this for years. What will be different for third wave companies is the way they define value and build the corporate culture and support systems to increase such value and how they measure the results (we deal with the measurement issue at greater length in Issue 7). Treacy and Wiersema define customer value as

> ...the sum of benefits received minus the costs incurred by the customer in acquiring a product or service. Benefits build value to the extent that the product or service improves the customer's performance or experience. Costs include both the money spent on the purchase and maintenance, and the time spent on delays, errors, and the effort. Both tangible and intangible costs reduce value.

They also note that price, product quality, product features, service convenience, service reliability, expert advice, and support services can either create or destroy value for the customer. The value added or destroyed depends on how much the value exceeds or falls short of customer expectations.[3]

Building the Operating Model

Issue 1 addressed the need to identify core competencies, but core competencies alone do not determine profitability. They must be turned into winning products and services. Whereas core competencies are the springboard, the chosen value proposition and its accompanying operating model enable a company to align its processes and systems and ensure that its management culture and performance measures fulfill its promises to the customer. Figure 2.2 shows the links in the operating model.

FIGURE 2.2

The Operating Model

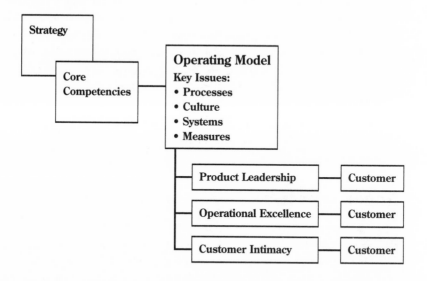

FIGURE 2.3

The Operating Model and the Value Chain

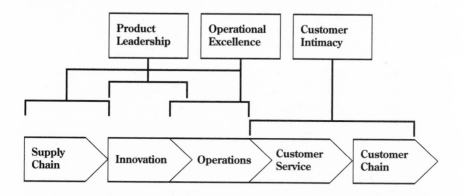

A closer look at the operating model shows how each of the three variants focuses on a different part of the value chain (see Figure 2.3). Shank has defined the value chain as "the linked set of value-creating activities all the way from basic raw materials through component suppliers to the ultimate end-use product delivered into the final consumers' hands."[4]

Although the three operating models bear similarities, each one is constructed to meet the needs of its (different) target customers. Porter notes that cost is generated by performing activities (steps within the value chain) and that cost advantage arises from performing particular activities more efficiently than competitors do. Performance of activities, then, constitutes the basic ingredients of competitive advantage.[5] The particular value proposition dictates which activities should be undertaken, and the operating model should be designed to ensure that they are performed more effectively. Thus, as Figure 2.3 illustrates, product leaders will focus on innovation activities; firms pursuing operational excellence will focus on minimizing costs throughout the supply chain and internal operations; and companies pursuing customer intimacy will focus on customer service and delivery.

Product Leadership

Companies that present themselves to the world as highly innovative must make innovation synonymous with their culture and a set of competencies that enables them to create exceptional products that sell quickly. They must measure their success in these terms. For example, 3M, which has over 60,000 products, subscribes to a primary measure known as the rule of "30 from 4"—that is, 30 percent of its sales in any year must come from products released in the previous four years. This and other mottoes such as FIDO ("first in, destroy others") help to drive the company.

Above all, companies pursuing a product leadership strategy know that to be first to market defines their success. In many industries, product life cycles and development times are shrinking rapidly. For example, fax machines, semiconductors, personal computers, and software packages have life cycles measured in months rather than years. The shorter the cycle, the less time there is available for profitable sales, and thus the fewer funds for further development. It is a vicious circle. The only way to win is to be first to market and so get the maximum length of time to reap the returns on investment. All later entrants inevitably must compete on price. According to Chris Meyer,[6] there is only one rule for these companies: "The competitor who consistently, reliably, and profitably provides the greatest value to the customer first, wins. There are no other rules."

Companies that fail to build on their core competencies and extend their leadership position soon feel the competitive effects. Lotus Development, for example, had a huge market lead with its 1-2-3 spreadsheet, which was largely synonymous with the IBM standard PC. But Lotus failed to develop its graphical capabilities. The result: Microsoft's Excel and Borland's Quattro gained a 52 percent market share within three years.

Product leaders achieve a number of benefits. For example, they have the opportunity to set industry standards. This happened with Microsoft's Windows products, Intel's microprocessors, Toshiba's laptop computers and Sony's Walkman. They also have the first option to engage the best distribution channels. It took years for the PC clones to be recognized by most major computer dealers who stocked the market leaders.

Market leaders dominate their markets by being innovative and fast. Superior development speed enables them to develop and deliver more generations of product. Thus the learning capacity of their knowledge workers is enhanced with each complete cycle. If one company takes two years to complete a development program against four years for a competitor, the first company's engineers have twice as many learning opportunities as those of competitors.

State-of-the-Art Products

Research[7] shows that innovation leads to market dominance. The following table summarizes a study of over one hundred technically related firms that confirms the correlation between the market leaders and the strongest innovators.

Position of Firm in Its Industry	Percentage of Sales from Products Introduced in the Past 5 Years
Leader in industry	49.1
Top third of industry	33.8
Middle third of industry	26.9
Bottom third of industry	10.7

Some firms believe that innovation cannot be planned, that it is inspirational or happens at random. But successful companies do not believe this. Their innovation record is based on a fine-tuned interconnecting process between competencies and customers. Boeing, for example, changed all its previous product design methods for its 777 plane by involving eight airlines in its design process. The result was a more flexible internal passenger layout and large numbers of initial orders. Customers who were involved in the process became committed to the product.

Continuous innovation of technology, especially proprietary technology, is critical if companies are to maintain their leadership positions. Olympus is a case in point. Developing "small in size" as a distinctive feature allowed Olympus to introduce the Stylus, a highly successful compact camera. Firms such as Olympus, locked into functionality-driven markets, must compete by creating products with distinctive features.

While these features do not create permanently differentiated products, they do create temporary first-mover advantages for the firm. To identify zones of technological advantage, such firms spend considerable effort on technological reviews.[8]

Many companies carry out exhaustive market research before releasing new products. This is not surprising given that less than 10 percent of all new products that start development programs are ultimately successful.[9] But for many new products with short life cycles, such expensive research is too onerous and is often not worth pursuing. Moreover, for revolutionary products like the Sony Walkman, such research is largely worthless because customers have no concept of the usefulness of the intended product. When products are the outcome of a well-founded core competence, then the costs of market research can often outweigh the benefits. Sony was simply driven by the market. If yellow products sold well in one market, they made yellow ones. If "beach" products sold, then they made more of these. If the competence platform is fast and flexible, and feedback information systems are good enough, then successful product families can be market driven. Of course, Sony also kept evolving its competencies as well as its products. Over ten years it reduced the weight of its Walkman four times, improved battery and disk-drive technology, and introduced better headphones.

Speed to Market

Profitability can be seriously affected by the length of the product life cycle. For example, a six-month delay in a life cycle of ten years means that only 5 percent of sales might be lost (although leadership could be sacrificed), but if there is the same delay within a two-year cycle, then 25 percent of sales could be lost. The only time when delays are acceptable is when a product really is revolutionary and will have no competition for some time, but such cases are becoming increasingly rare.

The secret of success in fast product development is concurrent engineering, which is reported to have cut product development times by 20 to 70 percent, boosted the productivity of knowledge workers by 20 to 100 percent, and increased sales by five to fifty times.[10] Motoo Suzuki, director of passenger car development at Mitsubishi, has said that his three thousand engineers produce three times as many new car designs as their eight thousand counterparts at Chrysler. "There is no secret to it," he says. "We bring in our suppliers and marketing people from the start, and do it together. They bring in the budget cutters."[11] (Chrysler's methods have improved, however, since this comment was made.)

Operational Excellence

Some customers buy on the basis of low cost and convenience of purchase. To respond to these preferences, competence platforms must include effective management of the supply chain and high levels of efficiency in managing inventories and logistics, but above all, suppliers must use market-driven (or "target") costing to ensure that their operating processes are fast, are efficient, and meet tough cost targets. Robin Cooper[12] has noted the demands of this approach: "Firms that adopt a confrontational strategy must become experts at developing low cost, high quality products that have the functionality customers demand.... Cost management, like quality, has to become a discipline practiced by virtually every person in the firm. Therefore overlapping systems that create intense downward pressure on all elements of costs are required."

Low Costs, High Quality

Many second wave companies have been driven into the wilderness in their vain attempts to manage costs by focusing on volume and capacity within the production process, or on contribution margin analysis within the sales process. In their efforts to compete, these companies have allowed designers to build advanced (and often unwanted) features into products with little thought as to the potential cost and quality problems. This has been particularly true of first-generation products—the assumption being that the market would stand a price premium and that later product generations could be produced at higher volumes and lower costs. Being first to market was adjudged the primary goal; cost management was someone else's problem. Japanese manufacturers have shown their ability to achieve consistent low cost and high quality. However, their success has been achieved not by ramping up volumes each time the business cycle is favorable, but by pursuing long-term stable production processes and relentlessly eliminating constraints and non-value-adding work.

Most exponents of operational excellence have one primary objective in mind: *keep operations simple.* They typically reject variety, relying on their own judgments to bring the best value products and services to the customer. Dell, for example, eschews a wide variety of products in favor of highly selective ranges, which enables them to keep high inventories, focus logistics and service operations on a small but high-volume range of merchandise, and, of course, offer the customer low prices. Procter & Gamble has also taken a leaf out of the book of simplification. When it slashed the number of product varieties in its hair-care range and thus the number of choices for its customers, it held its breath. But the strategy of simplification and price reduction on the remaining products was successful. P&G's market share for these products grew by five points.[13] The same principles of simplification also apply to buildings and equipment. Each McDonald's restaurant, for example, looks and feels the same to the customer whether it is sited in Moscow or Manchester, and Southwest Airlines always chooses the same standardized fittings for its Boeing 737s. In these organizations, employees are well trained, know exactly what to do, and thus keep waste and costs to a minimum.

In the third wave, external relationships—particularly with suppliers—will become important factors in the drive to reduce costs and speed up cycle times. Many companies are now learning this lesson, often with spectacular results. One such case is Chrysler.

In the late 1980s Chrysler was a basket case. Its development program was $1 billion over budget, it had an unfunded pension fund of $4.5 billion, and in the fourth quarter of 1989 incurred a loss of $664 million. Its turnaround since 1989 has been one of the biggest recent success stories of corporate America. Development times and costs have plunged, and its profit per vehicle has jumped from a miserable $250 in the 1980s to $2,110 in 1994, a record for any American auto company. New research by Jeffrey Dyer puts much of this change in fortunes down to its development of supplier relationships and its adoption of target costing.[14]

Prior to these changes Chrysler chose component suppliers on the basis of competitive tendering, and relationships were typically characterized by mutual distrust and suspicion. But a benchmarking exercise with Honda suggested that a different approach was worth trying. Honda's development teams were drawn from all functional disciplines and had cradle-to-grave responsibility for each vehicle. Selection of suppliers was on the basis of quality and cost targets. They were awarded long-term contracts covering the vehicle's life cycle and were intimately involved in design and cost problems. Chrysler's new management team, led by president Robert Lutz, set out to emulate Honda's methods on the new LH development program with, as it turns out, remarkable success.

It first created cross-functional teams, one for each product group. Then it built new relationships with suppliers based on trust, continuity, and coordination; the suppliers were given significant responsibility for designing components or systems. This enabled many design, engineering, and prototyping tasks to be carried out simultaneously, thus cutting time and cost. Previously, design and building of prototypes was carried out by different suppliers, often leading to "who is to blame?" disputes when quality problems arose. Management then turned its attention to target costing, initially on a trial-and-error basis. Barry Price, Chrysler's executive director of platform supply for procurement and supply comments: "We would involve suppliers and tell them, 'I've got X amount of money... Can you supply it for that cost?' Usually their response would be no, but at least they came back with some alternatives."

This approach has radically changed the cost management mentality at both Chrysler and its suppliers. Chrysler's focus on cost instead of price creates a win-win situation for both partners. Under the old regime, they simply pressured suppliers into reducing prices. Chrysler managers started to experiment further by inviting suppliers to put forward cost improvement ideas. In 1992, this evolved into a supplier rating system known as SCORE (an acronym for supplier cost reduction effort), which rewarded suppliers according to the number of ideas they proposed and savings made as a result of their implementation. For example, suppliers receive a $20,000 credit for every part removed from a system. Since 1993, Magna International, a supplier of seat systems, interior door and trim panels, and engine and transmissions systems, has submitted 213 SCORE proposals, of which 129 have been approved, resulting in cost savings of $75.5 million. Magna's sales to Chrysler have more than doubled from $625 million to $1.45 billion. As of December 1995, Chrysler had implemented thousands of ideas that produced annual savings of $1.7 billion both for the company and for its suppliers. SCORE has been a tremendous success not only in cutting costs but also in building trust and confidence between Chrysler and its suppliers. The exchange of knowledge and ideas that the system facilitates is a lesson in how knowledge sharing can lead to lower costs for all participants in the value chain.

Third wave companies will forge closer links with strategic suppliers and customers. Wal-Mart's success is based firmly on its computer links between stores and suppliers, and Federal Express has built tracking systems that enable so-called virtual post offices to be available at both ends of the transaction so that sender and receiver can monitor deliveries. Many firms now will accept orders only via computer links. Technology is also transforming how companies link with their distribution channel partners to jointly expand market share and improve quality and service. For example, Frito-Lay's investment in world-class information systems enables managers to "see" across the value chain so that marketing, sales, manufacturing, logistics, and finance can be viewed as an integrated whole.[15] It also provides managers with information on customers, suppliers, and competitors. The primary source of this information is FL's own employees. They collect data on stores' sales and on the performance of competitors' products. This information is then analyzed to produce scheduling and inventory requirements and promotion plans.

Some firms are now moving even further toward integration with their suppliers via virtual computer networks. McDonnell Douglas,[16] for example, has built a network whereby designs, technical drawings, contracts, and competitive bids can be shared with suppliers. The savings in time and cost have been dramatic. Moreover, each participating supplier need not invest in special technology. A secure network group within the broad structure of the Internet is all that's needed. McDonnell Douglas's software partner, AeroTech, manages the network ensuring that all data is secure and that all participants can communicate effectively.

Excellent Service

While it is essential for companies pursuing a strategy of operational excellence to achieve low cost, they must also make transactions easy for their customers. GE's electrical appliance division and Caterpillar's service operation show how the manufacturer-dealer-customer relationship can be dramatically improved by the imaginative use of technology.

GE reinvented its electrical appliance business around the idea of a virtual warehouse.[17] Traditionally, the GE sales force would endeavor to meet its end-of-quarter targets by offering special deals that the distribution partner often didn't need. The knock-on effect was felt by consumers who were pressured into buying the model stocked by the dealer rather than their own preference. Dealers were also badly mauled by low-price multibrand stores such as Circuit City, which competed on the basis of a wide product range with excellent stock availability and low prices (via its bulk-purchasing capability). GE's innovation was to connect the dealer directly to its own computerized stock lists so that the dealer could take a customer order, place the order directly with GE's warehouse, and have the product delivered within twenty-four hours. Thus in the eyes of the consumer the dealer's stock comprised not the "back room" but the stock in GE's own warehouse. In return for this service the dealer had to commit to giving GE 50 percent of its business, and the 12 percent savings on distribution and marketing costs enabled GE to reduce costs and increase margins to competitive levels.

Caterpillar is another company that has used technology to improve customer service by providing a "seamless" service through its dealers to the final customer. Its worldwide computer network integrates all information from dealers and can schedule and ship parts within twenty-four hours. Caterpillar is also testing a new direct-link computerized system that will cut the combined inventories between company and dealers, save time to repair, and improve customer loyalty. Through remote sensors on its earthmoving equipment, local centers can monitor the condition of any machine part. If a problem occurs, the local field technician's portable PC is alerted. The technician then logs into the global information system, sources the part, and agrees with the customer on a suitable time for fitting. Within hours of the alert the part has been fitted and the prospect of machine downtime avoided. Furthermore, the company's database has been updated with valuable information from which designers can learn how to improve future products.[18]

Customer Intimacy

The final set of customers want customized products and high levels of service. Firms pursuing this approach of customer intimacy have one objective in mind—to keep customers for life. Recent research has shown a strong *negative correlation* between market share and customer satisfaction.[19] According to one source, "One way to increase customer satisfaction is to deliver products designed to better meet the needs of more homogenous targets, rather than trying to deliver a product designed to meet the needs of a larger group of people."[20] This is exactly what companies pursuing customer intimacy set out to achieve.

According to Frederick Reichheld, customer loyalty has done wonders for investors. Credit card company MBNA has based its core competence on building a base of loyal customers. Notes Reichheld:

> Since becoming a separate company in 1990, MBNA's return on equity has approached 30 percent after taxes, and earnings per share have grown at 18 percent per year. Since 1982, MBNA has surged from thirty-eighth to second place in total bankcard balances. To what does Charlie Cawley, MBNA's founder, attribute this extraordinary performance? The answer is printed in large letters on the cover of his annual report: "Success Is Getting the Right Customers…and Keeping Them."[21]

At MBNA a 5 percent increase in the retention of customers grows the company's profits by 60 percent by the fifth year.[22] Clearly, loyalty-based strategies work. While many credit card companies rely on broadbrush mailing programs, MBNA targets specific affinity groups such as sports clubs, universities, and other associations, usually comprising members with above-average earnings. Currently the company produces Visas and Mastercards for 4,300 such groups, usually with personal logos, and the average balance held by its cardholders is three times the national average.[23]

Customization

Technology is enabling companies to offer personal customization as never before; and the more it is offered, the more people want it. Take Levi-Strauss.[24] A woman who wants a perfectly fitting pair of jeans can now go to one of Levi's Personal Pair outlets where a computer will pick out exactly the right size. The woman's specifications are sent to Levi by computer, and her made-to-measure jeans arrive a few days later. The price premium is modest—just $10 more than standard. Levi plans to introduce the system to nearly 200 stores in America by the end of the decade. This approach is part of the company's strategy to reestablish its brand against tough competition from the private-label producers. Moreover, this level of customization and delivery is becoming global.

Take also The National Bicycle Industrial Co. of Japan (which makes bikes for Panasonic). It can assemble by hand over 11 million possible varieties of custom-made bicycles in lots of one, and deliver via air express to any address in the world. Though it uses modern technology, the manufacturing process remains craft based. The factory looks like a traditional workshop with employees hand-wiring gears and silk-screening the customer's name on the frame. The company has transformed mass production into flexible *personalized* manufacturing.[25]

Andersen Windows is another example of a company that has reconciled mass production with mass customization. Until recently Andersen made a range of standard windows in large batches, but more and more customers demanded unique designs. Trying to keep up with demand was a nightmare. The product range increased from 28,000 to 86,000 and fifteen page quotes were not unusual. An increase in errors damaged the company's quality reputation. The answer was to issue distributors and retailers an interactive electronic catalog and design package. Now dealers can process orders in one-fifth the time, and the direct links with Andersen's production system mean that turnaround time has improved and error rates have plummeted. Although the product list has grown to 188,000, fewer than one in 200 van loads contains an error. The company can now produce in lots of one and exactly satisfy customer requirements.[26]

USAA, a loyalty leader with a staggering 98 percent customer retention rate, has built its entire business around loyalty management.[27] USAA sells insurance to particular groups such as military officers, who are often moved either nationally or internationally at short notice. Military officers are not very profitable customers for most insurers, but USAA has a 95 percent share of their business. The system is underpinned by a centralized database and telephone sales force that customers can access from anywhere in the world. This system, rather than a distributed network of agents, keeps contact with the customer and thus a long-term relationship is created. Investment in detailed customer profiles that help employees to tailor products and services precisely to customer needs has enabled USAA to target a number of highly segmented markets. For example, it prepares special policies for boat owners. But more than this, it has used its depth of information on customers to provide financing packages for particular needs and to offer other products (such as cars and jewelry) to the customer base.[28] In 1995, revenues increased 7 percent to $6.6 billion and net income surged to $730 million.[29]

Deep, Long-Term Relationships

Companies that compete primarily on long-term relationships with their customers cannot succeed without total commitment to their workforce. In other words, the bonds between supplier and customer are, more often than not, bonds between *employees* and customers. As one article commented: "In companies that are truly customer-oriented, management has designed (or redesigned) the business to support frontline workers' efforts and to maximize the impact of the value they create. New job definitions and compensation policies are critical parts of these redesigned systems. So are new organization structures and systems. The product is economic performance that is startling compared with the performance of traditional industry competitors."[30]

Perhaps IBM in the 1960s and 1970s was the arch exponent of creating and maintaining this kind of value proposition. Customers totally depended on their equipment and expertise, and this dependability, together with a commitment throughout IBM's workforce to providing excellent service, built a rich seam of profitability. While building customer relationships and sustaining them over extended periods is a tough assignment in any business, in a large airline it is especially difficult. To have done so is the measure of British Airways' achievement over the past ten years. In a recent interview,[31] its chairman, Sir Colin Marshall, noted that the extra competitive edge that these policies have generated has added about 5 percent to BA's revenues, or about $400 million per annum. He also notes that "anyone can fly airplanes, but few organizations can excel in serving people. Because it's a competence that's hard to build, it's also hard for competitors to copy or match." BA's mission statement sets out its creed: "To ensure that British Airways is the customer's first choice through the delivery of an unbeatable travel experience."

BA organizes its business around seven "brands," which represent its various customer segmentations (Concorde, First Class, Club Europe, Club World, Euro Traveller, World Traveller, and Domestic Shuttle Service). These brands are managed rather like those of a consumer-goods producer and refreshed by BA's own initiatives at periodic intervals. For example, first class and club class passengers can enjoy the innovative arrivals facilities at many U.K. airports, where they can receive overnight messages, use showers, have breakfast, and so on. These facilities are used by 200 people per day and have unquestionably played a part in boosting premium business. The sleeper service introduced on transatlantic flights has increased first-class bookings by 25 percent since its introduction in February 1995.

While other airlines are setting out to cut costs, BA is enhancing services. Moreover, while other carriers more readily give customers an upgrade to a higher class as a "sweetener," BA will not dilute its brand segmentation by having two passengers in the same segment paying vastly different prices.

BA keeps a constant check on its own performance through its marketplace performance unit. This unit is completely separate from, and therefore independent of, the marketing, selling, and operating side of the business. Its role is to measure performance through the eyes of the customer and compare BA's standards with those of competitors. Employees are totally involved in the service package. Says Marshall, "Our employees want to be proud of their product and they want to feel that they are making a difference to customers. When competitors surpass our product, and especially when customers tell them so, our employees become upset. They are very vocal in letting management know about such situations. They want to be part of a winning team."

Brand Loyalty

Another way to build customer intimacy is through brand identity and ultimately brand loyalty. Enhancing the brand identity almost becomes the operating model itself, and a company's processes (especially that of marketing), culture, systems, and measures are geared to achieving this goal. For companies such as Coca-Cola, Phillip Morris, McDonald's, Disney, and Guinness, the value of the brand equity equates closely with the value of the business itself (IBM's brand value crashed in the early 1990s at the same time its profits fell through the floor). Some companies, however, have built closer relationships with customers through involving them more directly with brand images. The Body Shop and Cadbury are two examples.

The Body Shop has associated itself with animal rights, aid (through trade) to the third world, and a variety of other causes. Its *profits-with-a-principle* philosophy involves both employees and customers alike, and its brand image is thus constantly reinforced. It recruits employees who passionately believe in these values, and it attracts a large following of equally impassioned customers (especially among the young) who support these causes. The result is a clear identity in the marketplace and a loyal customer base based on deep-rooted conviction—a tough relationship for competitors to beat.

Cadbury has involved its customers in a different way: by opening a theme park known as Cadbury World and treating visitors to a historical guide to chocolate making. This British theme park has quickly achieved international recognition and now attracts 450,000 visitors each year, greatly adding to the brand awareness of Cadbury's products and undoubtedly contributing to Cadbury being named Britain's most admired company in 1996. Both The Body Shop and Cadbury have set out to identify the customer with the brand and build a relationship that cannot be achieved by media marketing alone.

Evolve the Model Continually

Ask any manager today if his or her company is "customer led" and the reply is likely to be yes. Listening to the voice of the customer is of course important, particularly when it comes to service and efficiency, but few customers have real foresight. In a recent interview Hewlett-Packard CEO Lewis Platt noted:

> Most of our customers have a hard time describing their needs and possible solutions. Sometimes they don't suggest a solution because they don't understand what it takes to meet their needs; other times, they assume certain limitations exist. The trick is to really listen to customers and turn what they say into something actionable. If we can get that imaginative understanding, we can almost figure out how to meet a customer's needs or even go beyond.[32]

In other words, market surveys are of little help in predicting the future. Managers must work it out for themselves. What demand was there ten years ago for global computer networks, video conferencing, or telephone-based insurance services? Sony created a whole new market for portable hand-held music systems. It anticipated that customers would buy them once they could appreciate the benefits, but Sony did not ask customers if they wanted them.

Every market leader is a target for imitation and is vulnerable to imaginative competitors willing to challenge the existing rules of the industry. Competencies and operating models must be constantly improved even if this means denying easy short-term profits. How many companies would introduce new products long before existing *profitable* products have reached their "sell-by" date? Hewlett-Packard, Motorola, Intel, and Canon do this regularly. They compete with themselves to stay alive. Too many companies spend the valuable time of their best people supporting yesterday's products and starving tomorrow's opportunities of essential resources. GE goes further than most with its policy of shedding any business, whether profitable or not, that does not fit its vision of the future. Canon believes in "creative destruction." Even though

Canon's first laser printer had more than 80 percent of the market, front-line managers did not hesitate to support the development of a printer based on bubble-jet technology accidentally created in its own labs. The fact that the new printer would sell at half the price and generate lower margins was no barrier.[33]

Well-thought-out value propositions can last for a number of years, sometimes for decades. But the third wave economy carries many new traps for today's unsuspecting high flier. How will retailers such as Wal-Mart deal with home shopping, and PC/TV companies such as Hewlett-Packard and Sony with the all-in-one home entertainment center? Strong core competencies and improving operating models are the best protection, but managers cannot afford to lower their guard.

Issue 3

Knowledge Management

*Leverage
Knowledge for
Competitive
Advantage*

In the information age, a company's survival depends on its ability to capture intelligence, transform it into usable knowledge, embed it as organizational learning, and diffuse it rapidly throughout the company. In short, information can no longer be abstracted and stored at the corporate level, it must be distributed and exploited as a source of competitive advantage.[1]

Christopher Bartlett and
Sumantra Ghoshal

IT IS RATHER IRONIC THAT AS THE INFORMATION age finally closes in around us, organizations are becoming more dependent on *people* than ever before. Even today's most powerful computers can't match the intelligence of a worm. Their increasing ability to capture, process, and distribute highly structured information is a wonder of the age, but businesses still require the intelligence and experience of human beings to turn that information into useful knowledge and good decisions. As Peter Drucker noted, "knowing how a typewriter works does not make you a writer. Now that knowledge is taking the place of capital as the driving force in organizations worldwide, it is all too easy to confuse data with knowledge and information technology with information."[2]

While this has long been the case, the difference in the third wave is that advanced technology has dealt organizations a new deck of cards with which to leverage people's knowledge onto a much higher competitive plateau. Whether it be improving competencies and processes, facilitating more decentralized decision making, improving customer support, winning important orders, or reducing mistakes and missed opportunities, the application of knowledge is playing an ever increasing role in organizational success.

Consulting firms such as McKinsey and Andersen Consulting are reorganizing their processes around knowledge management systems; service firms such as the Swedish insurance company Skandia AFS and Canadian Imperial Bank of Commerce are similarly rethinking their business practices; and manufacturing companies such as Hewlett-Packard, GE Lighting, Dow Chemicals, and Monsanto are beginning to capture and utilize their knowledge assets in more purposeful ways. All these companies and many others have appointed knowledge managers whose roles are to identify, protect, and maximize knowledge-based assets or "intellectual capital." These roles are not peripheral—they have full management support and form a central plank of strategic and competitive programs.

Like any other investment program, however, knowledge management can be expensive: it requires large investments in technology, systems, and people. McKinsey & Co. has long dedicated 10 percent of its revenues to developing and managing intellectual capital, and industrial chemicals company Buckman Laboratories spends 7 percent of its revenues on knowledge management.[3] Rather like total quality management, however, cost is just one side of the equation. Managers must also question the cost of not knowing: How much does it cost when an organization continuously loses what people know, fails to inform people of valuable experience elsewhere, or is too slow to respond to a customer problem?

The promoters of knowledge management are not helped when the fruits of their efforts go unrecognized on the balance sheet. This condition may seem surprising because many companies have begun to recognize that long-term success depends on the accumulation and productive use of knowledge-based or intellectual assets. But how can managers be fully cognizant of the value they are creating (or destroying) if intangible assets are not measured? To many accountants this is an intractable problem. How do you value intellectual capability, skills, competencies, and the strength of the customer base? How can you audit numbers that don't derive from market-based transactions? These may be hard questions to answer, given the present state of accounting practice, but they will not disappear. Far from it. As intangible assets increasingly dominate corporate worth, investors and managers will increase their demands for more information on these assets. These concepts are discussed in more detail in Issue 8.

Knowledge-based competitive advantage can occur in many ways. For example, hotels can now create personal profiles of guests and ensure that their special needs are looked after across their global network.

Credit-card companies can monitor spending patterns and detect potential fraud or misuse. Maintenance engineers and medical practitioners can solve problems using special knowledge-based diagnostic systems. Among the smart products arriving on the market are clothes that react to temperature changes, cars that can inform drivers about tire pressures and road traffic problems, and television guides that can suggest a suitable viewing schedule for a user's particular tastes. Consumers will increasingly use computers for shopping, banking, investing, and communications without leaving the comfort of their own homes. The digital world is changing how we work, play, and interact with others. Soon this world will be virtual. We will be able to enter virtual shopping malls, virtual entertainment centers, and virtual investment banks.

The knowledge-based organization will also be able to monitor the performance of its key processes. For example, it will track how much value-adding work is being performed by its business units, teams, and employees; which services are valued by particular customers (and how much extra they will be prepared to pay); why customers defect; and which suppliers provide the best quality. In other words, when knowledge is applied to business processes it is the why, where, when, and how questions that will be answered—and not merely the final accounting result.

Although there is much talk of the benefits of managing knowledge, few companies have yet been able to tie tangible results to these programs. Indeed, many remain skeptical. It is hardly surprising that, at this early stage, there are more questions than answers. What are intellectual assets? How do we acquire and measure them? How do we improve the knowledge-based capabilities of our workforce and use this knowledge effectively in the pursuit of competitive advantage? These are some of the questions we will now address.

Managing Knowledge—The Problem of Definition

Knowledge management has been described as "making the most effective use of the intellectual capital of a business. It involves *wiring together* the brains of appropriate people so that sharing, reasoning, and collaboration become almost instinctive and a part of everyday work."[4] Looking at an organization as being knowledge-based represents one of the fundamental shifts to third wave thinking. Making this shift, however, means a complete overhaul in traditional management approaches (such as the recruitment, employment, and management of knowledge workers) and performance measurement (challenging such notions as return on capital and budgetary control). A recent article put these issues in perspective when it noted that "what's at stake is nothing less than learning how to operate and evaluate a business when knowledge is its chief resource and result."[5] Some companies now describe themselves as "learning organizations." According to David Garvin, such an organization is "skilled at creating, acquiring, and transferring knowledge, and at modifying its behavior to reflect new knowledge and insights."[6]

Defining Knowledge and Intellectual Assets

The new language of the knowledge-based company, intelligent enterprise and learning organization can be somewhat confusing. Terms such as "intellectual assets (or capital)" are frequently used interchangeably with "knowledge-based assets," "information-based assets," and "intangible assets." There are basic two distinctions to make. The first is *knowledge and learning,* which concerns how organizations and individuals acquire, disseminate and deploy knowledge, and how cultural and technological forces can help or impede this process. The second defines the *collective body of intangible assets* that can be listed, measured, and (with difficulty) valued.

Unlike information, knowledge itself is a fuzzy concept concerned with human cognition and awareness. Knowing a fact is little different from knowing a skill, but knowing how someone (perhaps a customer or competitor) might react to a piece of information requires human intuition and judgment. It is this combination of context, memory, and cognitive process that separates human knowledge from any other form (such as knowledge-based systems). Moreover, there are two types of knowledge: *explicit knowledge* (skills and facts that can be written down and taught to others) and *tacit knowledge* (skills, judgment, and intuition that people have but can't easily describe).

Quinn, Anderson, and Finkelstein suggest there are four *levels* of knowledge that need to be recognized: (1) Cognitive knowledge (or know-what) derives from basic training and certification; (2) advanced skill (know-how) translates book learning into effective execution; (3) systems understanding (know-why) builds on the first two and leads to highly trained intuition—for example, the insight of a seasoned research director who knows which projects to support; and (4) self-motivated activity (care-why), which drives creative groups to outperform groups with greater physical or financial resources. They suggest that the first three levels can also exist in the organization's systems, databases, or operating technologies, but the fourth can derive only from its culture.

Yet most enterprises focus virtually all their training attention on developing basic skills and little or none on systems or creative skills.[7] We will develop these important points a little later.

Intellectual assets are more readily definable. According to Quinn:

> Most companies see their patents, copyrights, and trademarks as assets, and many even carry them that way in their capital accounts, but at cost rather than market values. However, the majority of most companies' knowledge assets lie elsewhere, in the minds of researchers, engineers, production workers, marketing people, functional specialists, and managers. Others are embedded in the myriad software packages, databases, and information systems that codify and store the company's knowledge. Still others reside in the personal relationships, and shared knowledge patterns that cement supplier or customer continuity. The basis for almost all lies in the company's service capabilities and relationships.[8]

We can identify three types of intellectual assets:

- Human capital or competencies. These include the experience, skills and capabilities of people
- Structural or internal capital. These include patents, trademarks, and copyright; the store of knowledge in databases and customer lists; and the design and capability of information systems
- Market-based or external capital. These include the profitability and loyalty of customers and the strength of brands, licenses, and franchises.

According to Lief Edvinsson at Skandia AFS, human capital is the source of ideas and innovation but is useless without systems and channels to make it productive. It is structural capital that turns human capital into a productive and valuable asset. A *Fortune* article noted:

> Structural capital doesn't go home at night or quit and hire on with a rival.... It can amplify the value of human capital, marshaling the resources of the corporation—customer lists, talent from other departments—to support a new idea. Or it can subtract from human capital, as anyone knows who has watched the whole kludgy apparatus of his company—a rigid budget process, a snail's-paced MIS department, a turf-conscious manager—grind genius into gruel.[9]

Professor Dave Ulrich expresses the interplay between human and structural capital in a formula: "Learning capability is *g* times *g* or a business's ability to *g*enerate new ideas multiplied by its adeptness at *g*eneralizing them throughout the company."[10]

What Is Knowledge Work, and Who Are Knowledge Workers?

A recent article in *Sloan Management Review* made the following observation:

> Knowledge work's primary activity is the acquisition, creation, packaging, or application of knowledge. Characterized by variety and exception rather than routine, it is performed by professional or technical workers with a high level of skill and expertise. Knowledge work processes include such activities as research and product development, advertising, education, and professional services like law, accounting, and consulting…[and] include management processes such as strategy and planning.[11]

We take a wider view and include within our definition all workers whose jobs involve a significant element of knowledge work—that is, those who use and interpret information to make decisions.

Although knowledge workers appear in all guises, the commanding heights still belong to such professionals or specialists as researchers, software engineers, accountants, consultants, marketers, surgeons, and pilots. One of the key tasks for managers in the third wave is to release the pent-up productivity of these specialists by freeing them from the increasing burdens of administration and uncoupling them from strict cost controls that exert the wrong disciplines and provoke the wrong reactions. The time of specialists should be spent improving, sharing, and applying their knowledge for the benefit of the firm. A measurement system that encourages this productivity will likely have a major impact on corporate performance.

The rise of knowledge workers is changing the balance of power within organizations and creating new tensions and responsibilities between managers and workers. Knowledge workers no longer work simply for money; nor can they be driven by traditional financial incentive packages. Loyalty priorities will also change. First will come personal development, then one's professional loyalty, and only third will loyalty attach to the employer. Ghoshal and Bartlett suggest that a new "moral contract" will replace the traditional employment contract:

> In this new contract, each employee takes responsibility for putting in a best-in-class performance. In exchange, top management undertakes to ensure not the dependence of employment security but the freedom of each individual's employability. They do this by providing all employees with the opportunity for continuous learning and skill-updating that enhance their chances of finding a job outside the company. At the same time, they create a stimulating internal environment that not only

enables the employees to use their skills to enhance the company's competitive performance, but also motivates them to stay with the company, even though they could leave.[12]

This new moral contract is the essence of third wave management. It recognizes that knowledge and decision making no longer reside with top management but must be shared with frontline employees. Employees must increasingly look to their own education and ensure that their own development and knowledge is up-to-date and can create value for the organization. New responsibilities flow from this unwritten contract. Employees must act as entrepreneurs and decision makers; they can no longer wait for decisions to be made by remote executives. The elimination of waste and non-value-adding work and the improvement of processes and customer service are now their own responsibility—*even if such improvements mean the loss of a colleague's job.*

The change in management skills required to meet these challenges is even more dramatic. Webber[13] underscores the point: "If the job of the manager in the new economy is to eliminate fear, foster trust, and facilitate the working conversations that create new knowledge, then the authenticity, integrity, and identity of the individual turn out to be the most critical managerial assets." Managers cannot hide behind rule books and follow the tried and tested methods of their predecessors. As Webber goes on to say, "The new economy brings to center stage age-old human virtues and truths. The ultimate paradox of the new economy may be that it is not so new at all."

Sources of Knowledge

Organizations can aquire and improve their collective knowledge in various ways including learning by experimentation, from past experience (especially from past mistakes), from the experience of others, and by the acquisition of top individuals or even whole businesses. The leverage of knowledge is such that a few exceptional people can make an organization successful. Conversely, the loss of those people can cause it to decline (when the Saatchi brothers left the advertising company they built, the share price plummeted). It is therefore not surprising that high-profile knowledge-based companies like Microsoft, Merck, and McKinsey spend large sums of money and considerable amounts of time attempting to recruit the best brains available. And once the brains have joined the company, they are given intensive training, often under the guidance of mentors. This development is not confined to technical knowledge or laboratory experience. These organizations drive their top knowledge workers to solve real operational problems. Constant evaluation takes place. At Andersen Consulting only 10 percent of professional recruits go on to become partners—a process that takes nine to twelve years. Knowledge-based businesses are devoted meritocracies. Human resource managers will find themselves increasingly important members of the team as rivalry between firms will focus on acquiring the best potential "knowledge-stars" in the business. This is already happening in some investment banks and advertising agencies.

At one American steel company, Chaparral Steel, four primary learning activities create and control the knowledge necessary for its current and future operations. Three of these activities are internally focused: creative problem solving (to produce current products); implementing and integrating new methodologies and tools (to enhance internal operations); and formal and informal experimentation (to build capabilities for the future). The final activity involves importing expertise from outside.[14] These four sources of knowledge creation are illustrated in Figure 3.1

The experience of failure is perhaps the best method of learning, but it can be very expensive. According to Garvin,[15] "a productive failure is one that leads to insight, understanding, and thus an addition to the commonly held wisdom of the organization. An unproductive success occurs when something goes well, but nobody knows how or why." He quotes a story concerning IBM's legendary founder Thomas Watson, Sr., who called a young manager into his office after being told that he had lost $10 million on a risky venture. The young manager, thoroughly intimidated, began by saying, "I guess you want my resignation." Watson replied, "You can't be serious. We just spent $10 million educating you."

IBM's most successful computer, the IBM 360, arose from the failure of the Stretch computer that preceded it. Boeing's managers realized that despite much fanfare, the launches of the 737 and the 747 were far less successful than their predecessors, the 707 and the 727. The company formed a team to find out why this was the case and to document what lessons could be learned. At a later date members of this team were assigned to the launch of the 757 and the 767, which proved to be the most successful in Boeing's history. Unless past experiences are carefully analyzed, documented, and made readily available for future reference, such valuable sources of learning are lost.

Knowledge also comes from external sources, particularly suppliers, partners, customers, and other (often unconnected) organizations. The activity of looking at "best practices" within companies well known for excellence in carrying out particular processes is known as benchmarking. Customers are invaluable sources of information about competitive products and services, and suppliers can also provide useful feedback on the strength of a company's internal processes. However, learning will

FIGURE 3.1
Knowledge Creating Activities

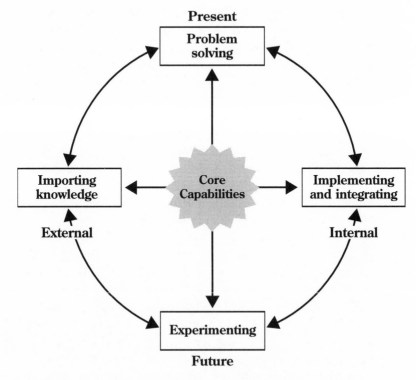

SOURCE: Dorothy Leonard-Barton, *Wellsprings of Knowledge* (Boston: Harvard Business School Press, 1995), 9. Reprinted by permission of Harvard Business School Press.

take place only if feedback is documented as it is received and not doctored to reflect personal views or biases.

Knowledge can also be shared between companies, particularly in joint ventures. Merck, for example, has formed separate alliances with both Du Pont and Johnson & Johnson. By pooling investments and sharing risks, each partner gains access to a wider group of knowledge workers, and by achieving critical mass in research may well achieve breakthroughs that on their own would be unlikely. According to Judy Lewent, Merck's CFO, "in creating a joint-venture company, you share as a partner but preserve an autonomous entrepreneurial view, a different outlook than if you acquired a company and brought it in-house. Du Pont Merck research is Du Pont Merck research. It is not Merck research."[16]

Managing Knowledge—The Learning Problem

Learning in the first wave agricultural economy was based on the teachings of the church and was concentrated on children up to fourteen years of age. In the second wave industrial economy it was taken over by governments and aimed at children and young adults between the ages five and twenty-two. In both cases such a learning process gave a person most of what he or she needed for the rest of his or her working life. In the third wave knowledge economy, however, learning will have to be continuous (some experts reckon that knowledge is doubling every seven years). In certain technology-based industries it is changing so rapidly that by the time some students reach their final year of study, the knowledge gained in the first year is already out of date. For companies to stay competitive and for workers to remain employable, they must engage in a continuous learning process.[17] But this poses a problem: How do people within complex organizations really learn?

The recent approach to managing knowledge has fallen into two broad camps or schools of thought. On the one hand we have the *information school*, which believes that knowledge is comprised of objects that can be identified within information systems; on the other hand we have the *behavioral school*, which sees knowledge management as a dynamic process within which skills and know-how are constantly changing. The information school, which has its roots in computing, artificial intelligence, systems management (especially groupware), and reengineering, sees excellent knowledge-based *systems* as the ultimate answer. The behavioral school sees the answer in first understanding human *behavior* and then winning the hearts and minds of key people. Its roots are in sociology, anthropology, psychology, and organizational behavior. The lines between these two schools of thought are somewhat blurred, but they are broadly representative of how knowledge management is now being approached.

The Information School

The information school, driven by groupware and the Internet, is currently in the ascendancy. Its advocates believe that useful knowledge comes from explicit "situational analysis"—that is, it is *objective knowledge*. They believe that this knowledge is a *resource* to be captured, analyzed, coded, and deployed for competitive advantage. While there is nothing wrong with this objective, the means of achieving it are open to question. Supporters see the problem as one of breaking down barriers to knowledge sharing in the same way reengineers see work flow as the barrier to productivity, and they emphasize system design and knowledge accessibility. They assume that if these can be improved, then benefits will flow to users. This, as we shall see, is where they part company with the behavioral school.

The information school recognizes that knowledge sharing is critical to success because intellectual assets, unlike physical assets, increase in value with use.[18] They believe in a sort of trickle-down theory of knowledge sharing and learning. In other words, if they pour enough information in at the top level (i.e., into their knowledge-based systems) enough sharing and learning will eventually pervade the lower organizational levels. Indeed, properly stimulated, knowledge and intellect grow exponentially when shared. If two people exchange knowledge with each other, both gain information and experience linear growth. But if both then share their new knowledge with others—each of whom feeds back questions, amplifications, and modifications—the benefits become exponential.

But professionals are not noted for their humility. They might respond to peer group pressure, but an external request for knowledge sharing is often given short shrift. Moreover, there is often little respect across professional disciplines even when people are working within a team with a common objective. There is also an unwritten hierarchy of knowledge work. Thus researchers (the thinkers) look down on designers (the artists) who look down on engineers (the real-world practitioners) who disdain accountants (the number crunchers). The difficulty of giving due credit to any one person or team for their knowledge contribution is also a problem.

The Japanese believe that knowledge sharing is essential to success. Indeed, their egalitarian style prevents the creation of knowledge prima donnas. Hirotaka Takeuchi, a Japanese professor of marketing, after conducting a survey into knowledge sharing in Japan, concluded that, "Innovation doesn't require genius. In the U.S. you hear people saying middle managers are dead weight, but these people play a key role in many of the Japanese companies we interviewed. Our corporate leaders are ideal driven. It's up to the frontline people to put those ideals into practice. When information is shared freely between top and middle management, knowledge spirals up and down the organization."[19] The Japanese style, however, is more akin to knowledge sharing by human interaction than to sharing through the deliberate creation of information-based systems.

Many organizations are now heading down the information systems path. Some have made heavy investments in knowledge-sharing networks such as Lotus Notes, and others have harnessed the power of the World Wide Web. However, the particular technology path chosen is not important provided its software design permits fast access to the required information. It is easy to install a networked information system, but much more difficult to distill its store of valuable information into easily accessible clusters of relevant knowledge. Early adopters such as the consulting firms have spent much of their time learning how to capture and codify information within their systems and make information clusters easily accessible to those who need them. Bain & Co. is a good example.

Bain & Co.[20] designed its system on two premises: first, it would contain only knowledge relevant to its business; and second, it would refer the user to a list of people to call if more information was needed about a particular topic. Each case team has an appointed case historian, whose job is to summarize the project (including the client problem, the approach to solving it, and the expected and actual results) in a *one-page document.* This summary is then entered onto the network; along with it are listed the case members involved. The information is deliberately limited so that anyone wishing to learn about a case must call the case members, thus encouraging not only computer networking, but also human networking. The experience of Bain & Co. demonstrates that the store of knowledge is far less important than its level and quality of use. In other words, what matters is the *productivity* of the knowledge-based system. The early experiences of many firms have not been good. Despite large investments in equipment and training, and despite exhortations from top management, few specialists have given such systems their full commitment.

The exercise of peer pressure and the recognition and rewards attached to the individual contribution for the "good of the team" are crucial factors in the adoption of knowledge-based systems. At Merrill Lynch's mergers and acquisitions group,[21] for example, individuals work on many different projects with different colleagues over the course of a year. Sometimes known as *spiders' webs*, these quick but informal responses to client situations work well, but all participants provide a confidential evaluation of one another, thus building up a picture over time of individual performance. Such spiders' webs are not dependent on geography. Computer networks with voice and video permit any number of participants across any number of countries. Such network systems and the knowledge they contain not only improve productivity, but also bond professionals to the organization by providing opportunities to expand and combine their knowledge.

Andersen Worldwide's experience is typical.[22] Andersen has recently linked its 82,000 people in 360 offices across 76 countries on a system known as "Anet." Data, voice, and video links are all available, and Andersen's professionals are able to form instant groups of professional expertise around any particular client problem. This problem-solving capability is supplemented with an extensive and well-cataloged database and with CD-ROMs that are regularly distributed around the various offices. But the initial response was disappointing. Usage picked up only when senior managers started to recognize professional contributions in all promotion and compensation reviews. Moreover, to stimulate a cultural shift toward the new technology, each morning partners would deliberately pose questions on employees' e-mail files that required immediate response. Of course even among professionals the herd instinct takes over. Once key influencers begin to use a system and sing its praises, other professionals witness this peer endorsement and begin to use it themselves.

Monsanto's agricultural group has also invested heavily in a "knowledge management architecture" using a Lotus Notes database. For example, its on-line customer and competitor database is used by all 600 employees and includes continuously updated company profiles; reports from salespeople and attendees' notes from conferences and conventions; an in-house directory of experts; and regulatory news, all cross-indexed by company, technology, and so on. According to project director, Bipin Junnarkar, "The focus shifts from 'How do I get the information I need?' to 'How do I exploit the information?'"[23]

Some Early Lessons

Most companies that have tried to manage the knowledge process have quickly realized that information input does not necessarily translate into knowledge output. Building knowledge-based systems, no matter how ingenious, does not mean that people will use them or, if they do use them, that the benefits will justify the costs. Information overload is a serious problem as designers have encouraged more communication via e-mail and more information is thrust upon users by service providers. Users are realizing that information "just in case" is both wasteful and time consuming, causing a decline rather than an improvement in performance. What they need is information "just in time," and this has caused designers to rethink their systems. The new approach is to enable users to design their own information screens with direct links to those information sources they find valuable. Thus they are separated from the barrage of (largely irrelevant) information that was previously aimed at them even though their interest in it was minimal.

Even within consulting firms packed with powerful knowledge workers, managers have had great difficulty getting wide use of networks and knowledge sharing. Some have had more success applying peer pressure and veiled threats, including the impact of nonconformance on pay and promotion. Lotus Development has gone as far as devoting 25 percent of the total performance evaluation of its customer support workers to sharing knowledge.[24] It is apparent that no matter how well the information system is designed, people are still reluctant to use it, and applying threats (particularly with knowledge workers) cuts right across the grain of third wave management.

Alan Webber[25] makes an interesting observation when he notes that it is through *conversation* that knowledge workers define the organization. Conversations, not rank or title or the trappings of power, determine who is literally and figuratively "in the loop" and who is not. At McKinsey & Co., the art of conversation has been wired into its business operations and has transformed the business into a truly interactive knowledge organization. The director of knowledge management supervises a network dedicated to providing "a marketplace of readily accessible ideas." On-call consultants are also available on a rotational basis (rather like doctors) to host conversations with or between staff members who are looking for ideas.

According to Professor Philippe Baumard of the University of Paris, understanding the differences between "knowledge" and "knowing" is an essential prerequisite in this new paradigm. Many organizations in their efforts to improve their knowledge base are simply processing more and more information. In Baumard's view, the development of intelligence capabilities should target the improvement of interpretational and sense-making skills, instead of pursuing the utopia and ubiquity of knowledge seen as a commodity. Such self-deception, he notes, "has its roots in the reproducability of information." His final comment is telling: "Making the simple complicated is commonplace; making the complicated simple, awesomely simple, that's creativity."[26] Baumard puts his finger on some of the key differences between the two schools of thought. Let's see how the behavioral school is progressing.

The Behavioral School

The behavioral school has been around for many decades, but recent research into organizational learning is providing some new insights into the problems of introducing knowledge-based systems. Edgar Schein of the MIT center for organizational learning has observed three broad but distinct subcultures running through organizations, each with its own tacit assumptions and values about what is good, bad, important, and irrelevant. This is particularly interesting when we consider how each cultural group sees the role of people within organizations. The first group—the "operator culture"—takes it for granted that people are the organization's most important asset and that they work more effectively in teams than individually. The second group—the "engineering culture"—sees people as problems (the most common source of errors) who get in the way of elegant solutions. And the third group—the "executive culture"—sees people as costs to be minimized; this group's priorities are financial results.

People within each of these cultures tend to share the same experiences, education, values, and assumptions. Thus miners, fishermen, accountants, assembly-line workers, and salespeople tend to have more in common with each other (even on a worldwide level) than with alternative cultural colleagues within their own organizations. Each of the three subcultures has gradually learned to tolerate and live with the others over the past hundred years or so (although not without turbulent periods), but when it comes to making radical changes in how organizations work (e.g., the imposition of major learning initiatives), the latent culture clashes come straight to the surface.[27] Failing to understand the different cultural perceptions is one of the principal reasons why initiatives such as reengineering or knowledge sharing are rarely successful.

Running in parallel (and sometimes cutting across) these subcultures are *communities of practice*. These are small subgroups of people who have mutual respect, share some common values, and generally get the important work done. A community of practice has been defined by Brook Manville, director of knowledge management at McKinsey, as "a group of people who are informally bound to one another by exposure to a common class of problem."[28] Communities of practice are usually small groups (no more than fifty) who've worked together for a period of time. They are not necessarily a team, a task force, or any other authorized group. They are peers in the execution of "real work." What holds them together is a common sense of purpose and a real need for each to know what the others know. Communities of practice can be found in every part of an organization, and most people belong to more than one. Companies operate through communities of practice, especially when they are interwoven within core competencies and external alliances. A community of practice in one partner will typically find affinity with a similar group in another partner. Until new ideas are safely embedded within these groups, it is safe to assume that real learning has not yet taken place. This is why classroom teaching is rarely as effective as learning on the job. In other words, the age-old systems of apprenticeship and mentoring remain the most effective methods of learning.

According to Schein, organizational learning is a three-step process. First an idea is articulated by academics (let's take McGregor's Theory X and Theory Y); then it is picked up by members of the consulting community, who sell the program to their corporate clients; and finally the program is implemented within the firm. But this is where its success or failure depends crucially on its acceptability to the communities of practice. If, for example, members of the operator culture recognize the need for real change in operations, they will attempt to learn from the consultant's prescription, but as they will likely find it incomplete or ineffective, a learning consortium emerges. The community of practice now takes over the problem, gives its stamp of approval, and the task is completed. Managers have great problems trying to understand and build any meaningful systems around this process of learning.[29] Indeed, sharing knowledge outside the community is extremely hard to enforce.

It is likely that one of the reasons why many laudable initiatives fail is because they hit these invisible barriers. Take, for example, a new reporting system (such as activity-based costing) or a new quality program. It is unlikely that either the finance or quality people will share the same community of practice as divisional managers or frontline operators. Salespeople or engineers, for example, instead of seeing such initiatives as improvements to operating capability, may well see another "flavor of the month," with more work for no extra reward (in their eyes any benefits will accrue to someone else). The battle is not with the design of new ideas and initiatives, but with cross-cultural commitment.

According to Brown and Gray, the key lesson from the behavioral approach is that learning is about work, work is about learning, and *both are social*. In other words, communities of practice are social groups built around informed participation. Consider what happened in the product design group at National Semiconductor. A community of engineers who specialize in phase-lock loops (PLL), a critical technology in some of National's most important products, began to conduct reviews of new chip designs. Groups from elsewhere in the organization would come to the PLL community to solicit its advice, and its reputation for excellence was second to none. But the PLL community couldn't simply publish the rules under which these reviews took place. The practice is embedded in the community, and the only way to learn is to become a member. Brown and Gray note:

> Organizations are webs of participation. Change the patterns of participation, and you change the organization.... At the heart of participation is the mind and spirit of the knowledge worker. Put simply, you cannot compel enthusiasm and commitment from knowledge workers. Only workers who choose to opt in—who voluntarily make a commitment to their colleagues—can create a winning company.[30]

After a new CEO (Gil Amelio) arrived at National in 1991, the company reorganized itself for growth and pursued a strategy of product leadership, with communities of practice as the centerpiece. In May 1994, the PLL community of practice was the first to be recognized in the company. Its charter was to make its know-how in circuit design accessible; to spread the word about notable product successes and failures; and to continue building National's PLL competence. The PLL community does not report to anyone; it is more of a members' club run for its own benefit, but it often executes the firm's most important work. Another successful community of practice at National focused on communication signal processing; it includes engineers from a variety of product lines. Carefully built over 18 months, this community has gained a powerful voice in the company's strategy. National now wants to extend the community program across the company and has created a community of practice council to provide advice and support for others.

Few managers recognize or understand these communities of practice. Their bonding is social as well as technical, and they are the veins and arteries of competencies and processes. This is where learning either takes place or it doesn't. But as Susan Stucky of the Institute for Research on Learning points out, communities of practice are not inherently good. They are simply a recognition of how things work in organizations, not how we would like them to work. The same observations will explain the social dynamics of a drug gang as much as they explain a successful product development team. She also notes that in a reorganization it's pretty easy to cut right through a community of practice and not even know you've done it.[31] There are many important lessons for the third wave manager in the current research into organizational learning, not the least of which is that people do not resist change so much as they resist *being changed.*

Leveraging Knowledge for Competitive Advantage

Making knowledge-based investments cannot be just an act of faith; such investments must ultimately bring financial rewards. Several firms have been pleased with their investment in knowledge-based approaches, notwithstanding the problems with definitions and measures. Most documented successes so far have been in deploying structural capital (especially knowledge-based systems) to improve customer service and relationships. Robert Paterson, VP at the Canadian Imperial Bank of Commerce, is a firm believer in this approach. CIBC created a model that looks at two key components of intellectual capital within its own competitive environment—innovation and initiative. Its goal was to identify customers' needs and develop relationships with its seven million customers and ultimately provide them with customized solutions. As Paterson notes, "If we can create human and structural capital at a rate that is greater than the rate at which customer expectations are increasing, we can create customer capital exponentially, and customer capital is what drives the creation of financial capital."[32]

American insurer Cigna Corporation,[33] has achieved a remarkable turnaround largely due to its investment in the accumulation and deployment of structural capital. In the two years from 1993 to 1995, the company turned a $251 million loss on its property and casualty division into an $87 million profit. Though reengineering helped improve operations, it did nothing for the quality and profitability of the risks the company was underwriting. Cigna achieved this improvement by giving its home-office managers the additional job of building and maintaining a knowledge base, housed in the same software that every underwriter uses to process applications. If, for example, a nursing home in California wants insurance, the system tells you the nearest earthquake fault and how dangerous it is; it gives guidelines for assessing risk factors like staff training or sprinkler systems; and so on. When new information comes in, whether it be from expert analysis, feedback from the claims department, or insights from the underwriters themselves, the "knowledge editor" evaluates it and, if appropriate, updates the database. Little new effort is required as most of this information is gathered anyway. In the past it just wasn't freely available for use in the business.

Chaparral Steel is a full working prototype of a third wave knowledge-based company. CEO Gordon Forward claims that "one of our core competencies is the rapid realization of new technology into [steel] products. We are a learning organization." Keeping out in front for Chaparral means leading the world in the low-cost safe production of high-quality steel. Dorothy Leonard-Barton explains the Chaparral story.[34] In its twenty-year history Chaparral has set world records for productivity a number of times and was the first American steel company to be awarded the right to use the Japanese industrial standard certification. Forward frequently takes competitors around the plant knowing that they can take little of its superior capability away with them. Like any true core competence, the Chaparral system can be seen only within an organic whole; it is constantly changing, continuously in a state of flux.

Chaparral's problems are solved where they occur, in the field, often using a whole network of expertise including suppliers and customers. Only two management levels separate the operators in the rolling mill from the CEO, and formal boundaries don't exist. Operators, not inspectors, report quality problems, and production workers do 40 percent of the maintenance tasks. Everyone is considered a salesperson. Decisions about production methodologies are pushed down to the lowest possible supervisory level, "where the knowledge is," and process improvements are immediately enacted without waiting for management approval.

Employees are encouraged to buy shares in the company, and 93 percent are now stockholders. The company makes a large investment in training and education, with formal apprenticeship programs and external training all part of the package. As Forward notes, "Expertise must be in the hands of the people that make the product." Incentive and educational systems are supported by a strong commitment to company values, which include: respect for the individual, tolerance of failure, and

FIGURE 3.2

The Inverted Knowledge-Based Support Structure

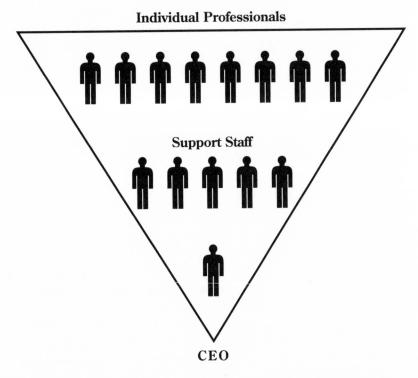

SOURCE: Adapted from James Brian Quinn, Philip Anderson, and Sydney Finkelstein, "Managing Professional Intellect: Making the Most of the Best," *Harvard Business Review,* March–April 1996, 76. Reprinted by permission of *Harvard Business Review.*

openness to ideas from the outside. It is the *total system* that gives Chaparral its distinctive advantage over other steel producers, including almost all other minimills.

Some service companies have gone even further by completely inverting their management and support structures (see Figure 3.2). In this model the center provides support services that leverage the self-sufficient professionals in the field. Doctors, consultants, and troubleshooters come readily to mind. But one can also see benefits for remote professionals in banks, insurance companies, and other professional sales and service operations.

NovaCare[35] is one of America's fastest growing health-care companies. Its professional knowledge is vested in 5,000 occupational, speech, and physical therapists. Working alone, their principal role is to provide customized health care for individual patients in 2,090 locations across 40 states. NovaCare has reorganized its entire management structure around the need to support its therapists. Its primary objective is to maximize a therapist's time with the patient; therefore it frees therapists from administrative and business responsibilities by managing contracts with external support facilities, scheduling and reporting their treatments, handling their accounting requirements, providing training updates, and increasing their earnings through the company's extensive marketing programs.

NovaCare's computer network is the backbone of the structure. It provides therapists with everything they need to know from compliance and billing to new treatments and changing care patterns. Knowledge about therapeutic care activities is collected and sorted into ten-minute blocks. This database can be accessed by various interested parties such as hospitals, government agencies, and even clients. Managers use peer and customer reviews to evaluate a therapist's work, and the evaluation forms the basis of a reward system. At NovaCare, therapists are top of the pile. Functional experts and line managers exist to support therapists by removing barriers, expediting resources, and generally acting as consultants. They never give them orders. Thus the old command and control system has been turned on its head, but the productivity improvements and the leverage effects on the organization's accumulated knowledge is immense.

Knowledge Management— A Long-Term Program

In the second wave organization, knowledge was assumed to be accumulated at the top and filtered down. In the third wave, knowledge is seen for what it is—universal. The new challenge is how it can be harnessed and used for competitive advantage. Many firms make large capital investments to support knowledge workers but fail to reap the rewards of higher productivity. Managers cannot force knowledge workers to be more productive. In fact, more often than not, knowledge is locked away inside remote departments, business units and especially communities of practice. In many cases this knowledge is fiercely protected not only from competitors, but also from colleagues in other parts of the business. In this way many islands of knowledge are created, resulting in the proverbial wheel being reinvented many times over.

Knowledge management is not just another competitive weapon to be extracted from the consultant's toolbox. It is a long-term program involving cultural change that goes to the heart of organizational management. The research into organizational learning is lighting the way.

Understanding the nuances of communities of practice and how to harness and spread their strengths is the key issue. The approach to IT investment must also adapt. Instead of proliferating knowledge-based networks concerned with the capture and distribution of information, organizations must now understand that knowledge sharing is as much a social activity as a technical one and that computer networks that facilitate this kind of dialogue are likely to be (and seen to be) more effective. McKinsey's efforts in this direction look promising.

Chris Argyris notes that "twenty-first century corporations will find it hard to survive, let alone flourish, unless they get better work from their employees...employees who've learned to take active responsibility for their own behavior, develop and share first-rate information about their jobs and make good use of genuine empowerment to shape lasting solutions to fundamental problems."[36] People and their attitudes remain at the center of the third wave company. This journey into knowledge management, as one recent article put it, "begins with technology and leads inexorably to trust."[37] In other words, to maximize the productivity of knowledge, bonds of trust need to be created between all constituents—between shareholders and managers, between managers and workers, between workers and customers, and between business partners. These are alien to the culture of the second wave economy (at least in Britain and America), and they represent one of the biggest challenges for aspiring third wave organizations.

Issue 4

Business Organization

Organize around Networks and Processes

For technologists, the lesson from reengineering is a reminder of an old truth: information technology is only useful if it helps people do their work better and differently.[1]

Thomas H. Davenport

SECOND WAVE ORGANIZATIONS WERE DESIGNED to be self-contained. They didn't need partners, nor did they look for them. They were driven from the center, and inevitably their corporate-wide skills and capabilities were diffused across a wide range of departments, divisions, and strategic business units. Skill sets and knowledge were duplicated and rarely shared. These autonomous units learned to look after their own interests first and foremost—after all, the careers of divisional managers were dependent on the performance of their own patch, not on events and results elsewhere.

But as knowledge has become the key competitive resource, second wave corporations have had little option but to devolve power and pass strategic planning down to the business units themselves. This process simply recognizes that competencies extend across divisional boundaries and increasingly involve external partners, but it changes the way group structures are managed. It is interesting to note that two of the great pioneers of the classic M-form multidivisional organization of the second wave—General Motors and Sears—were both soon in trouble when faced with emerging third wave competition. Old relationships determined by position and authority are giving way to new ones based on knowledge and mutual trust. But adjusting to this new world of work isn't easy, especially for those brought up under the old regime. Organizational evolution is creating a new form that is more likely to survive in the new world. Its structure, processes, and management styles are still evolving, but there are enough common features for us to recognize its broad shape. Some of these features suggest it is decentralized, networked, team based, and entrepreneurial. But above all it recognizes that *people* remain the critical determinants of success, and that people thrive within strong and cohesive *communities.* Success in the third wave organization will be based on the creativity and value-added work of knowledge workers and on a recognition that this very creativity can be greatly influenced by managerial attitudes and styles. The behavioral context has superseded the economic context for managing businesses. Issue 4 is concerned with how these developments affect organizational performance.

From Hierarchies to Networks

Second wave organizational models were predicated on the basis that *capital* was the primary economic resource and that the head office acted as banker and approval authority for budgets and investments across the group structure. Based on the military system of information flowing up the management hierarchy and orders flowing down, this hierarchical model was ideal for planning growth and could be used repeatedly to set up a new division, factory, or overseas business. It could also be extended vertically and horizontally, and it suited the accountants who wanted a structure for gathering, presenting, and controlling information. The head office was the home of strategic planners and functional experts who pontificated on future outcomes culminating in the rolling five-year plan and the annual budget. Thinkers were separated from doers, and it was assumed that all knowledge was captured and controlled from headquarters. (Figure 4.1 shows a typical second wave group structure with its hierarchical management layers.)

But the competitive pressures of the 1980s and 1990s forced managers to take a long hard look at their head-office functions. Their conclusions were predictable. They were too costly, too bureaucratic, and contributed too little in the way of added value. Jack Welch has followed the evolutionary path of GE's organizational structure. His comments are telling:

FIGURE 4.1

The Second Wave Group Structure

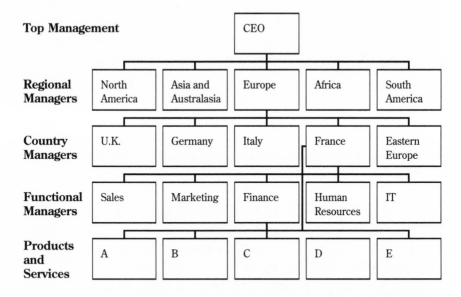

Top Management			CEO		
Regional Managers	North America	Asia and Australasia	Europe	Africa	South America
Country Managers	U.K.	Germany	Italy	France	Eastern Europe
Functional Managers	Sales	Marketing	Finance	Human Resources	IT
Products and Services	A	B	C	D	E

We had constructed over the years a management approach that was right for its time, the toast of the business schools. Divisions, strategic business units, groups, sectors—all were assigned to make meticulous, calculated decisions, and move them smoothly forward and upward. The system produced highly polished work. It was right for the 1970s, a growing handicap in the 1980s, and it would have been a ticket to the boneyard in the 1990s.[2]

The final and decisive blow was delivered to the hierarchical model by the advent of information networks. Communication, instead of being conducted up and down formal lines of authority, suddenly became instant, informal, and unstructured. Knowledge workers were able to assert their authority, and communities of practice were invariably strengthened as real power became diffused throughout the organization. It also became cheaper to buy in goods and services as the cost of handling external transactions fell in relation to internal costs, thus removing one of the key reasons for maintaining the hierarchy. Advances in information technology are also providing managers with alternative options, thus allowing them to mold the chosen structure to suit their own styles and strategic choices. For most large multinational companies, the networked organization is becoming the preferred model, and for knowledge-intensive businesses, it is the only model.

A networked organization is one where people, teams, and sometimes whole organizations act as independent nodes, form multiple links across boundaries, support one another, share common values, and report to a matrix of leaders who act more as coaches and mentors than line managers. Individuals and teams within the network gain their authority not from the hierarchy but from their skill and knowledge. One form of this model is particularly distinctive—the federal network. Charles Handy describes such a structure:

> Federalism [is not] just a classy word for restructuring. The thinking behind it, the belief, for instance, that autonomy releases energy; that people have the right to do things their own way as long as it is in the common interest; that people need to be well-informed; well-intentioned; and well-educated to interpret that common interest; that individuals prefer being led to being managed; these principles reach into the guts of the organization or, more correctly, into its soul—the way it goes about its business day by day. Federalism properly understood is not so much a political structure as it is a way of life.[3]

Federalism is not just another form of centralized control under which the center acts as banker to the divisions and subsidiaries. Nor is it simply a process of devolving power to satellite organizations that pursue their own strategic agenda. True federalism is much harder to achieve. It has to strike a new balance between size (think globally, act locally), between central planning and local decision making (shared vision, local flexibility and innovation), and sharing knowledge and experience across the enterprise.

The glue that allows all this to happen is technology. Federalism derives its real strength from spreading responsibility around the network. Forming project teams from different business units to bid for and undertake large contracts is just one example. Teams that deal with convergent technologies is another. The CEO is crucial to success. It is his or her missionary zeal that infuses shared responsibility for the common good. Ciba-Geigy, GE, Coca-Cola, BP, HP, Unilever, and Shell are among many large global corporations that have taken steps down this path. Figure 4.2 shows a typical large network with extensive interconnections.

However, perhaps the best example of the emerging networked organization is Asea Brown Boveri, a global electrotechnical company (mainly in the power transmission business) with 1,300 satellite companies and 215,000 employees. Since becoming CEO in 1988, Percy Barnevik has indelibly stamped his personal values and organizational design on the business and seen revenues rise from $17 billion to $30 billion and return on capital from 10 percent to almost 19 percent. In his previous role as head of Asea (the Swedish company that became the "A" of the ABB merger) he had increased sales four-fold and profits by a factor of ten.

FIGURE 4.2
A Networked Structure

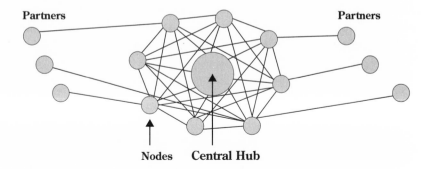

Barnevik's first task was to bring together all his senior managers and thrash out the new management policies and operating procedures. At the center of this review was a process of radical decentralization that proved to be quite different in form and substance from the divisionalization ideas of the second wave. Though the company was reorganized into a matrix of seven business segments and sixty-five business areas (not far removed from the traditional structure), the radical difference was the establishment of 1,300 companies as separate and distinct business entities—each with an average of 200 people and $25 million in annual revenues. Barnevik's idea was to create a federation of companies where employees would lose "the false sense of security of belonging to a big organization" and would develop the "motivation and pride to contribute directly to their unit's success." Each of the 1,300 companies is thus responsible for its own balance sheet (including cash management and borrowing) and each retains one-third of distributable profits after paying a dividend to the group.

Barnevik also made drastic changes to the management structure at group level. He reduced the previous eight or nine layers of management to just one intermediate level. At the corporate center, including the CEO and seven group executives, the total number of employees is less than one hundred. With such few layers of management and with each company responsible for its own resources and performance, individual company managers have little option but to help one another—and here is the key point—all the energy and resources of the corporate center are geared to facilitating cross-company cooperation, with computer networks and knowledge sharing being at the center of this process. For example, 90 percent of the annual R&D budget is used to support local centers of excellence, but expertise and knowledge is passed to others and leveraged across the corporation. And managers themselves also see benefits. Instead of spending their time dealing with vertical reporting procedures, they can concentrate their efforts on horizontal integration, learning from others, sharing strategic insights, and employing best practices wherever they exist.[4]

A few Japanese companies have taken the flexibility of the networked model even further by creating large numbers of small entrepreneurial companies that constantly change and adapt. One of the primary driving forces behind this idea is to simplify cost management. According to Kuniyasu Sakai, founder of the Taiyo Group, "It is the size of a company that matters. When a company gets too large it cannot respond in time. You need small flexible firms to survive. Breaking large companies into smaller independent units is a powerful form of cost management."[5] Another Japanese company, Kyocera, has created 800 small firms which it calls *amoebae* (after the unicellular organism that can constantly change its shape). Each amoeba is expected to form, expand, divide, and disband as circumstances evolve. However, whereas at the Taiyo Group satellite companies are wholly autonomous, at Kyocera they are part of a central network where the center holds the purse strings. Amoebae are essentially project teams of between five and fifty people who have profit responsibility, often for a specific product line or process. Promotion is based on performance, thus everyone is sensitive to competitive pressures.[6]

Retaining key knowledge workers in large organizations is central to long-term success. But many companies have difficulty keeping their high fliers, who often demand the freedom and resources that are not easy to provide. The result is often defection to a competitor who promises this extra support. 3M has tried to address this problem by allowing its 8,000 researchers to spend up to 15 percent of their time working on an idea without approval from management.[7] Some companies have adopted a different approach to retaining key workers by forming separate satellite companies that are partly owned and funded by the corporation and partly owned by the individual. Thermo-Electron is one company to successfully pursue this course. According to CEO, George Hatsopoulos:

> At Thermo Electron, we have been trying for many years to improve our understanding of how to stimulate growth as well as to attract, motivate, and retain individuals who can help us achieve it…. We developed a system that has had an enormous effect on our employees' attitudes and on the way they think about new opportunities. We repackaged the equity of some of our more promising businesses and began spinning off separate, publicly traded divisions. We call these promising businesses *spin-outs* to distinguish them from the more conventional spin-offs…. For investors, this approach has offered a means of participating in a particular technology as opposed to investing in the company as a whole….

From the outside, Thermo Electron, which keeps a majority interest in each of the spun-out companies, may look like a holding company. But we do a number of things to maintain an overall sense of cohesion among the various businesses. For example, for a nominal fee—a little over 1% of revenues—we provide much of the corporate infrastructure that these small companies need.... Today about 80% of our 12,000 employees work for our spin-outs.... Approximately 100 of our employees have options valued at $1 million or more.[8]

Though many organizations now use the power of information technology to redesign their organizational structures, too many make the mistake of making changes and waiting for improvements to follow. They believe that by choosing someone else's successful model they can simply introduce new structures, create federal networks or entrepreneurial enterprises, and wait for the dividends to flow from their newly "empowered" managers and employees. Such expectations, however, invariably lead to disappointment.

When asked what enables HP to adapt quickly to meeting the demands of the changing marketplace, CEO Lewis Platt replied, "If there's a single answer, it's probably decentralization."[9] Structures are important, but they will be effective only if well implemented and accompanied by other key changes—for example, in measurement and reward systems. One recent study by Majchrzak and Wang drew this conclusion:

> What counts is how well any one method is implemented. The implication: When redesigning their organizations, managers should not be overly influenced by what other units in their companies or other "best practice" departments are doing. Instead, they should ask their own employees what they would need in order to work well together. In addition, managers should consider the constraints and possibilities provided by technology, the work process, the existing organizational culture, and the organization's strategic mission.[10]

Strategic Business Units—An Emphasis on Processes and Teams

At the heart of the new business model lie processes and teams. Some companies, for example, have created a number of cross-functional teams that combine the functional talents of existing specialist areas to improve the flow of operations and customer service. Others have overlaid a horizontal process-based structure on top of their existing hierarchy, without actually making the physical and personnel changes necessary. But in the third wave a more formal move to the process-based model will be essential. How this model will be designed and how its management structure will work in practice will be determined by its chosen value proposition.

The New "Hierarchy"

The new organizational hierarchy has nothing to do with functions, departments, and management levels; it has everything to do with linking strategy, competencies, and resources to identifiable customer needs. These important linkages can be mapped or flow-charted. Figure 4.3 shows an example of such a competency map for a firm whose value proposition has been identified as customer service. The number of levels and the descriptive labels in the illustration are less important than the general flow of resources and the identification of where strategic priorities lie. Sometimes competencies and processes are indistinguishable where a particular process (such as innovation) is so important to the business. Processes and their subcomponents (activities), are, however, *where the work gets done*, and therefore rightly attract most management attention.

Many firms have adopted a process-based management structure in an attempt to align their operations with the needs of the customer. Davenport[11] has defined a process as "a specific ordering of work activities across time and place, with a beginning, an end, and clearly identified inputs and outputs: a structure for action." Driven by the TQM and reengineering movements, processes offer managers a clearer view of which work should be done and, when new technology is applied, how such work can be done faster and more effectively. Teams are integral to the process-based structure and "process owners" take charge of target setting and are accountable for performance. Business processes appear at two levels: major processes such as new product development and customer service, and smaller subprocesses that define the activities to be accomplished within the major processes.

One model now emerging for process-based manufacturing companies is that proposed by Womack and Jones[12] (see Figure 4.4), who suggest an organizational structure in which cross-functional teams are supported by highly specialized functional expertise. Functions in their view are where learning is collected, systematized, and deployed. Functions become centers of excellence, or fountains of knowledge, for marketing, finance, engineering, computing, and so on. They support frontline teams by carrying out benchmarking projects to find best practices, monitor competitive products and services, and provide essential feedback. Such feedback might include information on the latest developments in communications technologies, such as the Internet and video conferencing,

FIGURE 4.3

Customer Service Competency Map

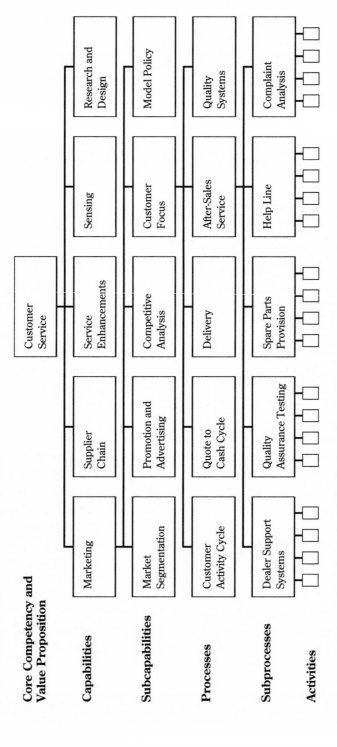

SOURCE: Adapted from Thomas E. Vollmann, *The Transformation Imperative* (Boston: Harvard Business School Press, 1996), 195. Reprinted by permission of Harvard Business School Press.

FIGURE 4.4

Role of Support Functions in the Horizontal Team-Based Structure

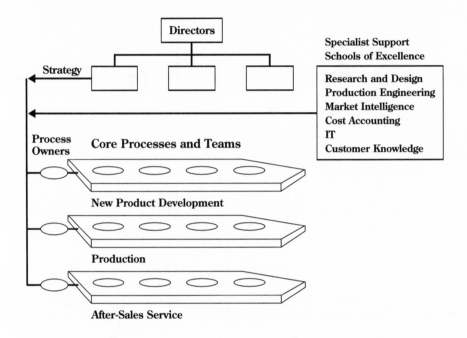

and on ensuring that the latest relevant research is quickly relayed to process managers. They act both as schools with an education and training role and as guardians of standards to ensure that best practice is being upheld in all areas.

Hewlett-Packard[13] provides an example of this approach. HP has recently invested in what it calls a Knowledge Links program, which is designed to leverage the value of its corporate staff. HP's Product Processes Organization (or PPO) is an internal consulting group whose services are "hired" by the company's highly decentralized business units. This fledgling group has already had one success in helping the deskjet printer business learn about market segmentation, and was able to link the experience and knowledge of the deskjet people with the requirements of their measurement group colleagues. Now the PPO group is placing its information on Web servers in the form of "war stories." Thus the technology network is now supporting the real knowledge network—the informal one where people talk to each other, but which is difficult to maintain in a highly diffused organization.

Most firms have concentrated on processes as a better way to deliver their existing products and services to customers. However, they often fail to make the crucial link between strategy, competencies, and processes.

Processes are the component parts of core competencies, and as competencies evolve and adapt so should processes. Jan Leschly, CEO of SmithKline Beecham, was convinced that a process-based structure was essential when he realized that a capability comes only by combining a competence with a reliable process. Notes Leschly:

> To be a leader in biotechnology, you first need the best cellular and molecular biologists in the world. But that isn't enough. You must also have a reliable, repeatable discovery and development process; otherwise products won't emerge regularly from the pipeline. These larger processes are themselves divided into many smaller ones—in the case of product development, more than 3,000 in all. Today each of these processes is charted and on the way to being repeatable and controllable.[14]

The real success in implementing processes, however, comes from the intelligent use of information technology. According the Xerox CEO Paul Allaire, "Today's information systems allow you to do things that weren't possible in the past, such as accessing information simultaneously from multiple locations and diverse functional groups. With that ability, you can enjoy the efficiency of a process orientation without losing the responsiveness of a divisional structure."[15] Before a complete piece of work can constitute a process, it must be capable of being flow-charted. Processes and their component activities also give accountants new opportunities to measure performance from the *inside,* that is, to understand why a process is not performing well by looking at its weakest links (a point that Issue 6 will examine further).

Figure 4.5 shows how a firm's information systems capability might appear. Within the IS capability might be five processes, each with a process manager and each accountable for its own performance. For example, within the new product development process would appear a series of activities such as specification, system design, programming, prototyping, and testing. As Issue 6 will explain, each activity can be tested for its value-adding content and thus form the focus of process improvement.

Process-based structures are an essential step toward the competence- and knowledge-based organization. They enable managers to ask new questions about the performance of their core competencies. Craig Weatherup, CEO of Pepsi-Cola, has no doubt about the value of this approach. He explains that much of his time is now devoted to discussions of core capability-building processes. "Whether it's new product development, single-voice communication, or coaching and support for sales, we're constantly asking, 'How do we leverage these processes for maximum advantage?' It's not as though we'd asked these questions before; they never came up. We were much too tactical and reactive."[16]

FIGURE 4.5
IT Process Map

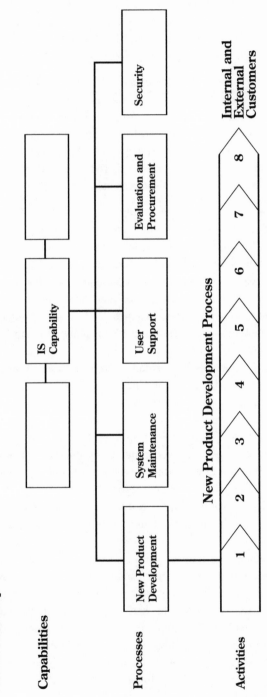

Capabilities

IS Capability

Processes

New Product Development System Maintenance User Support Evaluation and Procurement Security

Activities

New Product Development Process

1 2 3 4 5 6 7 8

Internal and External Customers

The Formation of Process Teams

Process-based structures are built around teams. Team working has of course always been a part of business organization, but teams in the third wave organization are the principal implementers of value delivery to the customer. However, creating effective teams is not a simple process of gathering people together and calling them a team. Many organizations support the team-based approach but fail to appreciate its nuances. In fact, as Majchrzak and Wang discovered, a badly implemented team-based approach can have severe *negative effects on performance.* They point out that most managers assume that structural changes by themselves will naturally lead to common understanding of, and a collective sense of responsibility for, customers' needs. But surprisingly few can define the type of collaboration they want employees to achieve, let alone the means they might employ to encourage such collaboration. Managers typically underestimate the power of the functional mind-set and how, unless it is tackled head-on (and quickly), team members will continue to carry out their old jobs albeit within a team-based system. Special attention must be paid to restructuring incentive systems, reconfiguring the work space, or redesigning jobs and procedures within the process-based units to encourage collaboration and collective responsibility.[17]

Effective teams have a number of essential characteristics, including a set of common values and objectives, a measurement and reward system set by them and *owned by them*, and the tools (i.e., information technology) and resources sufficient to fulfill their task. Their members must be dependent on one another, and they must rise and fall on their collective performance. Teams have leaders who take charge of and are accountable for *performance.*

Many team-based initiatives fail because team members bring their old functional mind-sets with them, particularly the measurement systems with which they are familiar. But to gain the full benefits from empowerment, teams must create their own sets of measures, and these should be directed at helping their own progress and not used solely to help top managers monitor performance. Such measures must track progress horizontally across the business from one process to the next and monitor customer-based performance (the customer may well be the next process team). Teams do, however, have boundaries that, if transgressed, should invoke sanctions. As Chris Meyer has noted: "The team and senior managers should also set boundaries, which, if crossed, will signal that the team has run into trouble serious enough to trigger an 'out-of-bounds' management review. Such an approach keeps managers informed without disenfranchising them."[18]

The Virtual Organization

Managers are accustomed to thinking of organizations as stable contractual bodies with physical locations such as head offices and operating units. However, technology is driving organizations in a new direction where they will be viewed as *systems* rather than physical entities. These new entities are becoming known as virtual organizations. Such an organization might indeed exist without any physical elements, merely comprising virtual value chains and a knowledge structure that links virtual inputs with market needs. Gant, an American garment brand acquired by Swedish investors, is such an organization. Gant has no proprietary assets (save for its intellectual capital). It consists of a small team that uses its knowledge infrastructure to coordinate market needs and channels with a constellation of independent suppliers. Hewlett-Packard is moving in the same direction in some of its operations. HP France, for example, has replaced some of its middle management with a centralized information platform that collects customer requests and relays them to teams of managers and engineers working from home who receive data via their electronic notebooks.[19]

There is little doubt that technology is opening up new opportunities for firms to cooperate more closely with their suppliers and customers up and down the value chain, thus reducing cycle times and lowering costs. However, the early movers in this arena are more interested in outsourcing their nonstrategic operations than in becoming a virtual hub of activities. The notion of a tightly knit, highly flexible company with a valuable core competence farming out its peripheral activities to external partners certainly has its attractions. Nike has often been hailed as a successful virtual organization that retains its design and marketing expertise in-house but subcontracts its manufacturing to its Asian partners. But, according to Chesbrough and Teece,[20] those organizations that succeed in their efforts to become virtual are crucially in strong positions of knowledge-based leverage vis-à-vis their partners. In other words, they call the shots and more often than not represent the largest customer and thus the principal paymaster of their virtual partners. Toyota is a classic example of a strong virtual leader that dominates its partners and can steer their research and development projects toward the strengthening of its own core competencies.

The successful virtuals have all invested heavily in their core capabilities. Few have survived by outsourcing everything. The competitive battle between MIPS and Sun Microsystems for the workstation processor market is a case in point. Sun had strong internal capabilities, whereas MIPS was attempting to compete as a virtual player, using the competencies of its partners (Compaq, DEC, and Silicon Graphics). Although

MIPS created a competitive design, it was incapable of holding its competitive position and when its partners' interest began to wane, the battle was soon lost.

British Airways has advanced plans to become a virtual airline, focusing on its core competencies of transporting people and cargo. To this extent it needs only to own its route structure and its brand and yield management system—everything else can be contracted out. Its plans include cost savings of $500 million per annum for the next three years. But the tough approach of new CEO Robert Ayling has set back the company's recent high levels of employee satisfaction. A satisfaction survey in May 1996 showed that less than one-third of staff had any faith in the "honesty of the management."[21] As the company's primary core competence built up over the past decade is based on customer service, which in turn stems from satisfied employees, Ayling is treading a fine line between hard-nosed cost cuts and future customer loyalty. Moreover, it hardly squares with the successful "people first" program of recent years.

A growing body of evidence, however, suggests that outsourcing can be a dangerous practice, particularly if it is not grounded in clear strategic thinking. It is doubtful whether such clear thinking is often in evidence. The Boston Consulting Group has studied more than one hundred major companies and has concluded that most outsource primarily to save on overhead and short-term costs.[22] Even when this is the chosen objective, many are disappointed with the results. A 1995 Deloitte & Touche survey of 1,500 chief information officers in the United States and Canada showed that only 31 percent believed their savings were significant. As the Outsourcing Institute in America reckons that 63 percent of U.S. companies now outsource some portion of their IT budgets (an estimated $40 billion or more will be spent on IT outsourcing in 1996), this is a significant finding. Problems start with a poor definition and fuzzy objectives. According to Eugene Prochnow, an outsourcing consultant with Deloitte & Touche, "you should *not* outsource what you can't define."[23]

Before spending $1.5 billion on its IT outsourcing contract, Hughes Aircraft CIO Mahvash Yazdi thought carefully about what to keep and what to contract out. Her advice is to prepare a watertight request for proposals. Her design team included procurement, human resource, and legal experts. After CSC won the contract and took over the jobs of the 950 staff, all seemed well. But the experience thereafter was unforeseen. According to Yazdi, after the deal was announced 25 percent of staff left, a third stayed, and another third "hated the change and still haven't gotten over it." There was also some resistance from the internal Hughes user base. The lesson is that outsourcing is ultimately not about processes and contracts but about *people*, but invariably the emphasis is on managing the contract.

The Organization as a Social Structure

The change to horizontal team-based processes has been driven largely by the business process reengineering movement. The emphasis has invariably been on short-term cost savings, especially reductions in people. Redesigning work flows using the power of information systems is the methodology, but there are serious pitfalls awaiting organizations that blindly follow this path. We noted, for example, in Issue 3, that reengineers can (unwittingly) slice right through a community of practice, thus rupturing one of the main arteries of value-adding work. The other pitfall is concerned with an understanding of how people work and particularly how they share knowledge.

The Reengineering Bubble

Professor Tom Davenport has blown the whistle on the reengineering charade. From a series of well-crafted ideas that were designed to show how technology could improve business processes in the late 1980s, the reengineering tidal wave grew into a $50 billion business in the mid-1990s. But the results have not been as expected. Even CSC Index—one of the pioneers of reengineering—has reported tales of woe, with 73 percent of companies surveyed saying that they were using reengineering to eliminate, on average, 21 percent of jobs; and of ninety-nine completed initiatives, 67 percent were judged as producing mediocre, marginal, or failed results. Nor have most of the high-profile success stories always been well grounded. Davenport notes, for example, that some firms—especially those that were the principal case studies in one of Hammer and Champy's best-sellers, *Reengineering the Corporation*[24]—had a revisionist view of their reengineering efforts, and none of the companies involved has been able to claim sustained success.[25]

However, Davenport is careful to point out that it is the hype and especially the colorful language of reengineering (e.g., "carry the wounded but shoot the stragglers") that has given these initiatives such a bad name. Remaining a staunch supporter of business processes, he notes:

> The most profound lesson of business process reengineering was never reengineering, but business processes. Processes are how we work. Any company that ignores its business processes or fails to improve them risks its future. That said, companies can use many different approaches to process improvement without ever embarking on a high-risk reengineering project.[26]

Work is a Social Activity

Process designers must also be aware that work practices and proce-dures cannot be simply designed on flow charts and implemented in the workplace without fully understanding how people actually spend their time. Many process designers only see the "authorized" or explicit work procedures and fail to see the "unauthorized" or tacit practices where much of the real work gets done. Consider the recent experience at Xerox. In the 1980s an anthropologist at Xerox's Palo Alto Research Center (PARC) made an interesting observation. Managers were trying to boost the productivity of field service staff, so, instead of simply accepting their descriptions of work activities, the anthropologist actu-ally followed the field staff around. He discovered that reps often made a point of spending time *not with customers, but with one another*. They would gather in common areas, like the parts warehouse or around the coffee machine, and swap stories from the field. Now imagine how this observation might be seen by a reengineering consultant—juicy pick-ings for increasing time on the job or with the customer. But this miss-es the point. The anthropologist saw these *social activities* as an extremely valuable part of the day; the reps were acting as a communi-ty of professionals, providing one another with valuable insights into improving their work and learning how to solve customer problems more effectively.

This insight changed the way Xerox designed processes and work practices. Managers turned conventional wisdom on its head and decid-ed to expand this knowledge transfer capability by providing engineers with two-way radio headsets, thus creating a "knowledge channel" through which problems could be discussed. But even this did not com-pletely capture such knowledge, so they went further and created an elec-tronic refinery known as Eureka, which organizes and categorizes a data-base of tips and war stories generated by field staff. Eureka operates as a free-flowing knowledge democracy, much like the natural, informal col-laborations among technical reps. Relying on voluntary information exchanges, any rep can submit a tip, the only incentive being to *contribute* to the well-being of the community of practice.[27]

The anthropologist made another interesting finding. When he accompanied a rep on a call, he asked to see the technical manuals that the rep consulted. The rep naturally produced the official company manual, but once the researcher gained the confidence of the rep, the "real" manual was produced. This was a dog-eared, hardly recognizable version of the original filled with notes and scribbles in the margin. Each rep was keeping two sets of books, the official and the improvised. Brown and Seeley suggest that this is how many of us approach our work, particularly in large organizations, and that what is unofficial remains invisible—except perhaps to members of our own trusted community. They also note that "processes don't do work, people do…when you're competing on knowledge, the name of the game is improvisation, not standardization …in the knowledge era, what's invisible is often most valuable."[28] In other words, when designing processes and work flows, the gaps and spaces are often the most valuable parts of the process where knowledge is exchanged. This must be recognized and accommodated within the process design; otherwise the informal, impromptu, inspirational ways that organizations really work will be lost—with fatal consequences for future performance.

The New Workplace

How people work, communicate, and share knowledge is also influencing the design of the workplace itself. Architects are recognizing that informal contact is important and are including kitchenettes, open offices with work units designed around meeting tables, and escalators instead of elevators. Alcoa's new offices are typical of the new breed. After downsizing and reengineering didn't bring the expected dividends, Alcoa—like many other companies—realized that the new management ideas of horizontal processes and team working didn't work well within old-style office buildings. CEO Paul O'Neill observes that the new office design will have "a lot of places where people can gather." His favorite place is the kitchen, where he notes, "it's like being at home in your own kitchen and sitting around the table."[29]

Work anywhere, anytime is the new approach. People are working from home, in their cars, and in their offices (including clients' offices). They work alone or in teams, in real space or cyberspace. It all adds up to a huge disaggregation of work. Technology is, of course, the common factor, and IT spending is already surpassing facilities and real estate as the second biggest operating expense.[30] "Hoteling" is another facility now growing in popularity. Consultants, salespeople, telecommuters, auditors, and many other workers who don't need a permanent desk are now accommodated in office meeting rooms that can be booked in advance with any requisite files and materials—just like a hotel. IBM reckons to have saved $1.4 billion of real estate expenses through this approach.[31]

Charles Handy sees a host of new challenges for organizations as they move further down the track of the virtual office and a transient workforce. He asks a simple question: "How do you manage people whom you do not see?" The answer is by trusting them. Trust is the critical element in the management of knowledge workers. Nor is he optimistic about the chances of success. He notes that "organizationally, we have to wonder whether a company is, in the future, going to be any-thing more than a box of contracts that some companies now seem to be. Is a box of contracts a sustainable basis for getting work done in our soci-ety, or is it not, in fact, a recipe for disintegration?"[32]

The Changing Role of Information Technology

The design of IT systems to support the needs of knowledge workers has improved by leaps and bounds over the past five years. We noted in Issue 3 how the mainstream consultants were now providing quick and effec-tive access to just the right amount of information to enable individuals to deal with a particular problem. However, while such approaches undoubt-edly improve productivity, they have not yet captured the *tacit* knowledge sharing that many sociologists believe is the main springboard for learn-ing and improvement. In other words, existing systems deal at the autho-rized level of information management—they have not yet penetrated communities of practice where much of the important knowledge-sharing takes place. However, the next wave of IT designs will begin to tackle this problem. Indeed, it is already happening at Xerox.

Xerox has launched what it calls Project Jupiter, which it terms "vir-tual social reality." Jupiter is a collection of audio, video, and communica-tions technologies to help communities form and flourish. According to Brown and Gray, Jupiter's real value is in supporting interactions that are richer and more focused than free-form electronic discussion groups, bul-letin boards—even the Web. It allows for flexible participation; users can be more or less engaged as they see fit. It provides context as well as con-tact: different programmable "rooms" and "objects" evoke different behaviors. They claim it is a network *place* rather than an electronic space, where people interact as a community. They note that "the most valuable knowledge often resides where we are least able to see or con-trol it: on the front lines, at the periphery, with the renegades. Companies that embrace the emergent can tap the logic of knowledge work and the spirit of the community. Those that don't will be left behind."[33]

The Changing Role of the CEO

The days of the CEO as hero are numbered, but he or she still has a cru-cial role to play in carving out organizational success. With strategy and key decisions being increasingly devolved down to operational level, the CEO's role is becoming one of setting the right purpose and direction, behavioral context, operating standards, and ensuring that all actions are aligned with broad strategic goals. He or she must see through the cultural layers of the organization and ensure inasmuch as possible that people and teams have similar perceptions, values, and assumptions about key organizational issues. Thus one of the primary qualities a CEO must possess is the ability to communicate and foster trust between disparate groups and coalitions. But how many CEOs have ruptured this self-evident truth by acts of betrayal paraphrased as "essential downsizing"? Trust between managers and workers that has taken years to build is often blown away in one reckless act of restructuring combined with poor communication, leaving in its wake cynicism and subterfuge.

One of the most frequent yet easily avoided causes of a breakdown in trust is poor communication. In 1993, Watson Wyatt Worldwide investigated 531 U.S. organizations undergoing major restructuring.[34] Wyatt asked the CEOs, "If you could go back and change one thing, what would it be?" The most frequent answer: "The way I communicated with my employees." Too often it seems that communications consultants encourage top executives to package their messages on videos, in newsletters, and at conferences. They believe that the assembled group wants to hear about changes in values and carefully thought out mission statements, when the reality is that they want to know how any changes affect their own jobs and prospects. More important, they want to receive these messages from people *they trust*, usually their immediate supervisors. They want to know the facts, not some flowery explanation of why change is necessary to meet competitive threats. The trouble is, of course, that the de-layering of recent years has seen the loss of many of these key supervisory figures who were essential to the successful dissemination of this type of message. There is a strong lesson here for the third wave manager.

The CEO stamps his or her mark on the organization by setting out a managerial philosophy including core values, rules of behavior, and measures of performance. For example, the policy at ABB is that individuals will interact "with mutual confidence, respect and trust...to eliminate the we/they attitude...and to remain flexible, open and generous." This code of behavior governs how managers act within the company, encourages them to develop personal networks and operating interdependencies, and rewards them for doing so. CEO Percy Barnevik and his executive colleagues carry the prime responsibility for translating these values into action through their selection and promotion of individuals, and they are quick to sanction anyone who crosses the line.[35]

Whereas the actions of second wave leaders were underpinned by a clear economic model that set the agenda for micromanagement, third wave leaders recognize that organizations are complex social organisms in which the behavior of key knowledge workers is sensitive to a wide range of stimuli and determines whether the all-important cross-fertilization of information takes place. Ensuring that creativity and value-adding work is maximized is one of the new challenges facing third wave executives.

Toward a New Managerial Theory of the Firm

Bartlett and Ghoshal suggest that we are moving toward a new managerial theory of the firm. Just as the multidivisional structure (M-form) set the standard for the second wave, a new model is now emerging that is likely to become the standard for the third. The classic second wave model was researched and well documented by Alfred Chandler in his 1962 book, *Strategy and Structure.*[36] In this model top management is the fountain of knowledge, the strategist, and the resource allocator; middle managers are the controllers and the frontline managers are implementers. Marvin Bower's observations added some interesting twists to Chandler's view. He saw middle managers in a far more influential role. He recognized that organizations were essentially political in their actions and decisions and that middle managers were the conduit between top managers and the implementers. What they proposed (e.g., new investments) was invariably accepted. Cyert & March articulated yet another perspective in their seminal work, *The Behavioral Theory of the Firm.*[37] They saw the company as a set of coalitions in which goal formation was achieved through a process of bargaining. The final agreements were held together by budgets and controls and were characterized by the avoidance of uncertainty.[38]

According to Bartlett and Ghoshal, what separates the new model from those described by Chandler, Bower, and Cyert and March is the switch from capital to knowledge as the scarce resource that determines (and constrains) strategic success. Unlike capital, knowledge (as we have already noted) is diffused around the business, and key knowledge workers are located far away from corporate headquarters—often in research laboratories, marketing departments, or IT operations. Third wave companies therefore need to create an environment in which these scarce resources are most effectively leveraged for competitive advantage.

In third wave companies knowledge workers are the key to success. Their social interactions and the resultant effects on behavior and performance are of paramount importance. In recognizing the importance of this social interaction, Bartlett and Ghoshal define the new organizational form in terms of three core processes: *the entrepreneurial process*, in which frontline operators become key strategists and decision makers, constantly creating new opportunities for the business; *the integration process*, in which middle managers provide a vital horizontal information-processing capability and leveraging task across the organization and with external partners; and *the renewal process*, in which top managers provide inspiration and a sense of purpose and frequently challenge the status quo—all essential elements in driving the organization forward. They note that the new model is "a process management orientation quite different from the classic one of ensuring that the allocation of resources matched the strategic priorities and that operating performance met the budgeted objectives."[39] GE, ABB, Toyota, Canon, and many others, are all moving toward the adoption of this business model. It looks set to become the standard in the third wave.

Issue 5

Market Focus

Find and Keep Strategic, Profitable, and Loyal Customers

Even in a mass market business, you don't want to attract and retain everyone.... The key is first to identify and attract those who will value your service and then to retain them as customers and win the largest possible share of their lifetime business.[1]

Sir Colin Marshall,
Chairman, British Airways

MOST SECOND WAVE COMPANIES PRODUCE AN annual plan that includes targets for market share and sales by market segment, channel, brand, and product. Sophisticated methodologies such as PIMS (Profit Impact of Marketing Strategies) and the Boston Consulting Group's growth/share matrix analyze the relationships between market size and growth, economic and technology factors, distribution channels, likely price movements, and the competitive strategies of key competitors. But conspicuous by its absence from these approaches is any method of evaluating whether customers—both existing or targeted—are *worthwhile*. In other words, there is little concern with which customers to keep, which have untapped potential, which are strategic, which are unprofitable, and which should be abandoned. Most marketing programs are simply aimed at replacing the 20 percent of customers the firm expects to lose each year without any consideration of whether resources would be better spent on keeping them than attracting the replacements. Reichheld has noted that a

50 percent cut in defections will more than double the average company's growth rate.[2]

Which customers, channels, and markets to keep and which to abandon are tough questions and, for sure, marketing people get precious little help answering them from their accounting colleagues. In other words, there is no meeting of minds between the marketer and the accountant. Take customer profitability. The best that most finance departments can achieve is some measure of gross profitability, but in a world where the fastest-rising costs are "below the gross margin line," such measures can be at best misleading and at worst disastrous. Ask any marketing manager or accountant which products, channels, or customers are really profitable after charging all the resources they consume, and you are likely to receive a blank look. Most of them haven't a clue. Yet important resource allocation decisions are made each day, whether it be millions of dollars of advertising or thousands of hours of sales and management time. Bain & Co. director Frederick Reichheld puts the problem in perspective:

> It is simply not possible to build or maintain a healthy business without learning how to get the *right* customers. In many businesses, the customers most likely to sign are precisely the worst customers you could possibly find.... One bank was surprised to learn that the wealthy, high balance customers it had always coveted were in fact less loyal and much less profitable than it had believed. Wealthy customers were sophisticated defectors. They took greatest advantage of average prices, were likely to prepay mortgages at just the worst times, and made maximum use of the implicit free options that most fixed-rate lending and deposit products offer.[3]...There is always a tension between commission sales and customer loyalty, because a salesforce paid on commission and hell-bent on customer volume generally finds that the easiest prospects to sell are the ones whose loyalty is low. By definition, customers with a high loyalty coefficient are hard to switch away from their current suppliers.... Most companies pay salespeople for conquests, not continuity.[4]

Issue 5 considers some fresh insights as to how managers can focus on acquiring and keeping the right customers.

Building the Value of Customer Capital

One of the principal assets owned by most companies is their customer base, but few firms either measure the changing value of customer capital explicitly or set specific targets for its improvement. If they did, what measures would they choose? We suggest they would be interested in tracking profitability, size and share of business, growth and potential growth, stability, satisfaction, loyalty and repurchase levels, organization-al learning capabilities, and the image-enhancing effects of dealing with market leaders. All these factors denote *value* in one form or another, and customers who fulfill most of these criteria would be equally highly val-ued by the competition. But which customer-related attributes do most organizations measure? The answer: market share and gross profit con-tribution. In a recent survey, a hospital executive summed up the mar-keting view when he said, "Cost is not our concern, it is revenues that we care about."[5] But as we will see, the traditional approach is no guarantee that the value of customer capital will be maximized.

The Mythology of Market Share

The pursuit of greater market share is built into the Western managerial psyche. That higher market share equals higher profits is the marketing counterpart of the accountant's belief that scale and speed is the only route to lower unit costs and improved competitiveness. It is so deeply embedded in corporate thinking that competitive success is judged by it, strategy is often based on it, and executive incentives are geared to its achievement. It is one of those immutable principles of management that is rarely questioned, but it has serious flaws, and the third wave manager should be on guard. Two traps await. One concerns the results of pursu-ing market share strategies in volatile industries where the business cycle rapidly ebbs and flows. The other concerns the long-term prof-itability of different groups of customers.

Recent evidence from two major studies suggests there is no causal link between market share strategies and profitability.[6] Moreover, those firms that have pursued stable production strategies have done better over the whole business cycle than those relentlessly chasing market share. The profits made in the upswing of the economic pendulum are more than wiped out in the downswing. During the recent market down-turns (1968–1970, 1973–1975, 1978–1982, and 1988–1991) the Japanese *gained more market share* than they lost in the previous upswing through adopting policies of stable production with steady expansion. Moreover, pursuing this reverse strategy leaves the manufacturer in a *stronger* posi-tion to compete during the next upturn.

The second caveat concerns the types of customers gained during periods of rapid sales expansion. One of the lessons of second wave success is that companies that build long-term *loyal* customers increase long-term profitability. They concentrate on keeping their good cus-tomers rather than chasing new ones. They appreciate that the likely consequence of an indiscriminate expansion in market share is the increase in floating customers, the type who look for special offers, absorb sales and management time, pay late, and return products at the drop of a hat. They are usually not worth the effort.

When marketing people talk about the correlation between market share and profitability, they generally mean *gross profitability*. Few accounting systems can tell them whether the same conclusion can be drawn at the net profit level. In particular they fail to distinguish between the profitability of new customers and the profitability of existing ones. As Reichheld notes,

> Accountants have developed sophisticated techniques for appraising capital assets and their depreciation; they have learned how to monitor the constantly changing value of work-in-progress; but they have not yet devised a way to track the value of a company's customer inventory. They make no distinction between sales revenue from brand-new customers and sales revenue from long-term, loyal customers, because they do not know or care that it costs much more to serve a new customer than an old one. Worse, in most businesses, accountants treat investment in customer acquisition as one more current expense, instead of assigning it to specific customer accounts and amortizing it over the life of the customer relationship.[7]

Let's now turn our attention to how we find long-term, profitable customers.

Wrong Assumptions about Customer Profitability

Because accounting systems gather, record, and report costs and profits by function and department, determining exactly which customers are profitable is an effort fraught with problems. The best that most accounting systems can achieve is some measure of gross profitability, but as a general rule many costs classified as "fixed" actually vary with customer demands. In fact some studies show that up to 60 percent of sales value is taken up in customer-driven costs.[8] As a general guide, consider the level of SG&A costs as a percentage of sales in the following range of industries. These costs contain a substantial element of customer-driven, especially marketing, costs:[9]

Perfume, cosmetics, toilet preparation	53%
Retail stores	43%
Telephone and telegraph apparatus	38%
Electronic computers	36%

One way of dealing with the problem is to simply ignore it. Accountants do so by tracing only the variable costs to products, measuring success by the resultant *contribution margin* (the sales revenue generated by the product less its associated variable costs). But contribution analysis encourages and reinforces the mentality that there is always a good reason to add or retain a customer, and seldom a good reason to abandon one. Equally, there is always a valid reason to accept a price that generates a contribution to overheads (however vaguely they are defined).

Recent research has shown that once the full cost of supporting customers is taken into account, the majority of customers (usually around 70 percent) are *not profitable at all*. In fact the studies carried out by Professors Cooper and Kaplan at the Harvard Business School have led them to the so-called 20-225 rule, which states that in some companies 20 percent of customers account for 225 percent of profits, which of course means that the other 80 percent "lose" 125 percent of profits.[10] Such a high-level revelation is not as shocking to accountants as it might appear. Most of them probably have a rough idea that this might be true. The problem is that they have no idea which customers make up the 20 percent and which make up the 80 percent. Nor do customer size or other intuitive signs of profitability help.

What is the Value of a Customer?

Customers can buy once and be worth very little or they can buy consistently over a lifetime and be worth a fortune. The impact of retention levels on profitability and thus on customer value is immense. Tom Peters provides the following anecdote to illustrate the long-term effects of customer profitability:

> Grocer Stew Leonard got me started on this. He says, "When I see a frown on a customer's face, I see $50,000 about to walk out the door." His good customers buy about $100 worth of groceries a week. Over ten years, that adds up to roughly $50,000.... Average lifetime auto purchases will total about $150,000, not including repair work. Given the remarkably low dealer loyalty of car buyers these days, might it not make a difference if dealers and their employees focused on this big number?[11]

Over the past ten years, Frederick Reichheld developed a model of the economics of customer loyalty that is worthy of our attention. He believes:

> The loyalty-based business model effectively explains success and failure in the business world. In most of the industries we've studied, the companies with the highest retention rates also earn the best profits.

FIGURE 5.1
Lifetime Customer Profitability

Annual Customer Profit

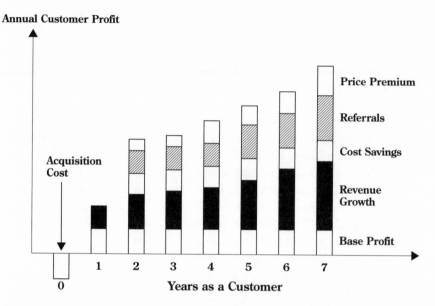

SOURCE: Frederick F. Reichheld, *The Loyalty Effect: The Hidden Force Behind Growth, Profits, and Lasting Value* (Boston: Harvard Business School Press, 1996), 39. Reprinted by permission of Harvard Business School Press.

Relative retention explains profits better than market share, scale, cost position, or any of the other variables usually associated with competitive advantage.[12]

Based on an analysis of various service companies, Reichheld suggests that there are certain common features that determine longer-term customer profitability in the service industry (see Figure 5.1). Specifically, by identifying and measuring six factors, companies can, over an appropriate time period that will vary from company to company and perhaps even customer to customer, form a clear view of the long-term profitability of their customers. The factors are these:

1. The *cost of acquiring a customer*
2. The *base* (or gross) *profit* from the goods or services provided to the customer
3. The profit from *increased purchases* arising from the additional spending of satisfied customers
4. The *reduced operating costs* of serving loyal customers
5. The profit from transactions with new customers who have been *referred by loyal customers*

FIGURE 5.2

Which Markets, Channels, and Customers Are Worthwhile?

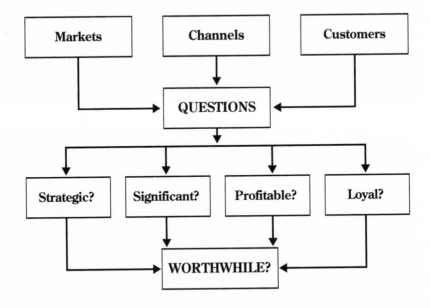

6. The profit from the *price premium* charged to loyal customers who
    are less sensitive to price.

It is vitally important to stress that the Reichheld model is not based on
point-in-time calculations. Such information then allows companies to
understand the lifetime value of their customer base and might, for example, give them some idea as to just how large an investment in customer
loyalty would be worthwhile.

So how can managers set about finding which customers add to the
capital base and which detract from it? Clearly, finding answers to these
questions is worth some effort.

Which Customers Are Worthwhile?

We have argued that decisions concerning customer retention and aqui-
sition determine long-term success. Thus managers must determine
where resources should be applied to maximum effect. This is a painstaking process. It requires a framework. Professor John Whitney[13] suggests
that the framework should encompass three principles: *strategy, significance,* and *profitability* (see Figure 5.2). We would add another—*loyalty.*
Some customers are strong on one element but weak on others.

These questions should be considered by representatives from different functional areas. For example, sales managers will likely have one view, order processing and debt collection managers will have another, and finance and IT managers may have yet another. The data must be analyzed into manageable blocks including, for example, customers by country, area, channel, size, product group, and type of service. The objective here is to filter out customers who are absorbing resources that could be applied better to those more in tune with the company's core competencies and with potential to grow.

Which Customers Are Strategically Important?

This question asks whether a customer is important over the long term. Do such customers fit neatly with our core competencies and thus are we in a better position to serve them than are our competitors? If they do not fit the strategy of a particular business unit, can they be switched to others in the group that better meet their needs? This review might also reveal deeper problems. What if we discover that few, if any, customers are aligned with our competencies? In that case, should we attempt to change our customers or our strategy?

Does one customer influence others? Dealing with one customer in a particular area or technology platform can be the gateway to many others—whether a community, territory, a group of companies, or perhaps an economic web. Can we work with a customer to break into a web? As we noted earlier, webs are now forming around customer databases, particularly those held by credit-card companies. Can we market our products and services to these "captive" customers through the web gateway?

Many other strategic relationship questions spring to mind. Is the customer likely to grow? Can we learn from the customer? Can we follow a particular customer into a new market opportunity? Does the customer have special technology or excellent systems from which we can benefit? Unless we ask these types of questions, the underlying importance of customers will remain unrecognized and their potential unexplored.

Which Customers Are Significant to Our Business?

How important is the customer in terms of the percentage of total revenue and gross profit? For example, does the customer figure in the top 20 percent? Size is not always correlated with profitability. The warning signs are usually there if you look close enough. For example, do large revenue-generating customers place onerous demands on sales, production, and management time? Do customers place thousands of small one-off orders or demand special promotions and extra stocking arrangements, all of which might offset the benefits of volume purchases?

Size is *significant,* however. In other words, large customers *should be* the largest contributors to profits and are not easy to replace. With these customers it is important to spend time investigating possible improvements in terms of trading. For example, can multiple small orders be combined in some way to reduce costs, or perhaps computer links established to speed operations and reduce handling costs?

Moreover, size does not relate just to the current level of business. It can also signify huge untapped potential. Are we the customer's number-one supplier, or are we low on the list? Acquiring this knowledge provides some guidance as to how we might structure future deals with this customer.

Many companies have a long tail of small customers who are neither strategic nor significant and must be questionable on the test of profitability. They clutter up the accounts-receivable ledger and are expensive to administer. Clustering them together through a central distributor with logistics systems more geared to their needs would be a sensible approach.

Which Customers Are Profitable?

Activity-based costing (ABC) techniques are now employed by many firms to give an alternative view of customer profitability and cost behavior. ABC attempts to charge costs to products, channels, and customers for the resources they consume but efforts at implementation have achieved mixed success. Even if ABC approaches prove too difficult to implement, it doesn't mean that managers cannot make intelligent "guesstimates" of customer profitability. Answering questions such as whether customers pay on time, whether they demand extra (free) services, special promotions, and extended credit, whether their orders are well prepared and right the first time, whether they demand high working capital support (such as high stock levels), and whether in general they are difficult to deal with, can take you a long way toward understanding whether customers are profitable.

The following profit statement (see Figure 5.3) is a useful guide as to how we might evaluate customer profitability for a manufacturing firm. It attempts to identify all *customer-sustaining costs*—that is, those costs that are incurred to support a particular customer. A similar statement can be prepared at different levels including channel, market, and country.

Nor, as we noted earlier, must we examine customer profitability just over the short term. The important measure is the *lifetime profitability* of a customer. Trends are also important signals that can inform us about the likely direction of future profits.

FIGURE 5.3

Customer Profitability Statement

Revenue		xx
Less: Cost of goods sold	x	
Returned Goods	x	
Discounts and allowances	x	
= Gross Margin		xx
Less: Sales cost	x	
Promotion cost (excluding media advertising)	x	
Channel managers cost	x	
Product development cost	x	
Direct warehousing cost	x	
Customer transport cost	x	
Financing costs	x	
Postsale service cost	x	
= Net profit		xx

The Customer Evaluation Guide

Whitney[14] suggests that all these decision criteria can be brought together in a matrix showing the strengths and weaknesses of each customer, channel, segment, or other grouping (see Figure 5.4). Such an assessment should be performed every year or so depending on the pace of change in the market.

This approach, while not being rooted in numerical accuracy, has the benefit of being reasonably fast and directs the attention of managers to the right questions. Instead of discussions about market share, market-based promotions, discounts, and other special offers, questions are now being asked about the central issues of strategy, significance, and profitability. Each decision point can then address further questions of resource allocation. What action shall we take based on this analysis? For example, which channels should we expand and contract? Which customer groups are profitable and how can we increase profits in targeted areas? In the search for new customers, the marketing department can benefit from understanding better which potential customers are likely to be worthwhile and which are likely to be a waste of time.

The benefits of this type of structured analysis are potentially

FIGURE 5.4

The Customer Evaluation Guide

Strategic	Significant	Profitable	
yes	yes	yes	These are the customers that you need to keep at all costs. Pour resources into them.
yes	yes	no	Work on the profitability problem through a mixture of pricing, service, delivery, etc.
yes	no	yes	Consider other channels to reduce costs (e.g., distributors). If business is low but potential is high, work hard to increase.
yes	no	no	Being strategic is not enough. Try other ways to improve scale and profits. Otherwise exit while leaving a way back in.
no	yes	yes	If customer does not fit your chosen competencies, then don't provide any special attention. If they demand special offers and management time, exit.
no	yes	no	This is the acid test. Size is not enough. Exit fast before your profits are drained even further.
no	no	yes	Your real profits lie with strategic and significant customers. Spin off to a distributor.
no	no	no	The easiest decision. Just say goodbye.

SOURCE: Adapted from John O. Whitney, "Strategic Renewal for Business Units," *Harvard Business Review,* July–August 1996, 91.

immense. The marketing manager can directly link her spending with closely targeted customers; the sales manager can educate his sales force in the "business case" of the specific customer transaction; the accountant can provide meaningful reports on the profitability of worthwhile customers; and the support manager can make intelligent choices as to who to support with free services and who to charge. There is, however, one further dimension to the question of whether customers are worthwhile, and this is the question of customer satisfaction, which, as we shall see, is a minefield of misinformation.

Acquiring and Keeping the Right Customers

There is little doubt that long-term growth comes from loyal, profitable customers who fit neatly within a company's core value proposition. Therefore it is worth whatever it takes to find those that fit your criteria for good customers and ensure that the marketing effort is aimed at attracting them—and not, as so often happens in practice, aimed at the world in general like a trawler's net designed to catch whatever fish happen to be swimming by. Such efforts tend to churn up the so-called floating voters, who hop around looking for the best deal each time they have an order to place. Acquiring and keeping the right customers is worth the effort.

Once analyzed, the customer base must be purged of those that are not worth keeping or not worth the effort to turn into desirable customers. New customers that fit the chosen criteria should replace them. But good customers are a valuable commodity, and alert competitors will be chasing their business. The standard satisfaction surveys (the major mechanism of checking whether customers are likely to remain) are, as we shall see, a poor indication of continuing support and commitment.

It would be hard to find a company that doesn't acknowledge "customer satisfaction" to be one of its primary goals. Indeed, the pursuit of customer satisfaction has led many companies to turn themselves inside out and upside down in an effort to find some magic formula that outwits the competition. But is customer satisfaction really the right objective? After all, customers can be "satisfied," but their repurchase levels can be miserably low. The link between satisfaction and repurchase (or loyalty) can be tenuous and sometimes downright misleading.

The Customer Satisfaction Trap

Let us begin with a closer look at this whole notion of customer satisfaction. Most of us, at some time or another, fill in questionnaires and answer market research surveys that solicit our views as satisfied or dissatisfied customers. Whether we encounter them on a flight, in a hotel room, or at a car dealership, the questions are similar. Are we satisfied with the particular product or service? The boxes to be ticked are clearly marked and the ranking system obvious. Now imagine for the next few minutes that you are the person responsible for the completion and analysis of your

FIGURE 5.5

The Third Quarter Customer Satisfaction Index

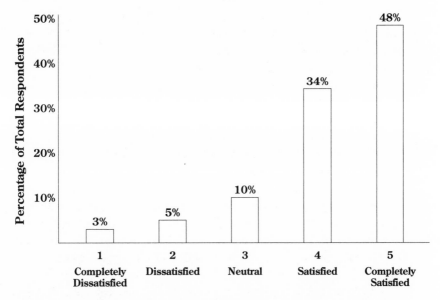

SOURCE: Thomas O. Jones and W. Earl Sasser, Jr., "Why Satisfied Customers Defect," *Harvard Business Review,* November–December 1995, 90. Reprinted by permission of *Harvard Business Review.*

organization's satisfaction indexes. Suppose further that there is a pervasive and not unrealistic belief that satisfied customers determine your entire organization's profitability. Your most recent chart, covering responses relating to the third quarter, is shown in Figure 5.5.

You review the findings with senior managers. You, and they, are delighted. Of your customers, 82 percent are satisfied and 48 percent are actually crazy about the services you offer. Congratulations are in order! In fact, you have hit your 80 percent satisfaction target. For the final quarter, the new target is to attain 90 percent of responses in the 4-to-5 range. Meanwhile, you devote your energy to sorting out the 18 percent who are either indifferent to you or dissatisfied.

Is this an unrealistic setting? A deliberately fabricated straw man that can easily be dismembered? Company after company performs some variant of this type of analysis (remember what we are discussing here—the causal chain that links satisfaction to profitability). If companies rely exclusively on satisfaction surveys to give them clues to profits, they run a real risk, because to a large extent these surveys may be asking the wrong question. The real question is *not* whether customers are satisfied with the existing level of service. Rather, it is whether the value they receive will keep them loyal. In other words, satisfaction indexes report (necessarily) what customers *say;* profitability comes from what customers *do.* If customers fail to return to repurchase products or reuse services, they are giving the company the thumbs-down signal. They are acting in a way that says the value they receive isn't up to the mark. But in survey after survey, report after report, between 60 percent and 80 percent of all lost customers say they are either satisfied (scale of 4) or even very satisfied (scale of 5) *prior to defection.*

We should understand that satisfaction surveys *in isolation* can be an insidious trap and a potentially lethal tool as far as predicting profitability is concerned. Satisfaction in itself is a temporary feeling and very difficult to measure in a meaningful way, which is precisely why we use such simple—and simplistic—rankings. Far worse than this, as we can now begin to see, it is likely to be the wrong measure. Without wishing to overemphasize the point, we might stress that excessive devotion to satisfaction indexes would be mitigated if the traditional questions were turned around. Instead of asking how satisfied their customers are, organizations should ask how many satisfied and profitable customers come back for more.

Let's return to the satisfaction chart and reinterpret the findings. Suppose, instead of presenting the data as showing an 82 percent level of satisfaction, you argue somewhat differently; for example, by saying that only 48 percent of your customer base was completely satisfied with your service (the percentage that gave you a 5), you are by implication reporting that more than half your customers are less than totally satisfied. Xerox's views on these questions are relatively straightforward. High levels of customer satisfaction lead to greatly increased loyalty and *increased customer loyalty is the single most important driver of long-term financial performance*, a point confirmed by Dave Illingworth, the first general manager of Lexus US, who stated emphatically, "The only meaningful measure of satisfaction in this industry is repurchase loyalty."[15]

So far the thesis seems reasonable. Satisfaction leads to loyalty, and loyalty drives long-term profitability. We might even term it the conventional wisdom. But when Xerox plotted *satisfaction indexes* against *loyalty rates* it dealt conventional wisdom a severe blow. Until 1991, Xerox's goal was to achieve 100 percent of scores in the 4 or 5 category (i.e., it was looking at satisfaction scores in isolation). Its subsequent analysis of repurchase behavior (specifically the repurchase of Xerox products in the ensuing eighteen months) showed that *a totally satisfied customer was six times more likely to repurchase than was a merely satisfied customer who had awarded a score of 4.* The result: pandemonium in the ranks of the satisfaction surveyors. Indeed, as a result of this analysis, Xerox invested in service levels designed to turn 100 percent of its customers into *apostles* (the company's term for customers awarding it a 5) by 1996. The Xerox experience had profound implications. Simply satisfying customers who have choices is not nearly enough to ensure loyalty. What is needed is *total* satisfaction.

Because creativity breeds imitation, a veritable body of literature has been spawned to examine this link between customer loyalty and satisfaction. Among the most impressive work to.date is that conducted by Jones and Sasser,[16] who, using vast amounts of data provided mainly by the J.D. Power organization, have scrutinized more than thirty individual companies and analyzed data from five industries with different competitive environments and different types of customer relationships. The researchers chose automobiles, personal computers bought by business, hospitals, airlines, and local telephone services as their industries. Their satisfaction rankings are similar to those used by Xerox (i.e., a 1–5 scale); they measure loyalty primarily by the customer's *intent to repurchase*. This measure is attractive because companies can capture the required information when they measure satisfaction, making it easy to link incentives and satisfaction to analytic use, and because repurchase can be measured at any time in the relationship. But perhaps its main advantage is as a strong indicator of future behaviors (i.e., although the measure may overstate the probability of repurchase, the degree of overstatement is consistent, thus enabling reasonably accurate predictions to be made). However, there are at least two other ways of measuring customer loyalty—by either primary or secondary behavior.

Primary behavior involves the accumulation and analysis of data on recency, frequency, amount, retention, and longevity; but because some customers may stay on the list for years without making purchases or using services, it is unlikely that recency, frequency, and amount of purchase will prove to be better measures of loyalty than are retention and longevity.

Referrals and recommendations are, as we have noted, among the most important determinants of loyalty and, though described as secondary behavior, should be incorporated into the analysis when possible.

Now let us see what Jones and Sasser found. The graph showing the link between satisfaction and loyalty for the different industries is set out in Figure 5.6. The industries appearing toward the upper left of the graph operate in environments often characterized by some or all of the following features: proprietary technology, high switching costs, powerful loyalty programs, and dominant brand names. The industries themselves are often regulated monopolies. Those industries appearing toward the lower right on the graph are usually highly competitive with low product differentiation and low switching costs. Because many substitutes are available, customers are often indifferent to the pull of brand names.

FIGURE 5.6

The Satisfaction-Loyalty Relationship

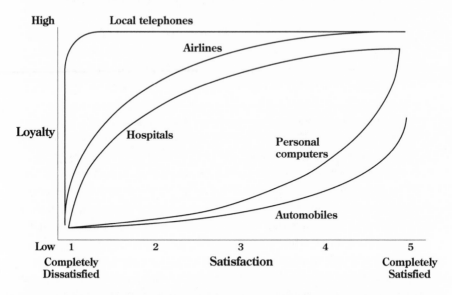

SOURCE: Thomas O. Jones and W. Earl Sasser, Jr., "Why Satisfied Customers Defect," *Harvard Business Review,* November–December 1995, 90. Reprinted by permission of *Harvard Business Review.*

As we would expect, the relationships in general support our intuition. For example, local telephone customers remain loyal no matter how dissatisfied they are (and they certainly seem to be dissatisfied). They have nowhere else to go. But the study's authors argue that in examining other actual or virtual monopolies one sees the curve snap into the shape of a highly competitive market *when the source of the monopoly's hold disappears.* This phenomenon has recently shown itself in the United Kingdom, as British Telecom has lost thousands of customers each month to cable companies—new entrants into the residential telephone market. Had these same customers been completely satisfied with BT, and had BT understood the link between loyalty and satisfaction, such wholesale defections might have been prevented.

In markets of intense competition, the study finds a huge loyalty difference between satisfied and completely satisfied customers. A slight drop from complete satisfaction creates an enormous drop in loyalty and profitability. The auto companies are beginning to understand the importance of loyal customers and indeed now use retention rates as performance targets. Ford, for example, has set the bold stretch targets of increasing customer retention—the percentage of Ford owners whose next car is also a Ford—from 60 percent to 80 percent. Each additional percentage point, Ford reckons, is worth a staggering $100 million in profits.[17]

Of the three less extreme markets, the most dramatic movement in the curve occurred in the business PC market. There is an important lesson here for manufacturers. When the time for replacement arrives, the satisfaction of the actual end user, as opposed to the centralized buyer, may have a big influence on loyalty. So also must hospitals and airlines be on their guard. It may well be that, at the moment, patients have little freedom in their choice of hospital, but when the time to exercise choice arrives, or when insurers are in a better position to widen their menu of hospitals, the graph shows that the curve quickly snaps. Customers who have put up with years of mediocre service on monopolistic airline routes will quickly take their revenge when the situation changes. Complete satisfaction, rather than another round of frequent-flier miles, is the only way of keeping them. The comparatively recent business history is replete with examples of how IBM, Digital Equipment, Amex, and numerous telecommunications, transportation, and airline companies have suffered dramatic losses in profitability from defecting customers through the speedy advent of deregulation, new technologies, loss of patent protection, and decline in brand dominance. And you can be pretty sure they were experts at measuring customer satisfaction! Jones and Sasser summarize their findings by noting: "In the final analysis, the company that will survive and flourish over the long term is the one that continually works to understand the relationship between satisfaction and loyalty for each of its customers, for each of its business units, and for each of the industries in which it competes."[18]

If we now turn our attention back to the customer evaluation guide, we can begin to see how satisfaction reports can help to direct valuable resources. For example, if a customer that has been identified as strategic, significant, and profitable indicates anything lower than a 5 on the satisfaction index, managers should spend time and effort solving the problem. Moreover, the overall satisfaction scores become less meaningful when this analysis has taken place because the majority of "completely satisfied" customers may also be the biggest loss makers! In other words, we need to know which customers we want to keep and ensure that *they are totally satisfied* with our products and services.

Defections Analysis

One way of learning about the strength of a company's value proposition is to ask those customers who move their business to a competitor. Such information is fresh and highly relevant compared, for example, with market research, which tends to be general, impersonal and after the event. That most companies don't perform this type of analysis only shows that few people look at the causes of failure. Indeed, they have been taught throughout their lives to concentrate on success.

Identifying defecting customers is not as straightforward as it might appear. If a customer closes an account, of course, it is clear notification of defection. But what if the customer's purchasing pattern simply begins to show negative signs? Perhaps a company's purchases are slowing down or merely remaining static even though its business is growing? If customers you have identified as worthwhile are beginning to order more from competitors, then it will show itself first in the declining pattern of their purchasing. They will be unlikely to dissolve their accounts completely (unless some particular event causes it) but will become less committed to one supplier. Knowing and measuring the market share of a particular customer is an important indicator of loyalty and profitability, and a negative shift will be a clear sign that all is not well.

To glean incisive information from defectors is not easy, and unless it is done by someone with the knowledge of the business, such information is likely to be useless. Interviews with defectors should be conducted by experienced managers, who can best build a picture of the causes of dissatisfaction and take remedial action. Deere & Company, which has an impeccable loyalty record of 98 percent, uses retired employees to conduct these interviews. USAA is another firm that places loyalty at the heart of its corporate strategy. The company encourages its sales force and all employees to key any information concerning customer complaints or suggestions for improvement into a shared database that is analyzed quarterly. As patterns are detected, the CEO makes a report to the board. Understanding the root causes of customer defection is a company's best early warning system that its value proposition is not functioning properly. Third wave companies must create suitable information systems to build these sensors into their core competencies. Otherwise they will be vulnerable to competitors who are better organized and more alert.

Why Marketers and Accountants Must Connect

Marketing people need the help of accountants and accountants must *learn how to help marketing people.* What use are customers, even the very satisfied 5s, if they are unprofitable and of marginal strategic value? Accountants can help marketers understand which customers to keep (and what level of resources to commit) and give them an idea of how much they are adding to or subtracting from the value of customer capital. Professor Whitney's guiding principles of customer value—strategy, significance, and profitability—can serve as a framework for this analysis, and Reichheld's analysis of long-term value must be part of it. But care should be taken in assessing profitability. Many customers create

extra work and unwarranted costs such as undue demands on management time, credit problems, extra staff training due to their high staff
turnover, and so forth. Moreover, many of these costs (e.g., the use of
technical people to help with demonstrations or other types of support)
are not easily identified within accounting systems. However, many customers are hassle-free. Customer profitability analysis over the right
period clarifies the economics of the customer relationship, and the
strategic fit identifies customers that must be retained.

Issue 6

Management Accounting

Manage the Business,
Not the Numbers

Management accountants must become effective members of the management team; they have to spend less time dealing with financial accounting, auditing, and tax issues. More of their time must be spent learning about product and process technology, operations, systems, marketing, strategy, and the behavioral and organizational issues relating to the implementation of new systems and processes.[1]

Robert Kaplan

MANAGEMENT ACCOUNTANTS AND THE techniques they use have long been under attack for failing to adapt to the new competitive environment. While they may listen sympathetically to the problems of the frontline troops, they have found few reasons to depart from their traditional methods of reporting. They are naturally suspicious of the clarion calls for change and see virtue in caution, consistency, and control (mixed, it must be said, with a degree of creativity). That they hold these views with such conviction is perhaps not so surprising in a world of management fads and short-term fixes that dazzle one minute and fizzle the next.

But as the third wave tightens its grip the news from the front line is not good. Global competition, decentralization, and the rise of knowledge-based assets have changed the emphasis from cost control to cost reduction, and from vertical to horizontal reporting—unfamiliar territory for accounting systems. Even one of accounting's most cherished principles (to match income with expenditure) is struggling to cope. The key investments of the third wave—better service, higher quality, extended customer loyalty, and increased knowledge—are not so easily matched with their future income, and unlike hard-side investments such as plant and buildings, these soft-side investments are treated as fixed costs and immediately written off. Where third wave managers see value, accountants invariably see cost. Inadequate accounting is not the cause of poorly managed companies, but the two often go together. As one recent article noted about a midsize waste recycling company, Safety-Kleen, "the main purpose of the cost accounting system was to help the accounting department keep the books, not to help operations do its job."[2] Accounting in the third wave must return to its roots and *service the needs of its customers*, that is, hard-pressed operational and process managers.

So what is it that accountants must do to delight their customers? There are many target areas from which to choose, but we have selected two that should be high on the list. In a recent survey, U.S. management accountants cited these as the two priorities likely to increase most in importance:[3]

1. Product and customer profitability—helping managers determine which products, services, and customers are profitable. (As we have already dealt with customer profitability under Issue 5, the focus here will be on products and services.)
2. Process improvement—helping managers improve the performance and reduce the costs of business processes.

Issue 6 proposes some possible pathways toward a more supportive view of the role of management accounting in the third wave company.

Product Profitability

To understand the problems confronting accounting systems today, it is necessary to trace some of the changes that have taken place through the twentieth century. The second wave view of costs and competitiveness is deeply ingrained, and its impact on strategic decision making has been profound. We begin by explaining the traditional cost mentality.

Competitiveness and the Traditional Cost Management Mentality

Second wave companies were built on the premise that bigger was better. Fueled by the great energy-based technologies of coal, oil, and electric power, and driven by large factories filled with high-powered machines, second wave manufacturers soon learned that the route to improved competitiveness was scale and speed. While this was clearly understood by early business leaders such as Henry Ford and Andrew Carnegie, they also realized that quality mattered, and that the way to achieve higher quality was to train workers, pay them well, and balance processes so that work flowed according to customer demand.

Henry Ford introduced the Model T in 1908 and the first moving assembly line in 1913. The car came in nine body styles but each rode on the same chassis, which contained all the mechanical parts. Assembly-line workers were responsible for simple repetitive tasks, leaving the design, product engineering, and quality to functional specialists. Productivity rocketed and the rest, as they say, is history. But Henry Ford was even cleverer than historians imagined. He knew he had to sell the car at around $500 to achieve his targets, and this led to his innovative production methods and overwhelming need for simplicity in production and maintenance. Thus he offered a single color (black) and only a few styles, enabling him to constantly reduce costs.

Ford's accountants didn't need to work hard to calculate the unit cost of a car. It was simple. Divide the *total costs* by units produced. Nor did Ford believe in the notion of fixed and variable costs; in his mind *all costs were variable*. Meetings held to discuss cost reductions would focus on reducing the number of parts and improving their quality, increasing the proportion of work done right the first time, and reducing the cost of inventories. Ramping up production volumes to recover the fixed costs of functions and departments was never considered. Ford was a brilliant marketer first and a brilliant producer second. Levitt quotes a most revealing section from Henry Ford's 1923 book, *My Life and Work*:

> Our policy is to reduce the price, expand the operations, and improve the article. You will notice that the reduction of price comes first. We have never considered any costs as fixed. Therefore we first reduce the price to the point where we believe more sales will result. Then we go ahead and try to make the prices. We do not bother about the costs. The new price forces the costs down. The more usual way is to take the costs and then determine the price; and although that method may be scientific in the narrow sense, it is not scientific in the broad sense, because what earthly use is it to know the cost if it tells you that you cannot manufacture at a price at which the article can be sold? But more to the point is the fact that, although one may calculate what a cost is, and of course all of our costs are carefully calculated, no one knows what a cost ought to be. One of the ways of discovering...is to name a price as low as to force everybody in the place to the highest point of efficiency. The low price makes everybody dig for profits. We make more discoveries concerning manufacturing and selling under this forced method than by any method of leisurely investigation.[4]

Is this is not the most articulate exposition of what we now know as *target costing*? How is it that the Ford Motor Company and most of Western business subsequently ignored this dictum and left the way clear for Japanese manufacturers to use it to devastating effect in world markets?

Ford's strategy was, in contemporary language, one of operational excellence. He designed for manufacturability; increased his production speed by controlling his supply chain (mostly by acquisition); and questioned every aspect of the work performed to ensure that it added value to the product. In the 1920s, Ford's total business cycle from mining the ore to shipping the car was three and a half days. By the 1960s, with the added complexity of multiple products, no American auto company could manage this same cycle within five or six weeks.[5] By the time Ford reached peak production volume of two million identical vehicles a year in the 1920s, he had cut the real cost to the consumer by an additional two-thirds.[6] The ultimate expression of Henry Ford's business success was the Fordson tractor production system with its carefully balanced processes operating to customer demand—a system which would become familiar to many some thirty years later, when Taiichi Ohno, founder of lean production at Toyota, based his system on the Fordson model.

The Increase in Variety

Ford's primary competition was to come from General Motors, which, recognizing that competing on cost was too difficult, began to offer customers a variety of products "to fit every purse." But competing on the basis of more variety also increased production complexity and, with the need to maintain low unit costs, GM began to decouple its processes. For example, GM produced engines in one plant and chassis in another, thus leading to a patchwork quilt of disparate and unbalanced production processes. GM managers reasoned that the only way to reduce unit costs was to run each separate process at its maximum speed and capacity, which in turn led to the need to maintain essential buffers between processes to ensure continuity of production. Thus production was made for inventory rather than for real customers, a position that led to waste, write-offs, and poor quality. The task of the marketing department was to persuade customers to buy (often unwanted) products at discounted prices, while at the same time ensuring that a "contribution" was made to fixed costs. And the accountant's primary role was switched from the management of process costs to the management of inventory and its valuation for the purposes of financial statements.

This complexity gave accountants other headaches, as the proportion of indirect costs to sales started to rise. They became mesmerized by the recovery of fixed costs. Their models of competitiveness focused on the relationship between costs, volume, and profits. Students learned from break-even analysis and capacity planning how to compute the "optimal" production volume and mix, and the "economic order quantity." Even more insidious was the "contribution margin" approach, which invited managers to increase the range of products and extend the list of channels and customers on the basis that each additional sales unit would contribute to the ever-growing pool of fixed costs.

There we have the crucial switch in emphasis. Which comes first, the fixed costs to be recovered or customers whose needs for products and services need to be (profitably) satisfied? Of course, second wave accountants did not see the question this way. They simply opted for the first solution by default. Thus from Henry Ford's price-led costing, we arrived at cost-led pricing—and the mentality that says we must recover fixed costs by increasing product and customer volumes.

The Collision between New Ideas and Old Systems

While American and British managers were pursuing strategies based on maximizing scale, Japanese manufacturers were concentrating on maximizing work flows. Ohno's lean production techniques at Toyota gradually spread to other firms, and by 1980 they produced more variety in smaller quantities, at higher quality and at lower cost than their Western rivals. They did it by designing and managing flexible processes to satisfy customers, not by pushing output through rigid processes, regardless of customer wants, merely to satisfy top-down accounting cost targets.[7]

When Western firms tried to copy the techniques of lean production, their accounting and reward systems often reported negative results. Initiatives such as just-in-time production and quality programs were brought into disrepute. Standard cost efficiency variances, for example, encourage the recovery of all direct labor hours, no matter what the consequences might be for quality or other hidden costs (such as high or unsaleable inventories) of the finished output. They encourage long production runs and large batch sizes, whereas JIT and TQM programs emphasize production to demand and high quality. The result is invariably more waste, more indirect labor costs needed to patch up poor quality, higher inventories, and a mad scramble at the end of each accounting period in an effort to hit volume and efficiency targets, all of which leads to *higher costs* and fewer satisfied customers.

GE and Harley-Davidson discovered these conflicts when they introduced JIT systems in the 1980s. As H. Thomas Johnson points out, the clash occurs as soon as plant personnel begin to spend time eliminating waste and increasing flexibility, not just producing output. In a JIT system, employees expend extra effort to train and to do things right the first time, pitching in wherever need arises, pursuits that traditional labor reporting systems usually classify as nonchargeable time—that is, time not "earned" producing output. Hence doing what it takes to send customers the *right* output on *schedule* can reduce the department's efficiency rating. That's the clash.[8]

The Increase in Complexity

Many companies today have hundreds and in some cases thousands of products (3M has 60,000!) and tens of thousands of customers in different countries who are reached through a multiplicity of sales channels. The complexity is immense. Where should managers place their efforts? Which products and markets should they expand and which should they contract? Which work supports winning products and customers and which supports loss makers? Do costs support the company's strategy or strengthen its core competencies? These are questions that go right to the heart of business success, but traditional accounting systems, even with the benefit of powerful computers, cannot answer them easily.

Most business managers understand intuitively that a very small number (say 20 percent) of events in a business account for most of the results (perhaps 80 or 90 percent). Indeed, the Italian economist Vilfredo Pareto taught us this in the nineteenth century, and Peter Drucker reminded us what the real implications of this meant in 1963, when he said that "while 90 percent of the results are being produced by the first 10 percent of events, 90 percent of the costs are being increased by the remaining and result-less 90 percent of events." In other words, "economic results are, by and large, directly proportionate to revenue, while costs are directly proportionate to transactions."[9]

Consider the implications of this view of costs for a typical company. It means that a handful of customers produces all the profits (we noted in Issue 5 how Kaplan's rule suggested that 20 percent of the customers might produce 225 percent of profits); a few salespeople produce the bulk of "good" orders; a small number of products, services, and distribution channels produce all the profits; and a small proportion of the work done in the research labs, the factory, and the office actually adds value to customers. We have noted that traditional accounting systems make no attempt to connect indirect costs with revenue streams (other than by largely arbitrary methods of allocation) and thus managers have little hope of discovering which costs are worthwhile and which are not. When work audits are carried out or where specific research is conducted, the results invariably show that between 20 and 50 percent of work is either unnecessary or of poor quality.[10] Figure 6.1 shows the likely relationship between costs and profits.

FIGURE 6.1

The Relationship between Costs and Profits

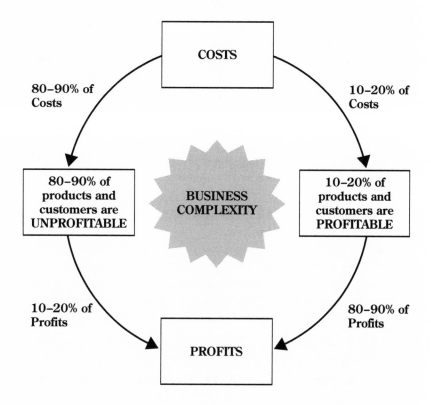

An obvious question now arises: How can managers identify those 80 to 90 percent of products and customers that absorb all the costs but contribute very little to the success of the business? Or phrased in a slightly different way: Which products and customers are profitable?

The Rise of Activity-Based Costing

To answer the question of which products and customers are profitable, it was clear that accountants would need a better understanding of the causes of indirect costs and how they were used to support products and customers. Traditional costing systems (such as standard costing) were concerned primarily with questions of control and inventory valuation rather than of cost reduction and improvement. And with the inexorable rise of indirect costs driven by variety and complexity, these methods were providing increasingly distorted results. John Hoffecker, a cost accounting specialist at KPMG, went as far as to say, "It's better to have no cost system than a standard cost system because it is so inaccurate."[11]

By the mid-1980s U.S. companies John Deere, HP, and Textronix and European companies Siemens, Ericsson, and Kanthal were experimenting with different transaction-based approaches to product costing. These ideas were then taken up by Harvard academics Robert Kaplan and Robin Cooper and became known as activity-based costing (ABC). ABC analysis presents a clearer picture of product costs through a better identification of the costs of activities (such as machine setups or purchase orders) consumed by products. Using ABC, many indirect costs could be more clearly related to the products and customers that consumed them, giving managers a more accurate picture of product and customer profitability. While this data helped designers better understand the cost implications of their design options and helped managers improve their product mix decisions, ABC was initially seen as no more than a better method of cost allocation that was of marginal benefit in improving profitability. Two crucial breakthroughs were required before it could fully deliver on its initial promise.

These breakthroughs came in a seminal article by Cooper and Kaplan entitled "Profit Priorities from Activity-Based Costing," in which they explained the causes of costs in terms of the production hierarchy and excess capacity.[12] They noted that costs were caused at four different levels:

1.   individual unit level (labor, materials, energy)
2.   batch level (setups, material movements, inspections)
3.   product-line level (engineering specifications, process engineering, engineering change notices)
4.   facility level (building costs, plant maintenance, administration)

Similarly, sales costs were caused at the brand, channel, and customer level. Cooper and Kaplan asserted that all costs could be attributed to one of these levels and that, consequently, *only by changing the capacity constraints at each level could costs be controlled.*

This hierarchical view of cost attribution provided managers with new insights about how to link activity costs to operating capacity and, by comparing actual usage with budget, how to derive useful information regarding excess capacity costs. Managers realized that because batch or product-line expenses didn't vary at the unit level, they could not be controlled at that level. This was in stark contrast to the traditional costing system that lumped all these costs together (as fixed) and charged them to products according to the volume (or cost) of direct labor expended. Kaplan and Cooper's work went a long way toward explaining the impact of variety and complexity on total costs, and it enabled organizations to optimize their work flows according to their mix of products and customers. These insights, for example, explained how two factories with identical physical outputs might have completely different cost structures. Kaplan and Cooper used the example of a pen factory to illustrate their point. Suppose one factory produced one million standard pens of one color and another produced the same number of pens but in 2,000 different colors and varieties. It is hardly surprising that the second factory would have much higher levels of expenses to support its product mix and multiple production runs. But these expenses are not incurred at the product-unit level; they are incurred at the batch, product-sustaining, and facility levels.

Of course, this simple example does not mean that pursuing a policy of product variety is necessarily wrong. Competitive imperatives may demand this approach, but ABC makes it clear to designers and managers that prices should reflect these extra costs; otherwise, these products will be unprofitable. Traditional systems fail to reveal these important differences. Kaplan and Cooper note that high-volume products should be produced in facilities optimized to perform unit-level activities, whereas low-volume, high-variety products should be produced in facilities that are finely tuned for batch and product-sustaining activities (such as a job shop with skilled, versatile employees and general purpose equipment).[13]

The second theoretical breakthrough was equally important. Whereas traditional systems allocate all costs to products and services, ABC measures the cost of the resources *consumed* by products and services, *not the resources available*. A new equation was now visible: cost of resources supplied = cost of resources used + cost of unused capacity. Cooper and Kaplan explain the principle of excess capacity in relation to a purchase ordering department in which there are ten people (the resource supplied) whose aggregate cost is $25,000 per month and whose process capacity is 1,250 purchase orders per month (the activity performed), giving a cost per order of $20. But if only 1,000 orders are processed, excess capacity is 250 x $20, or $5,000. The manager is now aware of the extent of resource use and over a period of time can reduce or increase capacity costs. What was seen as a fixed cost under the traditional system is now seen as a variable cost under ABC.[14]

The ABC view of cost behavior challenged the conventional wisdom that the best approach to reducing product costs was to find cheaper suppliers, buy in greater bulk, install higher-performance machines, build more automated warehouses, spend money on industrial engineering studies to shave a few decimal points off hourly labor costs, and, ultimately, relocate production to regions with lower labor costs. Instead, ABC suggested to managers that many of their best cost reduction opportunities were within their grasp. For example, they should reduce setup times, improve plant layout, reduce the need for inspection, build close relationships with fewer, high-quality suppliers, use just-in-time inventory control, integrate buying and payment systems, question product variants that add little extra value to customers, and design products with fewer parts. The challenge to the traditional cost mentality could not have been greater.

But not all in the ABC garden is rosy. While a number of companies have used ABC with great success, many more have experienced disappointment. Indeed, Ness and Cucuzza reckon that up to 90 percent of ABC programs have stagnated or are floundering.[15] There are a number of reasons why ABC projects fail, including lack of management commitment, failure to set clear objectives, and poor links between ABC programs and other management intiatives, such as just in time, total quality, and reengineering. However, perhaps the most important reason for the failure of ABC is that it is often seen by the workforce as just another top-down accounting tool in the hands of the finance department. Let's see how Chrysler implemented ABC and avoided these pitfalls.

During the 1980s, when GM and Ford were desperately trying to meet the Japanese threat through a variety of conventional cost reduction programs such as investing in more automated factories and driving down supplier prices, Bob Lutz, president and chief operating officer at Chrysler, had other ideas. In Issue 2 we noted how he built new relationships with suppliers based on quality and innovation. But he was also keen to make fundamental changes in the company's management structure and costing systems. After first introducing team-based processes throughout the company in the late 1980s, he turned to ABC in 1991. He knew that the introduction of such a system would invite suspicion and that he would need the approval of influential people (across cultural layers and within communities of practice). His fears were well founded. Many objections were raised, including the inability to collect data. Also, by the time the system was introduced, the company was starting to generate good profits. This in turn caused a number of managers to question why such a new system was needed at all.

But Lutz persevered. His first decision was *not to give the ABC project to the accountants*. Instead, he gave joint responsibility to an operational controller and a VP in charge of continuous improvement. In addition, Lutz and CEO Robert Eaton became vocal advocates for the system. Next, Lutz educated the workforce. More than 18,000 workers, including some union officials and suppliers' employees, attended ABC courses. These courses explained the objectives of ABC and how to use the system. The message, reinforced with examples, is that ABC's purpose is to help employees make better decisions, not to get them to work harder or to eliminate their jobs.

The pilot was launched in 1991 at the company's high-volume stamping plant in Warren, Michigan, and it was immediately successful. The ABC numbers showed that the actual costs of some low-volume parts were as much as thirty times the stated costs, which suggested that outsourcing would be a better option for those parts, leaving extra capacity to make high-volume parts. The pilot also uncovered areas of waste and inefficiency that were successfully eliminated. Finally, it helped the plant redesign both its products and processes so that it could make parts for the company's next minivan model much more efficiently.

Lutz and his managers were so impressed that two-thirds of the way through the rollout they decided to introduce ABC into six other plants. Chrysler estimates that since 1991 ABC has generated hundreds of millions of dollars in benefits by helping simplify product designs and eliminate unproductive, inefficient, or redundant activities. And the benefits have been ten to twenty times greater than the company's investment in the program.[16]

While ABC helped managers better understand cost behavior and enabled product designers to learn more about the full costs of components, it was not the complete answer. It remained primarily a reactive cost management approach that dealt with costs already committed, whereas managers were looking for an approach that could support their competitive strategy, one whose numbers were derived from the market rather than from internal costs alone. Once again, the Japanese had gotten there first.

A New Approach—Target Costing

Japanese manufacturers have long used a price-led approach to product costing. Western firms tend to design a product, pass the specification to the accountants for pricing, and then ask the marketing people if the product can be sold at that cost plus the required profit margin. If the answer is no, they either redesign the product and go around the loop again, or they scrap the idea. The Japanese, on the other hand, have product costing systems that are market driven: For what price does the product need to sell in x months time (i.e., when it would be ready to market)? How much profit are we aiming for? Therefore *what is the allowable cost*? Price and profit margin depend on the market share required over the appropriate period of time.

Target costing is a structured approach to determining the cost at which a proposed product with specified functionality and quality must be produced in order to generate the desired level of profitability at the product's anticipated selling price.[17] Its aim is to encourage managers to reduce costs in accordance with specific targets throughout the life cycle of a product. Its focus is one of total cost reduction rather than one of departmental cost control, and its usefulness is predicated on the notion that market prices should influence costs, rather than the reverse. If the firm has a problem meeting the target cost, it attacks the problem either by redefining the product secification within new cost guidelines or meeting with their suppliers to work out a mutually acceptable way of reducing costs. (Often the solution is a combination of both approaches.) *However, what doesn't change is the target cost.* If the immediate suppliers have problems, they are encouraged to discuss them with their own suppliers and so on down the line. The whole supply chain is thus involved in solving the cost problem, the incentive being the guarantee of work to all concerned by the principal manufacturer.

Although the logic of target costing is undoubtedly compelling, its methodology is often painstakingly slow and involves many cost/function reviews with designers and suppliers. Olympus Optical,[18] the Japanese camera company, was a market leader in SLR cameras in the late 1970s, but watched with dismay as competitors introduced high-feature compact cameras that tore into its market share. Although Olympus introduced its own compact range, by the mid-1980s the company plunged into losses. In 1987, it changed its policy completely to concentrate on the features valued by customers and geared its target costs to meet these increasingly volatile expectations. Only when designers and engineers were able to convince managers that market price points could be met, would a camera be committed to production. Only 20 percent of designs were acceptable on the first pass. Those that were not acceptable were subjected to a feature/cost review. In other words, designers and marketers were asked if the "nice to have" features really justified their costs, or whether those features could enhance a product sufficiently to move it up into a higher price bracket.

The essence of target costing is its dynamic approach, which drives managers to look for continuous improvement and ways of reducing costs. It has been the so-called secret weapon of Japanese manufacturers through their period of global expansion. Only in recent years have Western companies begun to use its methods. Chrysler has done so with tremendous effect, and Mercedes-Benz is a devout convert. Conceptually it is simple to understand and its logic is compelling, but its methodology can test the patience of the most professional manager.

Kaizen Costing

Where target costing applies downward pressure on costs prior to the commitment of a product to the manufacturing process, *kaizen costing* continues this cost reduction program throughout a product's life cycle. It is especially useful if a product has an extended life, when there is more opportunity for cost reduction. Kaizen costing methods also focus on the quality of products and the safety of production processes.

Kaizen cost targets are agreed between managers and the workforce and are set within the cost budgeting system. The budgeted costs include the reduction targets so that subsequent variances will show clearly that particular targets have not been met. If variances are negative, the manager responsible will be called to account. Positive variances are rewarded, and groups of workers are singled out for praise. Use is made of charts and picture boards placed around the factory. At Citizen Watch Company, for example, such boards contain pictures of before-and-after improvements, noting the savings and naming the group or individual who identified the savings. For example, one set of before-and-after pictures covered a reduction in the time required to read a set of meters. The person reading the meters determined that the required time could be reduced by shifting them. Prior to the shift, reading each one required two minutes and fifty-eight seconds. After they were moved, a meter could be read in only one minute and thirty seconds.[19]

This example shows the real essence of the kaizen approach to process improvement—every suggestion that leads to improvement, no matter how small, aggregates with other improvements to make a huge difference to overall performance.

Both target costing and kaizen costing sometimes exert unbearable pressures on subcontractors and those employees responsible for achieving cost reduction targets. This can lead to the failure of suppliers, and to some employees (especially design engineers) experiencing burnout—a disposition not made easier when they see their colleagues in marketing and administration subjected to much less pressure. Nevertheless, these elements of the continuous improvement process have contributed to the success of many Japanese manufacturers over the past twenty-five years.

Process Improvement

As we noted in Issue 2, every value proposition has its own operating model and key processes that must continuously break new ground in terms of speed, quality—and, of course cost—if they are to achieve the objective of delivering superior customer value. This means keeping track of process costs, which in turn means being able to continuously review the component activities and take out or improve those that add little value to the final customer. Moreover, different operating models and their constituent processes may well demand different approaches. A firm that competes on the basis of product leadership (where innovation and speed are essential), for example, will have different cost management priorities from those of a firm that competes on the basis of customer intimacy or brand loyalty (where relationship building and brand identity are essential).

The Extent of Wasted Costs

While ABC is focused primarily on the production process, a far greater proportion of added value is generated within other areas of the value chain: research, development, sales, marketing, distribution, IT, accounting, human resources, administration, and customer service. These costs account for up to 25 percent of revenue in manufacturing companies and an even greater proportion of revenue in service firms. In fact, if we take sales, general, administration, and R&D as a proxy for these costs, they run into billions of dollars in most large companies (for example, Coca-Cola spends $7.9 billion on these costs, Microsoft $4.4 billion, Merck $4.6 billion, and IBM $22.8 billion).

According to quality expert Philip Crosby, 25 percent of nonmanufacturing work is routinely redone.[20] It has been estimated that for the typical service company, somewhere between one-quarter and one-third of its annual budget might be spent on work that is either of poor quality or irrelevant to the customer. Janet Gray reckons that "the biggest cost is rework, which is the service industry's analog to scrap." She notes that rework is especially insidious "because it is usually masked as real work. Employees appear to be doing work that is necessary and important—and they usually are—but how many times do they do it before it is right? How often must they fix something before they can add value to it?"[21]

Crosby and Gray are not alone in their views. Most quality managers understand the extent and cost of wasted work, but few know how to analyze it. The pressure to reduce costs invariably falls on process and departmental managers; but after they consult with their accounting colleagues, such reductions tend to fall on people, as people represent the lion's share of cost budgets. The result? Fewer and fewer people are left to cope with the same volume of work, resulting in declining morale, lower quality work, and dissatisfied customers. The problem is that accountants measure costs in terms of salaries, benefits, and supervision rather than in terms of the work people do. By looking at costs through a different lens—processes and activities—managers will be in a much better position to reduce costs without placing themselves under this constant pressure. An example will illustrate the point.

Suppose you have responsibility for approving the budget of a sales department for the following year. Cash is tight, but an increase is needed to meet more ambitious sales targets and, according to the sales manager, an extra twelve sales and three support people are required. The actual expenditure for last year and the budget you have been asked to approve for the following year are presented to you as follows:

Accounting View of Costs	Actual	Budget
Salaries and benefits (85 staff)	$3,000,000	$ 3,200,000
Extra staff costs (15 staff)		600,000
Department expenses	2,000,000	2,200,000
	$5,000,000	$ 6,000,000

The sales manager is quite persuasive and easily justifies his position. Your inclination is to accept the budget without much argument, but imagine your reaction if last year's actual costs were presented in the following way:

Activity View of Costs	Actual	%	
Marketing	$ 600,000	12	VA
Selling	900,000	18	VA
Traveling	600,000	12	VA
Order processing	900,000	18	VA
Chasing incorrect or late deliveries	800,000	16	NVA
Dealing with incorrect quotations	600,000	12	NVA
Attending meetings of no value	600,000	12	NVA
	$5,000,000	100%	

In other words, non-value-adding costs amount to 40 percent of last year's costs. How would this alternative presentation change your view? It would be strange if you didn't react by demanding to know the detailed causes of these non-value-adding costs and how they could be eliminated. Nor is it likely that you would approve any further increase in overall costs; the extra resources being requested are already in place—the non-productive work merely needs removing. In fact the reality is that you would be demanding *cost reductions* and dramatic increases in productivity.

While this is a hypothetical example, a six-month study at a U.K. sales division of Hewlett-Packard produced similar findings (35 percent of all costs were wasted). The study found that 76 percent of deliveries were incorrect, 53 percent of configurations were wrong the first time, and 45 percent of orders needed processing more than once. The exercise paid for itself handsomely when HP "recovered" most of these wasted costs within a year or so. But how can these non-value-adding costs be derived more *systematically*? While the HP study was a one-off project where salespeople recorded their time using a variety of methods including "beeping watches," a number of sophisticated time recording systems and data-capture devices are now appearing on the market, improving the feasibility of more structured approaches.

Eliminating Unnecessary Work and Wasted Costs

In most service processes it is the improvement in the productivity and quality of people's work that matters, thus the key to improvement is finding out what people do, how well they do it, and how relevant it is to the customer. By looking at costs in this way, we can identify how much adds value and how much is wasted. In our earlier book,[22] *Transforming the Bottom Line*, we called such an approach a horizontal information system.

The objective of a horizontal information system is to look inside processes at the relevance and quality of activities and systematically report on their value-adding performance. Two fundamental questions must be addressed: (1) Is a piece of work (i.e., an activity) relevant to the needs of the customer, or can the process of which it is part be equally well performed (or improved) if it is eliminated? (2) Is the *time* spent by process workers consumed in adding value, and, if not, what are the causes of excess work? A horizontal information system recognizes that a great deal of work is involved in corrections, rework, and revisits and is caused by delays and bottlenecks, more often than not the result of inefficient upstream activities. Low levels of non-value-adding (NVA) work speed up processes, whereas high levels slow them down.

A number of steps are involved in the implementation of a horizontal information system:

- Take the total budgeted costs of the process (to include the costs of people, buildings, technology, and management), attribute these costs to each employee on some acceptable basis (e.g., prorata to their base salaries), and divide the resultant costs by their budgeted working hours to derive a cost per hour for each employee.
- List all the activities that comprise the process. Note which activities add value and which don't (a percentage scoring system can be applied).
- Either map employees' standard time to fixed activities and record *by exception* if they spend time outside these standards; or simply record all time by activity as it occurs on a daily or weekly basis.
- Build a picture of activity costs, looking closely at the percentage and causes of those that add no value. These are the signposts to productivity improvements and cost savings.

FIGURE 6.2

Converting Process Costs into Activity Costs

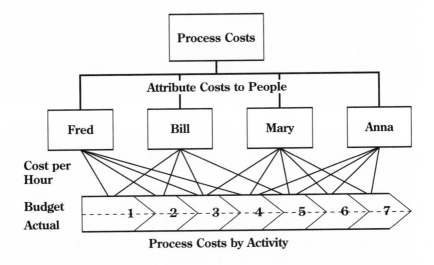

Process Costs by Activity

Such a methodology is familiar to most professional practices that compute the hourly cost of employees and use this as the basis for client billing. But, unlike professional practices, we are interested in applying employees' time (and cost) to activities to gain valuable insights into productivity and the amount of wasted time. The objective is not work study or time and motion analysis, but the eradication of years of clutter and debris from the work process, resulting in more satisfied customers and more secure value-adding jobs.

Figure 6.2 shows the links in the conversion process. The top half of each activity cost represents the budgeted cost at the outset, and the bottom half represents the actual cost once the non-value-adding time (and cost) has been analyzed. This can be viewed in two ways. First, the overall cost for each activity (and the whole process) can be compared and the potential cost savings noted. This might lead to a reorganization of work flow, or it might point the finger at the source of poor quality work that results in delays, corrections, and rework. Second (where appropriate), the cost per activity can be compared. For example, if the activity is order processing, the budgeted activity cost per order might be, say, $12, but the actual cost of value-adding time spent might be only $10 ($2 per order was spent on wasted time). This type of analysis can be useful in a number of ways. For example, it helps accountants compute customer and channel profitability more accurately. It also enables other comparisons to be made. For instance, one process or activity can be benchmarked against another, either within the same group of companies or with an external company. This is particularly useful if managers are considering outsourcing a particular process.

We noted earlier that the primary reason most ABC implementations fail is that ABC is seen as another top-down accounting system in which employees have little interest. The approach taken by a horizontal information system is different. It is a *bottom-up* approach that is *dependent on the involvement of employees*. Its objective is to improve work flow and achieve higher levels of productivity, both of which lead to lower costs, higher added value, and greater employment security. All employees have an interest in making their time more valuable, but few know how to do it. By a process of education and training and the use of imaginative software, they will become aware of which time adds value and which doesn't. They will also find that most non-value-adding time is caused elsewhere, often in so-called upstream activities; thus they have a vested interest in noting its causes and in eliminating its effects.

By continuously improving processes we will begin to see significant productivity gains, particularly from highly qualified specialists. These people dislike nothing more than being distracted from their work, but distraction is increasingly the case among all professionals. For example, who can say that the teacher of 1997 is more productive than the teacher of 1957 despite all the new technology?

Toward More Relevant Accounting Systems

Second wave managers believed implicitly that the way to improve competitiveness was to lower unit costs by increasing scale and speed. But doing the *wrong* things better, faster, or on a greater scale does not lead to improved competitiveness. Nor have accountants understood the behavioral impact of their systems and measures on managers and workers often encouraged (through reward systems) to strive for volume-based targets. Only by linking key business processes to strategic targets and continuously improving the organization and quality of work performed within those processes, will customer loyalty and long-term profitability be maximized. Traditional accounting systems not only fail to support this view of competitiveness, but also frequently undermine it.

CFOs and their departmental colleagues have never worked harder. They are spending huge amounts on implementing enterprisewide systems that can help them see across traditional functional boundaries and avoid the mass duplication of their old legacy systems. But are they spending their time and money wisely? Have they demanded systems that help them answer the crucially important questions confronting organizations in the third wave? We doubt it. There is little evidence of cost management systems that can measure process performance, product, and customer profitability or can link cost management to strategic objectives. Management ideas and accounting systems are colliding rather than connecting.

It would, however, be churlish to suggest that management accounting has not made progress over the past ten years. Certainly many initiatives have taken root—for example, Kaplan and Norton's work on the balanced scorecard (see Issue 7), which has breathed new life into strategic management information. Others include the piecemeal introduction of target costing and ABC. But it seems strange to us that organizations can spend hundreds of millions of dollars on new information systems without considering whether they will answer the key competitive questions of tomorrow—and sometimes even those of today.

Management accountants are not indispensable. Indeed much of their expertise is now codified in computer systems and databases. Most managers know their way around accounting reports and are more than capable of setting and monitoring their own performance measures. But IT has presented management accountants with new opportunities to improve the service they can offer their customers and make a significant contribution to strategic improvement and long-term profitability. But they must first ask the right questions and gear their systems to answering them. Some lateral thinking would not go amiss.

Issue 7

Measurement and Control

Strike a New Balance between Control and Empowerment

> The budget is the bane of corporate America. It never should have existed. A budget is this: if you make it, you generally get a pat on the back and a few bucks. If you miss it, you get a stick in the eye—or worse....
>
> Making a budget is an exercise in minimalization. You're always trying to get the lowest out of people, because everyone is negotiating to get the lowest number.[1]
>
> Jack Welch, CEO, GE

AT THE HEART OF THE SECOND WAVE organization lies the annual budgeting process. Executives typically spend weeks discussing strategic plans, analyzing competitive strengths and weaknesses, and deciding which investments to make, which factories or divisions to close or expand, which work to outsource, and how best to structure their organizations. The results of these deliberations are then taken over by the finance department and translated into an interlocking series of financial budgets for the forthcoming year. Thereafter these budgets become the primary force for controlling and driving management performance.

But do these budgets encourage the right management behavior and support strategic targets? We think it very unlikely. In fact, in many organizations the strategic direction and the budgeting system are often at odds with each other. Budgets invariably mirror the organizational structure of the firm and thus their focus is on the performance of functions, departments, cost centers and divisions. Managers are measured on their own particular piece of the hierarchy rather than on their attainment of · strategic objectives, and this divergence is reinforced by reward and recognition systems.

In most diversified firms, budgets are prepared by each strategic business unit (SBU) and submitted to the head office for approval. Indeed, in many cases budgets also form the basis for future funding. Managers of SBUs see themselves in competition for these funds, and performance against budget becomes a kind of league table where the winners are promoted and the losers are relegated. In this respect the budgeting exercise encourages each SBU to pursue its own separate agenda. But such an approach fits uneasily within the emerging third wave organization.

Issue 7 explores some of these conditions in more depth. It looks at the behavioral consequences of budgeting systems and examines some new approaches that attempt to align performance measures with strategic targets. In particular it examines one of the most difficult managerial challenges of the third wave—how to adjust the balance between central control and the empowerment necessary for the effective devolution of decision making.

Budgets and Behavior

In the 1920s, large organizations formed divisions in order to economize on the high costs of information needed to manage diverse product lines, extensive markets, and different technologies. These companies coped with complexity by placing the activities of each distinct product line, region, or technology into a separately managed compartment (i.e., division) and subjecting all divisions to the financial discipline of a strong corporate staff. According to Thomas Johnson, "The M-form perhaps more than anything else, has legitimated the use of accounting information—especially the use of ROI [return on investment] information—to control operating activities."[2] Johnson also notes that with the coming of the M-form, managers began regularly to delegate responsibility for achieving accounting results, and managing scorecard results rather than process results became standard procedure. In the 1960s, companies increasingly used accounting results not just to keep score, but also to motivate the actions of operating personnel at all levels.[3]

Each strategic business unit, whether it be a division or a separate subsidiary company, was handed its targets, and its performance was usually measured by some variant of return of investment. Following the original scientific management principles of Frederick Taylor, once the "best way" of managing the business was established it was locked in, and each successive management generation followed the same rules. The underlying thread was one of *control.* The head office did not like surprises. The plan was agreed and adherence was expected. But in the third wave economy such blueprints are no longer feasible. Markets change so quickly that local managers must think on their feet and make fast decisions. Organizations need to adapt to a new entrepreneurial environment where expertise concerning strategy, products, markets, and competition now resides with local managers and not with head-office staff. Henry Mintzberg[4] recently expressed his views on this process:

> Part and parcel of this so-called decentralization effort has been the imposition of financial measures—control by the numbers. If division managers met their targets, they were ostensibly free to manage their businesses as they pleased. But the real effect of this decentralization *to* the division head has often been centralization *of* the division: the concentration of power at the level of the division chief, who is held responsible for the impersonal performance. No wonder that now, in reaction, we have all this fuss about the need for empowerment and innovation.

Profit plans and budgets are now the most pervasive control systems in modern business firms. In a 1987 Umapathy survey of 402 U.S. firms, 97 percent reported using a formal budgeting program in their business.[5] According to Simons, there are two accepted truisms in management control literature. First, measurement is critical to management control. Second, participants focus a disproportionate amount of attention on any variable that is measured.[6] In Umapathy's survey, 67 percent of firms required written explanation of the causes of deviations.[7]

Most firms use budgets for target setting and to encourage managers to achieve performance levels. In a study of incentives provided to profit center managers in twelve American companies, Merchant observed, "The vast majority of profit center managers in the 12 corporations face the same budget contract: they are asked to make their budget targets and told that if they fail to do so, at least more years than not, they will face potentially severe consequences." He also observed that diagnostic performance measures were tied to incentive compensation by formula in all twelve of the companies involved in his study. The potentially punitive aspect was noted: "Managers who fail to achieve budget targets usually lose out on many rewards.... Often, even more important, the managers also lose credibility."[8]

Merchant speculates that managers choose highly achievable goals to improve the predictability of earnings forecasts, improve resource planning, ensure that only significant negative variances become a focus for superiors, provide a competitive compensation package, and allow organizational slack for the purposes of experimentation. Argyris further argues that superiors provide relatively easy budget goals to avoid the potential embarrassment of confronting inadequate performance.[9]

Accountants have long known that budgets can exert perverse effects on management behavior, but their focus has largely been on ensuring that managers are measured only against those revenues and costs that are influenced by their actions. Many studies have illustrated that "gaming" is rife. In his 1987 study, Umapathy found budget games and manipulation were widespread. He noted:

> Deferring a needed expenditure [was the budget game] used with the greatest frequency.... Getting approvals after money was spent, shifting funds between accounts to avoid budget overruns, and employment of contract labor to avoid exceeding headcount limits are the other relatively popular games. Almost all respondents state that they engage in one or more of the budget games.... Managers either did not accept the budgetary targets and opted to beat the system, or they felt pressured to achieve budgetary targets at any cost.[10]

The case of the Calgary General Hospital in Alberta, Canada[11] provides an insight into the perverse behavior caused by wayward budgetary measures. Calgary General is one of Canada's public hospitals where, in common with welfare states around the world, the government has been anxious to improve performance and, in particular, reduce costs. Alberta Health gives each hospital in its jurisdiction a budget within which it is expected to operate. There is no opportunity to earn extra revenue. Improvements must come from greater efficiency. Accordingly, Alberta Health produced a ranking scheme known as the Hospital Performance Index (HPI) as "a relative measure of a hospital's predicted resource utilization over its actual utilization when compared against all the hospitals in the group." An HPI score of 1 means that the ratio of predicted expenses for a hospital is the same as the average for all the hospitals in the group.

The HPI both assesses and rewards performance. Hospital budgets for the following year are adjusted according to how well a hospital performs, as measured by the HPI. Thus if a score of 1.05 is achieved and the provisional budget for the following year is $10 million, the new budget will be set at $10.5 million; if the HPI score is 9.5, the budget will be $9.5 million, and so on. The consequences are clear. The intention, of course, is to reward those who perform well and punish those who do badly, the overall objective being to raise performance across all hospitals. But in practice things do not always work out.

In April 1993, Calgary's daily newspaper printed the year's winners and losers according to the HPI scoresheet. With a budget cut of $2.9 million from its inpatient expenditure of $111 million, Calgary General was a major loser. When this was made known to the general public, you can imagine the effect on morale. Calgary General's managers saw pretty quickly that the problem was rooted in its palliative care units, which attend to the needs of the terminally ill; as it turned out, the terminally ill were not dying very quickly. Since the HPI rewards hospitals for fast throughput, this had a detrimental impact on its score, so Calgary General's managers drastically reduced the palliative care program to improve the hospital's rating for the following year. However, when Calgary General stopped receiving palliative care patients from other hospitals in the system, the knock-on effects were severe. Grace, another hospital in Calgary, suffered particularly badly when its HPI score declined and budget cuts placed its survival in jeopardy. Far from acting as an incentive for improvement, the HPI system devised by the accountants led to declining morale, job cuts, and much poorer service for palliative care patients in the Calgary area.

The motivational problems of budgets have been discussed by behavioral scientists for well over fifty years. From the 1930s onward, writers such as Mayo, McGregor, Maslow, Herzberg, and Argyris all argued in one form or another that human behavior is driven not by incentives but by working conditions, job satisfaction, and self-esteem. But by the 1980s the wheel had turned full circle and the views of economists were once again dominant. They argued that the evidence showed that individuals are innately self-interested and find disutility in effort. This served only to confirm the fundamental beliefs in the efficacy of financial incentives and thus give renewed credence to budgets and performance measures.

According to the authors of most management accounting textbooks, budgets change human behavior, compel managers to look ahead, force executives to think, remove unconscious bias, and search out weakness. But Argyris disagrees: "Strictly speaking budgets do not do these things.... Such unilateral and coercive activity will activate individual and organizational defensive routines that are overprotective and anti-learning."[12] Alfie Kohn, in one of the *Harvard Business Review*'s most discussed articles, posited this view:

> Whenever people are encouraged to think about what they get for engaging in a task, they become less inclined to take risks or explore possibilities, to play hunches or to consider incidental stimuli. In a word, the number one casualty of rewards is creativity.... Excellence pulls in one direction; rewards pull in another. Tell people that their income will depend on their productivity or their performance rating, and they will focus on the numbers. Sometimes they will manipulate the schedule for completing tasks or even engage in patently unethical and illegal behavior.[13]

To ask whether or not budgets act as a positive motivating influence on managers is, however, *not to address the right question*. Of far greater relevance is whether the divisional or SBU-level budget provides the right basis for performance measurement when strategic objectives now stress quality, speed, and innovation. Furthermore, as businesses operate in the third wave economy, managerial concerns switch from departmental and divisional performance to the improvement of core competencies, which more often than not extend across divisional and individual SBU boundaries. Mutual support and knowledge sharing become the crucial factors. But if performance continues to be measured against predominantly financial budgets in separate SBUs, then such cooperation and support is unlikely to be achieved. Francis Fukuyama has noted that "there is usually an inverse relationship between rules and trust: The more people depend on rules to regulate their interactions, the less they trust each other and vice-versa."[14] These dilemmas go to the root of the cultural divide between second wave and third wave companies, and crossing this divide is a major obstacle.

The Management Control Dilemma—The Balance between Control and Empowerment

Managers in aspiring third wave companies are faced with a difficult dilemma. On the one hand they want to devolve more decision-making power to frontline managers to give them more flexibility. On the other hand they are frightened to relax the tried and tested budgetary control systems that have served the company well for many years. Executives want to encourage enterprise and risk taking, yet they don't want unpleasant surprises. They want to invest in quality and longer-term improvement programs, but they don't want to sacrifice this year's results. They are keen to give divisional managers more autonomy, yet their executive information systems give them instant feedback on detailed variations from the original plan and thus encourage interference. They want to encourage cross-division and cross-company knowledge sharing and support, yet they don't want to change the product and service based strategic targets and financial plans for each SBU. And although they are not sure whether incentive plans really work, they are afraid to make changes lest they upset the performance applecart.

The shifting balance between fewer controls and greater responsibility has not been helped by a number of recent high-profile cases where traders have lost enormous sums on either legitimate or fraudulent trading. Losses of around $1.2 billion created by rogue trader Nick Leeson brought down Barings Bank (one of London's oldest and most respected merchant banks), and more recently it was revealed that a $1.7 billion loss at Sumitomo Corporation was again the work of one trader, Yasuo Hamanaka, who had been perpetrating these losses for an amazing ten-year period. This has prompted some commentators to suggest that the lax controls in many Japanese companies leave them vulnerable to this type of misappropriation. Certainly other scandals (in these cases "legitimate" foreign exchange losses) at Daiwa Bank ($1 billion loss); Kashima Oil ($1.5 billion) and Showa Shell ($1.6 billion) suggest that something is awry. Even these pale into insignificance against the scale of Japanese property loans that must now be written off.[15] Kidder Peabody, Sears Roebuck, and Standard Chartered Bank have also hit the headlines with internal control problems.

But such apparent breaches of control, though not excusable, miss the point. No one would suggest that financial institutions must relax controls when such huge sums are changing hands every day. What we are concerned about are situations when the behavior of operational managers is driven by budgetary controls rather than by the strategic direction of the business. This is particularly important in a decentralized business. As Goold[16] has noted,

> Decentralization can only work well if two conditions are fulfilled: [first] the center must be able to determine whether the business is on track with its strategy. Unless the center knows when to intervene, decentralization becomes abdication of responsibility, [second] the business heads must know what will be counted as good performance. Without clear goals, the whole concept of decentralized responsibility suffers, since the conditions under which a business head can expect to operate free from central intervention are ill-defined.

The control process should set clear goals and monitor performance against those goals. But too often it is financial budgets that perform this function. However, in recent years some companies have made giant strides to separate financial budgets from management control and performance measurement. IKEA, the large Swedish furniture retailer, is one firm that has recently abandoned its traditional systems of budgetary control. IKEA describes itself as a learning and problem-solving organization that trusts the intuition of its staff, and this belief has led to a more informal and less bureaucratic management structure. According to CEO Andres Moberg,[17] "we realized that our business planning system was getting too heavy; we can use the time saved for doing other things better." Now each region must merely keep within a fixed ratio of costs to turnover. GE and Northern Telecom have also taken such steps in many of their SBU's. The authors of a recent CAM-I report[18] noted that traditional budgeting has little to do with the new realities, time frames, and language of operational management. Some believe that it should be reduced to a role of financial forecasting and cash-flow management. There is a persuasive logic in this, yet the system persists and continues to exert significant power over resources and organizational behavior. Professor Tom Johnson goes even further: "Accounting-based control information motivates the work force to *manipulate* processes for financial ends. Global competition requires companies to use bottom-up information that empowers the work force to *control* processes for customer satisfaction."[19]

Many companies have taken tentative steps to cross the bridge between excessive control and strategic improvement without yet making it to the other side. Most large companies, for example, now include nonfinancial measures in their management reporting systems. Measures of speed, quality, and innovation have begun to appear, but in most cases, they remain subservient to financial measures where it counts—in the executive boardroom and on the computer screens of professional investors.

Strategic Control Systems

To make it across the divide greatly depends on how well executives and managers interact and how much they *trust each other*. As both Henry Mintzberg[20] and James Brian Quinn[21] have observed, grand designs with carefully specified plans seldom work. They argue that most changes proceed incrementally. Mintzberg draws a parallel between the potter at the wheel and the strategist. The potter begins to work with some general idea of the artifact to be created but does not see the detailed design or even the whole conception until the work is part way through. New possibilities constantly arise as work progresses. The present-day manager is often in a position similar to that of the potter, never quite knowing what opportunities might arise that require immediate changes to the plan.

Simons[22] argues that modern firms need four types of controls: diagnostic controls, beliefs systems, boundary systems, and interactive control systems (see Figure 7.1). He uses the term *diagnostic control system* to describe preset planning and strategic management systems. These systems are designed to keep the firm on a predetermined track but they are not sufficient on their own. In fact, if so-called empowered managers are simply left on their own to "get on with the job," and (as so often happens) rewards and punishments are associated with achievement, many will be driven to achieving targets come what may—no matter how inappropriate such targets might have become in the light of changing circumstances and even if their attainment means manipulating the numbers. The big six accounting firms have indeed observed a substantial

FIGURE 7.1

Controlling Business Strategy: Key Variables to be Analyzed

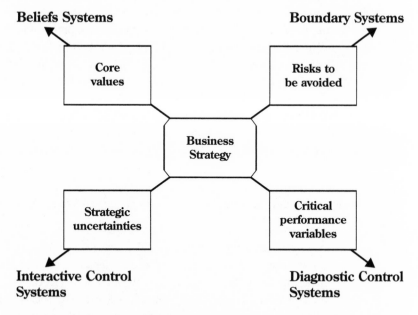

SOURCE: Robert Simons, *Levers of Control* (Boston: Harvard Business School Press, 1995), 7. Reprinted by permission of Harvard Business School Press.

increase in control failures in recent years as firms downsize and cut out many previous checks and balances.[23]

Beliefs systems are designed to ensure that the behavioral context within which managers work is rooted in the firm's core values. They draw managers' attention to mission statements and value propositions that define the style and manner of internal and external relationships. One article noted that successful firms

> are all having to grapple with structures that are almost formless compared to what went before. In some ways they start to resemble the old days of partnerships.... A partnership's central cohesion had little to do with strategy and much to do with shared beliefs and objectives.... It was not the office organization that made it successful. It was the relative freedom of the partners doing the work that created success.[24]

Boundary systems specify and clarify the rules of the game. These include codes of conduct, minimum standards, and ethical behavior. Many companies rise or fall on their reputation and thus these controls are meant to set the invisible limits to what people can do. They are especially important in organizations that have devolved responsibility and decision making and where the management system is based firmly on trust. Sometimes such trust can be abused. The department store group Nordstrom has a book of rules that states, "Rule #1: There are no rules." Some Nordstrom employees claimed that frontline supervisors were pressuring them to under-report hours on the job in an attempt to boost sales per hour. Settling the claim cost Nordstrom $15 million.[25] Team-based structures provide a stronger foundation on which to build the trust needed to be successful. Charles Handy[26] notes, "Freedom within boundaries works best when the work unit itself is self-contained, having the capability within it to solve its own problems."

Interactive control systems describe a different approach, one that relies even more on trust and continuous communication. Interactive systems attempt to understand why performance is good or bad and thus promote a real learning process. Diagnostic systems deal with *outcomes;* interactive systems deal with *processes*. Simons explains the difference:

> Interactive control systems are used to guide the bottom-up emergence of strategy. In the emergent model, individuals throughout the organization act on their own initiative to seize unexpected opportunities and deal with problems. Some of these actions will be tactically important; others will not. Successful experiments will be repeated and expanded. Over time, the organization will adjust its strategies to capitalize on the learning that resulted from testing these new ideas.[27]

Simons notes that diagnostic control systems facilitate *single loop* learning whereas interactive control systems facilitate *double loop* learning.[28] Single loop learning keeps a process within desired bounds; double loop learning leads to questions about the very basis on which strategies have been constructed. Chris Meyer notes the differences with a practical example:

> *Results measures* tell an organization where it stands in its effort to achieve goals but not how it got there or, even more important, what it should do differently. Most results measures track what goes on within a function, not what happens across functions.... An 8% drop in quarterly profits accompanied by a 10% rise in service costs, for example, does not tell a customer-service team what its service technicians should do differently on their next call.[29]

Harold Geneen, the former CEO of ITT, describes the exhilaration of participating in meetings which were subject to interactive control information:

> Not only did we learn and get help from one another, not only did we achieve speed and directness in handling our problems, but our meetings often were charged with such dynamism and enthusiasm that at

times we worked with a feeling of sheer exhilaration. Generating new ideas that were not on anyone's agenda, we came up with new products, new ventures, new ways of doing things.[30]

In interactive control systems, rewards tend to be based on contribution rather than on results. In this way they encourage information sharing and learning. Managers are also more likely to make their efforts more visible to superiors, whereas under diagnostic systems there is often little connection between effort and results. However, Simons is cautionary about the extended use of interactive control systems. He notes that the pressure of operating such systems on management time can be excessive and suggests that only one interactive system should be in use at any one time. All the others will be diagnostic, probably of a strategic control form.

The balance between the four control systems will of course be influenced by the company's strategy. For example, firms pursuing operational excellence will be keen to note that tight diagnostic systems are in place to ensure that waste, delays, and errors are kept to a minimum and that standards are maintained. Firms pursuing customer intimacy strategies will wish to empower their frontline employees to improve customer service and responsiveness. Beliefs and boundary systems will be particularly relevant to keep promises and commitments within the bounds of company policy and capability. Product leadership followers will be more relaxed in their control systems and more interested in encouraging creativity and knowledge sharing among knowledge workers. They will emphasize interactive controls.

Those firms that have taken significant steps down the empowerment road have realized that, given the same information as their supervisors, employees in middle and frontline positions usually reach the same conclusions as their bosses. More important, the arrangement allows frontline managers to fix problems at their own level instead of sending variance reports up the hierarchy and then waiting for top-down judgments. ISS International Service System is a cost-conscious Danish company that has grown from a local office-cleaning contractor into a $2 billion multinational business employing more than 10,000 people. The company's entire control process is built around founder and president Poul Andreassen's belief that people at all levels of the organization will make the right decisions if they are properly informed. Andreassen encourages the thousands of cleaning-team supervisors to run their operations as if they were independent businesses. To help them, he provides them with financial reports by individual cleaning contract. Once frontline supervisors are thoroughly trained, they are able to interpret the data and understand the business's economics. Andreassen finds that they use that information to control costs—even exerting pressure on middle managers to provide value for the overhead they generate. He could never achieve that kind of control through a controller's office.[31]

The four levers of control form an interconnecting web of management systems, styles, measurements, and controls. They act as the organization's eyes and ears and become interwoven into its culture. Such systems are essential in high-tech and service organizations where value propositions are built on creativity, quality, and employee-based service. The design and behavioral consequences of control and measurement systems become even more important once reward and recognition systems are based on them.

The Balanced Scorecard as a Strategic Management System

Controls and measures go hand-in-hand and, as Simons notes, "empowerment needs more controls, not less."[32] No employee can be properly empowered unless he or she is accountable for his or her actions. Thus any move toward more interactive controls must be underpinned by a solid framework of performance measures. But these measures will be very different from those emanating from the traditional budgeting system.

Performance measures should, as we have argued, be determined by how the organization chooses to compete, by its core competencies, and its value proposition. But it must also perform well financially, and it must build and use its knowledge base productively. Figure 7.2 shows some of the measures that companies might use and how they derive from the chosen value proposition.

In recent years a number of companies have begun to make serious attempts to put together a more balanced view of performance that includes many of the value proposition measures we have just outlined. These companies have been given support by the balanced scorecard approach of Kaplan and Norton,[33] who suggest four perspectives of performance: financial, customer, internal, and organizational learning (see Figure 7.3). These measures are derived from the firm's chosen strategy and are mutually enforcing. They are balanced in a number of ways: first between external shareholders and internal performance; second, between the past and the future; and third, between financial and nonfinancial. In compiling the balanced scorecard added weight can be placed on measuring that part of the scorecard that relates to a firm's value proposition.

Kaplan and Norton have discovered that since they introduced the balanced scorecard in 1992, many companies (for example, Rockwater and FMC) are using it to manage their strategic progress.[34] Rockwater

FIGURE 7.2

How Measures Relate to the Value Proposition

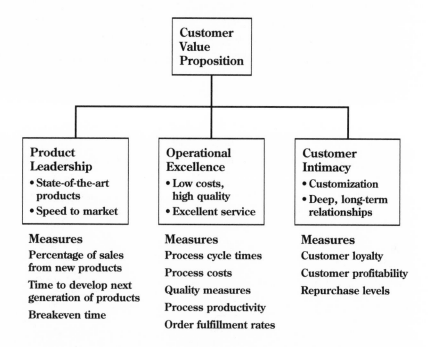

used the scorecard to translate its mission and strategic objectives into operational measures that employees could follow. The result was to structure new customer relationships and to identify a much broader set of important internal processes.[35] Kaplan and Norton note that none of the more than one hundred organizations they have worked with set out to develop a strategic management system, "but in each one, the senior executives discovered that the scorecard supplied a framework and thus a focus for many critical management processes: departmental and individual goal setting, business planning, capital allocations, strategic initiatives, and feedback and learning."[36] In terms of successful implementation they note four key areas: translating the vision, communicating and linking, business planning, and feedback and learning (see Figure 7.4).

Translating the Vision

Many companies fall into the trap of issuing lofty mission statements that sound grand but in reality are just words. Few managers take them to heart, particularly if their performance continues to be measured on traditional budgetary lines. Kaplan and Norton cite the case of a recently merged bank whose twenty-five executives had agreed on a new mission statement that committed the new organization to providing a "superior service to targeted customers." While formulating the customer perspective on the balanced scorecard, executives quickly realized that each had a different concept of "superior service" and "target customer." This led to a reappraisal of the marketing effort and a clearer understanding of the special capabilities they needed to achieve their real objectives.

Communicating and Linking

To make the system effective, top managers must achieve commitment from all SBUs and senior managers. They must, in simple words, "get the message across." Clear goals—both near term and long term—and a linking of management rewards to the chosen measures help. Measures must be customized for and chosen by each SBU to support its own competitive position.

FIGURE 7.3
The Balanced Scorecard

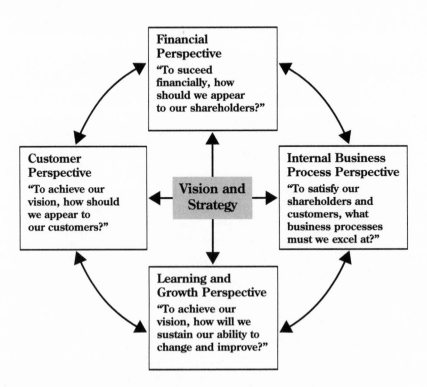

SOURCE: Adapted from Robert S. Kaplan and David P. Norton, "Using the Balanced Scorecard as a Strategic Management System," *Harvard Business Review* (January–February 1996), 76. Reprinted by permission of *Harvard Business Review.*

FIGURE 7.4

The Balanced Scorecard as a Strategic Framework for Action

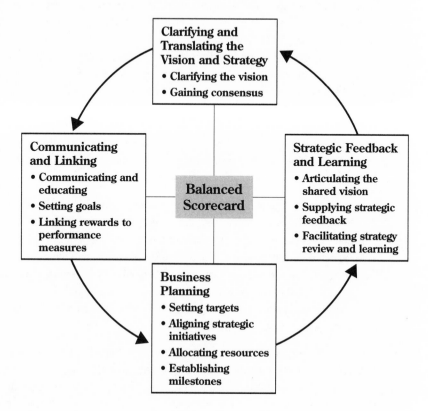

SOURCE: Robert S. Kaplan and David P. Norton, "Using the Balanced Scorecard as a Strategic Management System," *Harvard Business Review* (January–February 1996), 77. Reprinted by permission of *Harvard Business Review.*

Business Planning

Any strategic management system must be coordinated with the financial planning system, but this is rarely achieved and is a common cause of system breakdown. Once targets have been set and milestones agreed on, managers must then take the necessary action to achieve those targets. This is the real strength of the system. Managers will be encouraged to improve core competencies even though necessary investments might not improve short-term profits. In a well coordinated system such effects will be taken into account.

Feedback and Learning

As any line manager knows, understanding the causes of accounting variances can be a frustrating exercise. With a strategic management system, managers can constantly monitor progress and adjust plans according to actual events and competitive actions. In other words, such a system can benefit from what Chris Argyris called "double-loop learning," that is, feedback that links cause and effect and can lead to effective action through a process of learning.

This aspect of the balanced scorecard offers us a practical method of reinforcing Simons's four-way control system and thus finally *consigning the old budgetary control system to the scrapheap.* With frontline managers working within clearly defined strategic milestones rather than financial budgets, there is more scope for tactical changes midstream than any financial structure can normally permit. More important, there is the power of double-loop learning, which can tell managers *why* targets have been missed or exceeded. As Kaplan and Norton note,

> If an organization's employees and managers have delivered on the performance drivers—such as reskilling of employees, availability of information systems, development of new products—then failure to achieve the expected outcomes—for example, higher sales or multiple products sold per customer—signals that the theory embodied in the strategy may not be valid.... Managers must then engage in an intense dialogue to review market conditions, the value proposition they are delivering to targeted customers, competitor behavior, and internal capabilities.[37]

The balanced scorecard undoubtedly offers a more coherent approach to strategic measurement. However, as is the case with all measurement systems, if it is to stand a chance of being effective, users must have *ownership.* The balanced scorecard, for example, constitutes a predominantly top-down view of organizational performance. If such measures are simply rippled down the management hierarchy, they are doomed to failure. Even in horizontal organizations that revolve around process teams, the needs of these teams are often overlooked. But in today's competitive climate, it is the performance of teams that will ultimately determine the winners and losers. Teams do the real value-creating work. It is crucial that the right team-based measures are chosen and that the underlying information systems can track those measures. But whatever the measures chosen, some clear principles ought to guide their selection. In particular, *measures should always be derived from strategy, and as the firm's strategy changes, so should its measures.*

The Relationship between Head Office and SBU

While the balanced scorecard represents a significant step forward in the reconciliation of control and empowerment within strategic business units, the key question remains: How are these measures chosen and agreed on? The real tensions are often between the center and the SBU.

As we have noted, many companies have recognized in recent years that SBUs need to establish their own strategic plans and targets. Only then will they truly "own them" and feel accountable. This has led to various forms of strategic control whereby targets are negotiated between SBUs and the center, results are monitored, incentives are aligned, and interference occurs only if significant variations take place. Moreover, such plans can cover more than the typical twelve-month span of most financial budgeting systems. The success of any form of strategic control often depends on the clarity of objectives, the quality and timeliness of the monitoring system, and the degree of intervention from the center. In a survey of the top two hundred U.K. companies, Goold[38] found that only 15 percent claimed to have explicit strategic objectives or milestones as part of their control process.

However in a small number of companies he found that strategic control processes were quite advanced. These included BP, Ciba-Geigy, ICI, Natwest Bank, Pilkington, RTZ, Shell, and Xerox. Some operated with formal systems (i.e., with specific objectives and milestones) and others with more informal systems. Examples of specific targets include market share, new-product introduction dates, customer satisfaction measures, product quality levels, and acquisition timetables. The arguments for formal systems center around the ability to specify the right objectives and milestones that can be stretched and used as a basis for performance incentives. The central argument was put by a manager at ICI: "When we did not have a formal identification of strategic measures or milestones, there was a danger that long-term alarm bells were missed. There was a tendency to over-rely on financial information as opposed to strategic information about the businesses."[39] However, in a SBU with high levels of uncertainty and rapid change (such as occurs in the computer industry), specific targets can soon be inappropriate. It is then difficult to distinguish between variations that result from changes in the competitive environment and those that stem from poor managerial performance. Moreover, targets set at the SBU level do not resolve the problem of knowledge sharing across the organization. As one Digital manager put it, "Because of the separate accountability it was difficult to provide an integrated approach to large accounts. There were lots of boundary disputes. Instead of being strategists, the product people were being police officers, accountants, and lawyers. Now we are trying to encourage people to work together in a more flexible fashion."[40]

Goold also notes that where companies had adopted more informal control systems, there was a general view that performance measures were unclear. In any case, managers knew their performance was still tied to financial targets. Others saw relationships rather than systems as the way forward. A Nestlé manager reported that "you could achieve your monthly budget targets by disturbing the strategy; for example, by repositioning brands or changing media expenditure. But if you did, it would quickly be noticed by the product group director at the center, not through the formal control report, but through informal contacts with the country in question."[41] The key argument against formal controls, however, is one of inflexibility. For example, the dogged pursuit of preset targets (whether financial or strategic) may prevent managers from seeing and accepting new opportunities. As one manager noted, "Most of our success stories are not based on a disciplined strategy but on reaction to opportunity."[42] Nor is it always easy when things go awry to know whether responsibility lies with the manager or with the targets themselves.

Clearly, although setting strategic milestones must be a significant advance on pure financial targets, many problems remain, not the least of which is the question of how top management can encourage knowledge sharing and overall cooperative support across all the SBUs. Let's see how Asea Brown Boveri (ABB) dealt with these issues on its takeover of Westinghouse's North American power transmission and distribution business.

Prior to the ABB acquisition, Don Jans—then heading the relays division at Westinghouse—operated under a traditional M-form divisional structure with a mass of financially based hierarchical controls and measures. The ABB management style was a severe culture shock. From a highly structured and controlled business with many managerial layers, Jans suddenly found himself in charge of his own business within the ABB federal network of 1,300 companies. He now reported to only two people, one in charge of the worldwide relays division and one in charge of the American region.

As head of ABB's worldwide relays business, Ulf Gundemark saw his role as supporting Jans' initiatives, and, as if to prove a point, ensured that capital requests that took months (sometimes years) to be approved within Westinghouse were given the go-ahead in weeks. More importantly, Gundemark provided support for Jans's strategy, which would likely involve a short-term fall in profits before longer-term success could be expected. Jans also reported to his geographic manager, Joe Baker, who, while not wildly excited by a low-key profit budget, was persuaded by Gundemark to support it (but only after Gundemark agreed to provide expertise from one of the Swedish companies). One of the key elements in ABB's structure is to facilitate cross-company sharing of resources and expertise, and thus budget approvals always take account of resources elsewhere. At the group level, Goran Lindahl had overall responsibility for the performance of the American company.

Lindahl's role was one of building commitment and questioning the robustness of individual company strategies (by, for example, testing them against environmental legislation or potential trade barriers). He was also concerned to embed performance standards that would stretch the organization to achieve extraordinary results. This led him to adopt a fingers-in-the-pie style of management, which he contrasted with the more familiar management by remote control. Managing in this way, he had no problem making direct contact with Jans or other frontline managers to expand their horizons, encourage their initiatives, or help when performance was slipping off track. The interplay of clear strategic objectives defined by Lindahl, the close support and guidance offered by Gundemark and Baker, a groupwide system of information and performance league tables, and the entrepreneurial initiative that was expected of Jans, proved to be a potent mixture of strategic improvement and managerial control. Trust and commitment in key relationships both up the line and across the group were the crucial elements in reestablishing this successful business.[43]

Remote control management will no longer work in the third wave company. In decentralized companies where real authority is vested in knowledge workers rather than head office, managers will have to rethink their control and measurement systems. The balance is hard to achieve. The implementation of a balanced scorecard measurement approach is undoubtedly a major step in the right direction, provided local managers and teams are involved in setting and agreeing on targets. But the relationship between the head office and the SBUs remains a key unresolved issue. ABB's approach of building close relationships both up and across the group network based on trust and commitment must be the right way ahead.

Managers must also be wary of measurement systems and their behavioral implications. Aligning measures and rewards at individual managerial, SBU, and group levels is hard to achieve. "You can't manage what you can't measure" and "what you measure is what you get" may be neat managerial catchphrases, but managers will do well to keep measurement systems in their place. They should act more as a supportive framework to guide strategy than as the overarching report on which success or failure is judged. Such reports, whatever their structure and content, can rarely give their readers sufficient insight into what happened and why. Nothing beats insider knowledge.

Issue 8

Shareholder Value

*Measure the New
Source of
Wealth Creation—
Intellectual Assets*

The true value of a corporation is not in its physical
assets, but in the human
competencies, databases,
organization capabilities,
intangible images, and
ongoing coalition relationships (all services) that it
creates.[1]

James Brian Quinn

WHILE THE BALANCED SCORECARD
provides a more rounded view of managerial performance, financial results remain the primary measure of corporate success—especially in the
eyes of shareholders and executives. Return on
capital employed and earnings per share have long
been their chosen performance criteria, but when
stocks are changing hands at four or five times
their book values, what information are investors
relying on to support their decisions?

Valuation theory tells us that it should be the
present (discounted) value of future cash flows, but
most investors wouldn't have a clue what they are or
how to value them. Perhaps they look at asset backing or dividend yields, but these (like return on capital and earnings per share) tell them little about
managerial performance when capital is such a
small input to the wealth creation process, and key
investments in competencies, customers, and new
products are immediately written off in the profit
and loss account. They might be interested in market and economic value-added—measures that pur-
port to tell them more about real wealth-creating

169

performance—but as we shall see, these are too easily upset by short-term factors. The fact is that while investors undoubtedly look at a wide variety of indicators, they are denied information on one of the most crucial aspects of managerial performance—the changing value and productivity of *intellectual assets*—the brands, loyal customers, processes, and competencies that determine success in the information age. Issue 8 looks at the rise of intellectual assets and how both shareholders and managers are trying to come to terms with problems of their valuation and measurement.

The Rise of Intellectual Assets

Intellectual assets underpin up to 80 to 90 percent of many share values, but their worth (taking the difference between market and book values as a proxy) remains hidden inside the *invisible balance sheet*. Whether they realize it or not, investors are making huge bets on these assets each day without any idea of their underlying worth. Are these bets justified, or are they mere acts of faith? What do investors know about these assets—their existing and future returns, productivity, and how well they are managed and protected? It seems that neither executives, investors, nor accountants know what to do about them. Published accounts and their associated performance measures were developed for a tangible world in which assets can be counted and audited. But for a predominantly intangible world new measures of performance and value must be found.

These issues will not go away. The gap between market and book values is likely to continue widening (despite a number of short-term corrections). As we noted in The Challenge at the beginning of this book, services now provide almost 80 percent of added value (even within so-called manufacturing companies), and this added value is driven by the accumulation and productivity of intellectual assets. How well these assets are managed and measured will greatly influence success in the new economy. Our interest is measurement, but we are entering uncharted territory. In the intangible world measures are seldom supported by audit trails and transaction costs.

We noted in Issue 3 that intellectual assets can be divided into three categories: external structure (the value of brands, customers, and contracts); internal structure (the value of intellectual property, infrastructure, and culture); and competencies (the value of people's skills, learning capability, and management experience). Figure 8.1 shows some of these elements. We must also remember that intellectual assets can turn into intellectual *liabilities,* as many downsized companies have discovered when declining employee morale leads to a disaffected (and devalued) customer base.

Although the existence of these assets has been acknowledged for

FIGURE 8.1

Some Elements of Intellectual Assets

External Structure	Internal Structure	Competencies
BRANDS	**INTELLECTUAL PROPERTY**	**PEOPLE COMPETENCIES**
• Product brands	• Patents	• Professional experience
• Service brands	• Copyright	• Levels of education and skills
• Corporate brands	• Trademarks and design rights	• Training methods
	• Trade secrets and know-how	• Management education
CUSTOMERS	**INFRASTRUCTURE**	**LEARNING CAPABILITY**
• Individual customers	• Processes	• Knowledge sharing
• Sales channels	• IT systems and databases	• Communities of practice
• Distribution channels	• Communications systems	• Problem solving capability
	• Operating models	
	• Financial structure	
CONTRACTS	**CULTURE**	**MANAGEMENT CAPABILITY**
• Franchise agreements	• Management philosophy	• Entrepreneurship
• License agreements	• Recognition and rewards	• Leadership
• Other favorable contracts	• Management structure	• Growth record

many decades (accountants have always known them as "goodwill"), it is the recent explosive increase in their value that has set the alarm bells ringing within the investor, management, and accounting communities. A brief look at some figures will explain why.

The Brookings Institute has calculated that intangible assets grew from 38 percent to 62 percent of market values in the ten-year period from 1982 to 1992 across a range of American *manufacturing and mining companies.*[2] By 1997, average stock market values were over five times book values in America and three times book values in Britain. If we take a snapshot (1995–1996 year-end figures) of a few well-known companies (see Figure 8.2) and take market value as the aggregate value of tangible assets and intangible assets, the ratio of intangible to tangible assets is clearly seen.

In our sample, only Ford Motor has a preponderance of tangible assets, which of course reflects its history of heavy infrastructure investment in plant and equipment. GE's value represents its superb profit record and legendary managerial capabilities under the leadership of Jack Welch. Microsoft's value reflects its high brand image, people competencies (how would its value be affected if Bill Gates resigned?)

FIGURE 8.2

The Ratio of Intangible to Tangible Assets

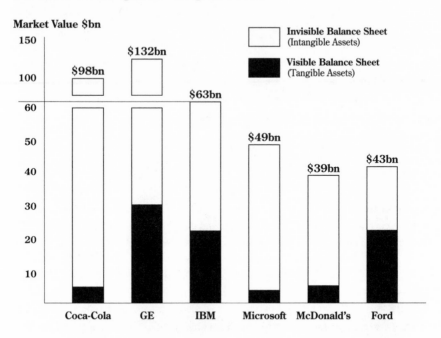

and worldwide customer franchise. The other three market valuations are also heavily dominated by brands. IBM's brand image has recovered well in recent years; and the Coca-Cola and McDonald's brands are two of the three highest valued brands in the world (the other is Marlboro). In fact, executives at Coca-Cola like to say that if the place was wiped off the face of the earth, they could walk right into the nearest bank, borrow $100 billion, and rebuild the company in a matter of months, just on the strength of the brand.[3]

Nor are these figures a figment of investors' imagination. They are regularly underpinned by acquisitions. Take Nestlé's acquisition of Rowntree Mackintosh in the late 1980s, when one brand alone (the KitKat chocolate bar) added $160 million to its net asset value, or IBM's $3.5 billion acquisition of Lotus when Lotus's balance-sheet worth was only $500 million. But in the absence of such market-based transactions, how can we value these assets? And how do we derive measures of how well managers have used them?

While there are still more questions than answers, a number of enterprising companies are making some headway, particularly in Sweden. But the emphasis, quite sensibly, is more on identifying and improving the value *and productivity* of intellectual assets than on trying to formulate and justify their balance-sheet values. Indeed some progress is also being made with methods of valuation—typically using scoring systems (especially in relation to brands)—though we believe these ideas can usefully be adapted to some other asset categories. Intellectual assets have long been treated as a soft currency not to be taken too seriously, but all this is changing as managers recognize how critical they are in the battle for competitive advantage, especially now that innovation, speed, quality, and customization have become its defining factors.

Apart from a few isolated examples, we cannot cite extended case studies showing how certain companies have successfully dealt with these issues. All we can do is look at recent experience and suggest some guidelines. We will first consider the problems facing external information users (such as shareholders and analysts) who must place heavy reliance on published accounts; then we will look at the same problems (and opportunities) from the perspective of internal information users (particularly senior managers) who are able to use more flexible and innovative approaches to the production and presentation of measurement data.

The External Perspective

Ask any seasoned venture capitalist what is the most important factor in building the value of a business and you are likely to receive the following three-part answer: *management, management,* and *management.* But if the real value of a company rests on the capabilities of its management, how are investors to judge such capabilities? Without the benefit of insider knowledge, investors inevitably have to rely on published financial statements, but these statements and the measures investors can derive from them need to be treated with great caution. Moreover, managers who are trying to satisfy demanding shareholders also need to be on their guard against decisions that might appear to provide short-term benefits but may also undermine future performance. Let's now examine the merits of some traditional measures (and their more recent variants) starting with the most familiar of all—return on capital employed.

Accounting Profits and Cash Flows

Return on capital employed (ROCE) is usually defined as profits after tax as a percentage of the total share capital of the business. Its popularity follows from the stewardship principle at the heart of Western capitalism. The ROCE ratio can be expressed as follows:

$$\frac{\text{Profits after tax}}{\text{Capital Employed}} = \text{Return on Capital Employed}$$

To improve the ratio, both the numerator and denominator are open to manipulation. Take the profit figure. One of the easiest ways to make quick improvements to profits is to reduce expenditures on discretionary and intangible investments. When sluggish sales or growing costs make profit targets hard to achieve, managers might try to prop up short-term earnings by cutting expenditures on R&D, promotion, distribution, human resources, and customer relations—all of which are, of course, vital to a company's long-term performance. The immediate effect of such reductions is to boost reported profitability, but at the risk of sacrificing the company's competitive position.

Some companies are also adept at massaging their capital employed. The U.K. conglomerate Hanson PLC, for example, has long been noted for its clever financial practices, as the following example will illustrate. The U.K. accounting system is virtually alone in allowing companies to write off goodwill immediately on acquisitions. According to author Terry Smith, it is still possible to find analysts who do not appreciate that the ability to write off goodwill is the perfect opportunity for acquisitive managements to reduce the CE in the ROCE calculation. Therefore a sluggish performance in terms of return on shareholders' money can be presented as a dazzling result using the standard return on capital formula. As Smith notes, "An investor who calculated Hanson's return on equity net of tax at 24.9% in 1994, and therefore concluded that its management was creating value based upon this measure, would be unpleasantly surprised when the cumulative goodwill of £4.9 billion written off was added back to the equity base to produce a much more pedestrian ROE of 11.6%."[4]

Traditional methods of calculating accounting profits and capital employed fail to make any concession to the huge changes that take place as companies move from the second to the third wave. In particular, they ignore any values and measures that give investors clues about the performance of intellectual assets, even though, as we have noted, these assets now dominate the value of many companies. However, some consultants and analysts have tried to compensate for these shortcomings by making adjustments to traditional accounting numbers. Both market value-added (MVA) and economic value-added (EVA™) are attempts to make accounting numbers more useful, and they have become extremely popular in recent years.

Market Value-Added

The idea of MVA is straightforward. It takes the total capital entrusted to management, aggregating the money raised through share issues, borrowings, and retained earnings, and compares the result with the current market value of shares and debt. The difference between the two is the MVA, which at a very simple level measures how well managers have fared with the capital resources available to them. Thus

MVA = Current market value of shares and debt - (Total capital raised + retained earnings)

A positive MVA means that value has been created for shareholders; a negative MVA suggests its destruction. GM provides an interesting example. In the 1980s, the market value of GM increased by $60 billion—one of the largest increases of any company in America over that period. On the surface, shareholders should have been delighted. But unfortunately, to achieve that increase in market value, GM had to raise some $70 billion, thereby, according to the MVA criteria, *destroying* shareholders' wealth by $10 billion!

One of the benefits of MVA is that it irons out a number of accounting distortions and shows management performance in a more realistic light. Let's again take U.K. conglomerate Hanson PLC, one of the United Kingdom's highest-flying stocks of the 1980s. While accounting results have consistently given shareholders a favorable view of performance, the MVA figures for 1996 showed that managers had *reduced* shareholders' wealth by £2 billion out of more than £20 billion entrusted to them.[5] Of particular interest is how the MVA calculation makes a series of adjustments to the accounting definition of capital (and income). For example, it recognizes some aspects of the "invisible balance sheet" by including R&D as an investment rather than an expense (and then amortizing it over an appropriate period) and by reinstating purchased goodwill previously written off. In all, up to 122 accounting anomalies are subject to correction.

The 1996 MVA rankings[6] show Coca-Cola and GE to be far ahead of other companies with accumulated MVA figures of $87.8 billion and $60.8 billion, respectively. Ford Motor was the biggest loser with negative MVA of $12.9 billion. One of MVA's staunchest supporters, Coca-Cola's CEO Robert Goizueta, summed up his role when he said: "I get paid to make the owners of the Coca-Cola Co. increasingly wealthy with each passing day. Everything else is fluff."[7]

The appeal of MVA lies in its simplicity. But is the difference between capital provided and the current market value of that capital always a good measure of managerial capability? It is certainly an easy concept to grasp and is undoubtedly helpful over an extended time frame (five or ten years), but as a measure of short-term performance (one or two years), it has serious drawbacks. Share values fluctuate for a host of reasons, not the least of which relate to economic factors both at home and abroad and the impact of good or bad news within a particular market sector. Indeed, empirical research has shown that "market movements" (as opposed to the performance of individual stocks) explain a large fraction of any change in the market value of an individual stock.[8] Consider, for example, what happens during a stock market "correction" such as occurred in October 1987, when many markets around the world fell by about 25 percent. How do shareholders distinguish the fall in MVA due to poor managerial performance during this period from the fall due to such an uncontrollable correction? The popularity of MVA has risen on the back of a long bull market, but its measurement sustainability has yet to be tested when stock markets are in retreat.

Economic Value-Added

An even more controversial measure of managerial performance is the profit-and-loss account version of MVA or economic value-added (EVA) defined as the (adjusted) after tax profit for the period less the (weighted average) cost of capital. Thus if a company has after-tax profits of $20 million, shareholders' funds of $100 million (with a cost of capital of 12 percent), borrowings of $50 million (with a net of tax interest cost of 4 percent), its EVA would be $6 million (profit of $20 million less equity cost of $12 million and debt cost of $2 million).

EVA goes a long way towards meeting some of the criticisms of published accounting information. For example, by deducting the full cost of capital from accounting profits, shareholders can measure the real underlying increase in the value of their wealth. Traditional accounting practice does not impute a cost for the use of shareholders' capital. Apart from the cash dividend paid, such capital is often seen to be "free" by managers, but it is certainly not viewed in this way by shareholders, whose real cost is the return they can get elsewhere on their investment funds (their "opportunity cost"). The cost of debt is easier to calculate, but it is the weighted average that counts, turning the spotlight on the optimal capital mix. This has caused some companies to reconsider their approach to raising capital. For example, until EVA was introduced, Coca-Cola was proud of its debt-free status, but under EVA it was penalized heavily for having too little (lower cost) debt. Taking on new debt lowered the company's cost of capital and has helped Coca-Cola maintain its position at the top of the American MVA rankings.[9]

In recent years a number of investors and top-management teams have argued that stock prices are more in tune with EVA than with accounting profits, thus suggesting that EVA is the elusive link between the real performance of a business and its market value. According to James Meenan, chief financial officer of AT&T's long-distance business: "We calculated our EVA back to 1984 and found an almost perfect correlation with stock prices."[10] This has spurred a number of companies to align their internal measures with EVA. Such companies as Coca-Cola,

Anheuser Busch, Quaker Oats, Eli Lilly, and Monsanto have all incorporated EVA measures, in some cases down to divisional levels. AT&T is now using EVA to measure the performance of its newly created operating units. Burton, one of Britain's largest clothing retailers, has adopted EVA at the level of the individual store. Says finance director Andrew Higginson, "The company used to pay store managers bonuses based on sales. That encouraged them to order stocks in the hope that they might shift them, and safe in the knowledge that they could always get rid of the stuff in a sale. It was good for sales figures, and hence bonuses, but lousy for profits."[11]

There are, however, a number of concerns about the overzealous use of EVA. We have identified four such concerns.

Calculating the cost of capital. Calculating the cost of capital for EVA purposes can be a tortuous and very imprecise science. According to recent research across a range of well-regarded American companies, there is significant variation in the way the numbers are derived, particularly regarding the cost of equity capital. The researchers caution that at best the cost of capital is an uncertain estimate.[12] Moreover, which capital figure should be used? Because EVA uses a company's book value of capital (as adjusted for a number of transaction costs over prior periods such as spending on R&D and goodwill) instead of its *market value*, it ignores the full cost of intellectual capital. Think of this another way. The opportunity cost for investors (arguably the best proxy for the cost of capital) is the return (both in percentage *and in dollars*) they would expect on a similar investment elsewhere based on the *current value* of their investment. How can EVA supporters claim to show the real increase in shareholders wealth without first deducting investors' full opportunity cost before deriving such a figure? The problem might be that if such figures were used, few companies would show a positive EVA. On the other hand, EVA profits are also likely to be understated, as it is unlikely that EVA adjustments take full account of costs that should be added back to reflect the full contribution they make to the value of intellectual assets.

The fluctuating capital base. The value of many assets can fluctuate according to a number of uncontrollable factors such as currency movements, changes in commodity prices, and share values themselves (this is why MVA/EVA tables ignore financial services and some utility companies). But many so-called trading companies now include a substantial element of financial services and commodity dealing (GE, Ford, and Marks & Spencer are all examples). Take Shell, the U.K. company with the highest MVA in 1996 (£28.4 billion). How is it that Shell also had the highest *negative* EVA for the two previous years (an aggregate figure of

£6.5 billion)? The answer is that the increase in its (unrealized) oil reserves during this period also increased the capital base from which the cost of capital is derived, and this extra capital cost overwhelmed its *realized* earnings for the year.

The impact on management behavior. Improving EVA means increasing (or at least maintaining) profits while working with fewer assets; lowering capital and operating costs, or investing in projects that beat the cost of capital. But, like most measures that have short-term profits as a core ingredient, managers are encouraged to "make the assets sweat" and reduce operating costs. While this is a fair maxim as far as it goes, when those assets and operating costs are critical (but unseen) elements of future competencies such as computer networks and communities of knowledge workers, then managers need to tread extremely carefully. These potential problems are accentuated if reward systems are linked to EVA performance.

Correlation with share prices. Its supporters claim a high correlation between EVA results and share prices, but recent research casts some doubt on these claims. Two U.S. professors of accounting, James Dodd and Shimin Chen, looked at 566 U.S. companies for which full figures were available for the years 1983–1992 and found that only 20.2 percent of the variations in stock returns could be correlated with EVA—a poorer correlation than that of the much criticized measure of return on assets (which of course uses no cost of capital calculation), which explained 24.5 percent of stock variations. In fact, as the two academics note, EVA is no more than a refined version of "residual income" (unadjusted profits less a charge for capital used), which was popular for a while in the 1960s. Indeed, using their numbers, they concluded that residual income and EVA measures were hard to separate in their correlation with share prices. They also note that more complete models (using regression analysis) resulted in an explanatory ability of 41.1 percent for EVA against 40.9 percent for residual income.[13]

While EVA appears to offer few really new insights into managerial performance, those companies that adopt it soon become its apostles. There is little doubt that by setting targets that must cover the cost of capital (however defined) as opposed to, for example, beating last year's results, managerial thinking and performance is more clearly aligned with that of shareholders. But like most measurement systems, the devil is in the detail, and if employed too rigidly (especially if also linked to rewards), these measures may lead to behavior and performance that damages longer-term success.

Measuring Intellectual Assets

Paul Strassmann, former chief information officer at Xerox, has spent many years looking at the productivity and value of intellectual assets. Keeping with the MVA and EVA terminology for a moment, he sees the relationship between the two in a different light. In his view EVA (or more accurately, *residual income*) is tantamount to the *return* on intellectual assets (i.e., after deducting the cost of tangible capital employed in the business, the remaining surplus *must be the return on intellectual capital*), and MVA is equivalent to their *capital value*. Of course, the relationship between the return on intellectual assets (or the *yield)* and the capital value can work both ways. Thus if we know that intellectual assets are worth $10 million and the residual income is $1 million, then the yield is 10 percent. Likewise, if we know that residual income is $1 million and the yield factor is 10 percent, then we can calculate the value of intellectual assets to be $10 million.

What does this tell us about real companies? The answer is confusing. If we take the companies in Figure 8.2 (1995–1996 figures), and use market value less book value as a proxy for intellectual assets, and post-tax profits less an estimated 12 percent cost of capital as a proxy for the residual income, we find the following results:

	Intellectual Assets	Residual Income	Yield
Coca-Cola	$ 91.7bn	$2.3bn	2.6%
GE	$ 102.2bn	$3.0bn	3.0%
IBM	$ 40.8bn	$1.5bn	3.7%
Microsoft	$ 42.8bn	$1.4bn	3.3%
McDonald's	$ 31.0bn	$0.5bn	1.5%
Ford	$ 17.6bn	$1.0bn	5.9%

This table shows that all the yields are fairly low and indeed would be unacceptable as returns on tangible capital employed. Alternatively, they might suggest that shareholders valuations are awry and do not properly adjust for the value of intellectual assets. The answer probably lies somewhere in between, possibly with the ineffective use and consequent poor productivity of intellectual assets, which are barely recognized and seldom nurtured by most companies.

Strassmann uses other ratios to support his ideas. For example, he believes that because the cost of managing information is now far greater for most companies than the cost of managing capital (he notes that 91 percent of American companies are now more information intensive than capital intensive), the productivity of intellectual assets (or *information productivity,* in his terminology) is of paramount importance. He derives an index of information productivity by first estimating the costs of management, which he assumes to be the aggregated accounting figures of sales, general, and administrative (SGA) costs plus expenditure on R&D, and comparing this with the return on intellectual assets. He reckons that SGA + R&D, by and large, fairly represents the costs of managing intellectual assets such as customers, brands, and competencies. Thus his calculation for information productivity is:

$$\frac{\textbf{Return on Intellectual Assets}}{\textbf{(Profits after tax - cost of capital)}}_{\substack{\textbf{Management Costs} \\ \textbf{(SG\&A + R\&D)}}} = \textbf{Information Productivity}$$

This ratio estimates *what percentage of management costs have been converted into intellectual assets as opposed to being one-time non-value-adding costs.* On this basis he notes that the high flyers are such companies as Intel with an IP index of 98 percent; Merck, 58 percent; Abbott Laboratories, 45 percent; and Coca-Cola, 38 percent. But he reckons that from his database of some three thousand companies, about 40 percent show a *negative return,* even though in some cases accounting profits (in the near term) look healthy, and directors' bonuses (based on those profits) are paid.

In Strassmann's opinion, information productivity indexes are especially sensitive in diagnosing deficiencies that would otherwise remain hidden. He notes that the information productivity measures of firms such as AT&T, Xerox, IBM, and General Motors started to nosedive years ahead of their decline as reported by their financial statements.[14] As with other accounting-based measures, managers are always capable of making quick-fix improvements by cutting the costs of management, but in so doing run the risk of cutting competencies and the value of intellectual assets. To compensate for this problem, Strassmann advocates looking at IP indexes over a complete business cycle.

Problems with Using Published Accounting Information

Published accounting statements were never designed for organizations that have their values underpinned by intellectual assets. Accounting figures are too aggregated, subject to manipulation, open to wide interpretation, and of course they fail to explain changes in the value of intellectual assets. It is therefore hardly surprising that shareholders and analysts who try to use them for measuring managerial performance (especially in service and high-tech companies) face many acute problems, particularly when market values, the cost of capital, and different time periods are brought into the equation.

The way out of this problem is surely for the accounting profession to move faster toward agreeing on new standards for including intellectual assets within published accounts. There would certainly be some advantages. For example, the accounting debate over purchased goodwill would largely disappear, and a more realistic valuation of shareholder funds would improve capital leverage ratios, making fund-raising easier and return on capital figures more meaningful. However, few companies would wish to parade their detailed intellectual assets (especially the *changing* value of their customer base) in front of competitors. But the main problem concerns the lack of any transaction-based audit trail. The thought of having to audit intellectual assets is enough to cause an outbreak of apoplexy among the accounting community.

Nor has the case for inclusion been helped by recent experience. Ever since the U.K. food conglomerate Rank Hovis McDougall (RHM) first included *home-grown brands* (as opposed to acquired brands) in its balance sheet in 1989 (at a sum of £678 million), the accounting and investing communities have been up in arms. The polarity of views within the accountancy profession is well captured by Foster: "At the one extreme is the purist creed, which holds that the balance sheet should provide an accurate summation of past trades and transactions from the formation of the company down to the present time. At the other is the conviction that it should approximate to a statement of value."[15] Suffice to say that the purists still hold the moral high ground. The view of bankers and analysts is no less hopeful—a recent U.K. survey showed that they simply saw the inclusion of intellectual assets as undesirable aspects of creative accounting.[16]

The Internal Perspective

It seems unlikely that we will see intellectual assets appearing in published accounts for many years, but that doesn't mean that companies should not begin to monitor these assets within their *management accounting systems*. In broad terms, the challenge is to measure organizational *capability* and then compare that capability with strategic objectives. While building a framework for monitoring the value of intellectual assets must be the way forward, once again the problems are daunting. For a start, "capability" is a forward-looking measurement concept, whereas accountants typically use only rearview mirrors.

Difficult though these problems are, it hasn't prevented some companies from trying to solve them. But the emphasis has been on devising

FIGURE 8.3
The Intangible Assets Monitor

External Structure Indicators	External Structure Indicators	Competence Indicators
INDICATORS OF GROWTH/ RENEWAL	INDICATORS OF GROWTH/ RENEWAL	INDICATORS OF GROWTH/ RENEWAL
• Profitability per customer • Organic growth • Image-enhancing customers	• Investment in IT • Structure-enhancing customers	• Professional experience • Levels of education • Training and education costs • Competence-enhancing customers
INDICATORS OF EFFICIENCY	INDICATORS OF EFFICIENCY	INDICATORS OF EFFICIENCY
• Index of satisfied customers • Sales per customer • Win/loss index	• Proportion of support staff • Values/attitudes index	• Proportion of professionals • Value-added per employee • Value-added per professional • Profit per employee • Profit per professional
INDICATORS OF STABILITY	INDICATORS OF STABILITY	INDICATORS OF STABILITY
• Proportion of big customers • Age structure of customers • Devoted customers ratio • Frequency of repeat orders	• Age of organization • Support staff turnover • Rookie ratio • Seniority	• Turnover of professionals • Relative pay • Seniority

SOURCE: Karl E. Sveiby, *The Intangible Assets Monitor* (http://www2.eis.net.au/~karlerik/ IntangAss/CompanyMonitor.html.) Reprinted by permission of Karl E. Sveiby.

a methodology to track *improvement* rather than value per se. In other words, by agreeing on a set of performance indicators and tracking these over time, managers gain a better understanding of whether and to what extent they are increasing or decreasing the intellectual asset value. Much of the pioneering research has been done in Sweden. Several Swedish companies known as the Konrad Group have evolved a methodology based on an Intangible Assets Monitor[17] (See Figure 8.3). In 1994, forty-three Swedish companies measured and reported at least some of their intangible assets according to the Konrad model. This model has the same three components we identified in Issue 3 (external structure, internal structure, and competencies). These are further divided into three indicators: *growth/renewal, efficiency*, and *stability*. Only one or two measures within each indicator should be selected and those will be determined by the business of the company. Thus Figure 8.3 is adapted for a knowledge-intensive company.

The Swedish consulting company Celemi adopted this model in 1994. Celemi is a young, fast-growing consultancy, the priorities of which lie with building a strong client base and creating a high level of internal competencies. Its intangible assets monitor was constructed with these in mind. Thus its external structure tracks its *reputation, image,* and *customer relationships*, extremely important for a growing consultancy; its internal structure tracks the strength of *patents, models, systems*, and *general management*; and its competencies track the *capabilities of its employees*, especially how well they could act in a wide variety of situations.

Of specific interest was the way Celemi's 1995 accounts reported on its customers. Celemi was particularly interested in tracking the contribution from three categories of customer:

- *Image-enhancing customers*, who improve the potential to find new customers and thus reduce marketing costs. These customers (usually well-known multinationals) provide excellent reference sites. They contributed 40 percent of revenues in 1995.
- *Organization-enhancing customers*, who demand state-of-the-art solutions that contribute to Celemi's own knowledge and development. These customers are particularly valuable if their projects involve a significant number of Celemi experts who can share explicit *and tacit* expertise with both their colleagues and the client's staff. Celemi was particularly pleased with the results of this group, which contributed 44 percent of revenues in 1995.
- *Competence-enhancing customers*, who help Celemi employees improve their individual knowledge and skills.[18] This group contributed 16 percent of revenues.

Overall, Celemi's revenues grew by 44 percent in 1995, of which 66 percent represented repeat business. The company also increased staff levels by 92 percent and the total competence of its experts (measured in terms of aggregate years of professional experience) by 43 percent, despite the large number of young recruits. It also invested 33 percent of added value in its infrastructure, including large investments in information systems and product development.

The Swedish insurance company, Skandia AFS is the fastest-growing division of the AB Skandia group to which it contributed $2 billion in revenues in 1995. It is perhaps the best known implementer of the Konrad model. Leif Edvinsson, its director of intellectual capital, has designed a

FIGURE 8.4

Skandia's Business Navigator

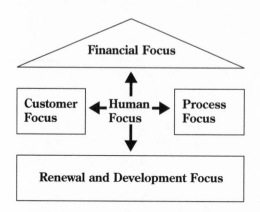

FINANCIAL FOCUS
- **Return on net asset value**
- **Result of operations**
- **Value-added/employee**

CUSTOMER FOCUS
- **Number of contracts**
- **Surrender ratio**
- **Points of sale**

PROCESS FOCUS
- Contracts/employee
- Administrative expense/ gross premium
- IT expense/ administrative expense

R&D FOCUS
- **Premium from new launches**
- **Increase in net premium**
- **Business development expense/ administrative expense**
- **Share of target employees**

SOURCE: Robert S. Kaplan and David Norton, *The Balanced Scorecard* (Boston: Harvard Business School Press, 1996), 212. Reprinted by permission of Harvard Business School Press.

"business navigator" (see Figure 8.4) that combines the Konrad methodology with the "balanced scorecard" approach of Kaplan and Norton.[19]

Skandia uses different terminology from Celemi and others to describe its measurement system. We can assume that "customer focus" equates to external structure, "process focus" to internal structure, and "human focus" to competencies. Skandia has issued a full report (twenty-two pages) on its intellectual capital as a supplement to its 1994 accounts. Under the "customer focus" perspective, the 1994 results showed market share to be 2.3 percent; number of accounts, 14,524; customers lost, 1.1 percent; fund assets per customer, SEK78,000; and the satisfied customer index (scale 1–5) to be 3.95.[20] While some companies would see the publication of these numbers as a free gift to the competition, Skandia clearly believes that customers and employees will be reassured and that the report will lead to long-term improvements and greater financial returns.

While the issue of valuation remains elusive, the Swedish approach creates a measurement framework that enables companies to monitor the systematic accumulation and use of intangible assets. Many of these indicators have strong links with our discussions on operating models and customer relationships. It is clear that strong, efficient, high value-adding processes and long-term, loyal, profitable customers represent a large investment and a significant component of corporate value. Recognizing these investments, at least in the internal management accounts, and including them in performance targets will undoubtedly raise their profile and make managers far more conscious of their performance obligations.

Measurement Approaches Based on Scoring Systems

While any attempt to value intellectual assets is fraught with problems, some progress has been made using scoring systems especially in relation to the value of brands. The brand-valuation technique developed by British company Interbrand Group (and used by RHM) is based on an earnings multiple which is determined by brand *strength*. The brand-strength analysis involves a scoring system based on seven key criteria (shown in Figure 8.5) together with their maximum scores.

When these seven criteria have been considered and scored, the final figure is converted to a multiple that is then applied to the *net profits of the brand*. Thus brand value = earnings multiple x brand profits.[21] Multiples range from 4.4 to 19.3. Take Gillette as an example. In 1995 the blades and razor brand had $2.6 billion in sales and $961 million in operating earnings. The first step is to estimate how much capital was employed to produce the brand. To do this, the median ratio of capital employed to company sales for each industry must be estimated. In the personal care industry this came to 0.38 ($38 of capital was needed to produce $100 in sales). Thus to derive capital employed, you multiply sales by the median ratio ($2.6 billion by 0.38), or $988 million.

The next step is to look at how much better than a generic brand this return is. A generic brand should produce a 5 percent profit on capital employed. So for Gillette this would produce a return of $49 million ($988 million x 0.05). The "premium return" is therefore $912 million ($988 million - $49 million), but before we can arrive at the final income figure and apply the multiple, two further adjustments are required. First, the figures are based on the weighted average of two years' earnings (with a higher weighting given to the most recent year), and from this figure tax is deducted. The final adjusted net income for 1995 was $575 million and its multiple (reflecting one of the most prestigious names in the personal care industry) was an impressive 17.9, giving a brand value of $10.3 billion.[22]

This methodology is, of course, highly subjective, but when brands are compared with one another, and when benchmark values are set in the marketplace, it is perhaps not difficult to see why such techniques have grown in popularity. According to Financial World, the leading brand values in 1996 were: Marlboro ($44.6 billion); Coca-Cola ($43.4 billion) and McDonald's ($18.9 billion).[23] However, these figures are intended to reflect asset values, which may or may not equate to market

FIGURE 8.5

Brand-Valuation Methodology

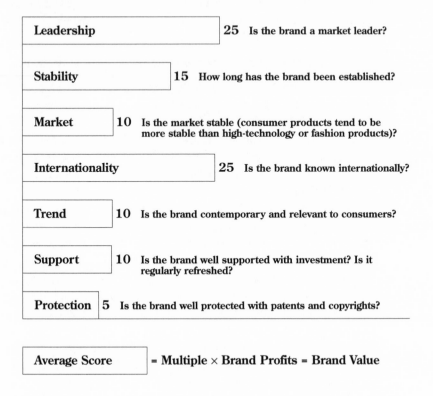

Leadership	25	Is the brand a market leader?
Stability	15	How long has the brand been established?
Market	10	Is the market stable (consumer products tend to be more stable than high-technology or fashion products)?
Internationality	25	Is the brand known internationally?
Trend	10	Is the brand contemporary and relevant to consumers?
Support	10	Is the brand well supported with investment? Is it regularly refreshed?
Protection	5	Is the brand well protected with patents and copyrights?

Average Score = Multiple × Brand Profits = Brand Value

values, particularly (as in the case of Coca-Cola and McDonald's) when the brand is synonymous with the company. Market values are typically higher anyway, as they represent not just a premium income stream, but also the accumulated cost and time it has taken to build the brand to its present-day level. This is understandable when you consider the longevity of consumer brands. Of the top twenty brands in America in 1925, no fewer than eighteen of them are still (more than seventy years later) the best-selling products in their categories.[24]

There seems no reason why such a scoring system cannot be devised for other categories and elements of intellectual assets. However, such methods are more appropriate to assessing strengths and weaknesses than to calculating market values. (Unlike brands, the profit contribution from other intellectual assets is difficult to segment.) We noted in Issue 5 how such an approach can improve the value of *customer capital.* In particular, we looked at strengths and weaknesses in terms of strategic fit, significance, profitability, and loyalty. In the case of *competencies,* such a scoring system would likely emphasize experience, skills, knowledge sharing, and learning capabilities. For *intellectual property assets* such as patents, copyrights and trademarks, measures would focus on the strength of protection and the length of their remaining lives. And for *infrastructure assets*, measures would concentrate on the strategic value of processes and information systems, how much value-adding content they produce, and how well they are managed.

While such evaluation systems are inevitably subjective, they might at least prompt managers to ask the right questions. Apart from the evaluation questions, which themselves might be quite revealing, other results-based questions spring to mind. Why has a particular index risen or fallen? What are the trends? What are the results of our previous actions? What new action should we take? This methodology also lends itself to graphical presentations of scores and trends, which might paint interesting pictures and patterns of performance over time. Such an approach would be particularly useful in measuring the performance or value of a division or strategic business unit with its own customer base.

Dealing with New Investment Proposals

Managers are not only concerned with measuring the performance of existing assets; they are also faced with evaluating new investment proposals. Though traditional methods of investment appraisal were developed for discrete project-based investments such as factories, product lines, and distribution operations, the type and mix of investment projects has radically changed. In the United States, for example, corporations now spend nearly three times as much on information technology as they do on other basic equipment, such as transportation, production equipment, and office fixtures.[25] But IT spending is rarely a discrete investment that can be subjected to financial analysis. It is merely a catalyst for *managing information*, and the real test is thus the *productivity of information*, not some outdated notion of payback or discounted cash flow.

Paul Strassmann has looked at the correlation between IT spending and profitability over many years and can find *no evidence whatever of any link*. He notes that "profitability and spending on computers are unrelated because they are influenced by the way a company is organized and managed and not by the choices of technology. Looking for a 'technology fix' to problems that are fundamentally managerial must end up in failure."[26] Nevertheless, managers still insist on reducing IT spending in their efforts to curb increasing costs, even though such spending averages less than 10 percent of the costs of managing information.

Despite these changes, most investments remain subject to hard and fast financial discounting tests. Factors such as training costs, market-entry costs, process improvements, and cross-functional benefits are difficult to calculate; many projects, taking the more prudent accounting approach, simply ignore them. But by ignoring the wider effects of investment decisions on the value of intellectual assets, managers will likely damage the future of their companies by underinvesting in their key resources. Clearly this is not their objective, but unless a framework (such as the intangible assets monitor) exists for making these implications explicit, then the full picture will not be revealed.

Future Directions

Although there are many differences between life in the second and third wave company, one thing remains constant: cash flow is the ultimate source of strength and survival. It is the oxygen of corporate life. We can devise all the measures we like, but if there isn't sufficient cash flow to pay wages, invest in new projects, and service shareholder dividends, the company will decline and become easy pickings for a more profitable competitor. The whole reason for emphasizing intellectual capital is that it is now the primary source of future cash flows, and managers must sensibly chart its progress. It will be a testing time for the accounting profession, whose traditional measures are becoming less and less useful as indicators of managerial performance.

The management literature is replete with examples of poor accounting measures. While the reported balance sheet is lacking information on its most important (intellectual) assets, the profit-and-loss account gives precious little indication of real managerial performance. Neither MVA and EVA nor other measures that use published accounting data fully redress the problem. Any measures that incorporate market values are subject to uncertain and uncontrollable changes that, more often than not are influenced more by economic and market factors than by managerial performance. However, MVA is perhaps the best measure of performance over an extended period. But EVA seems to be little more than a modern version of residual income (profits less an imputed cost of capital), which was tried and eventually discarded by many companies a generation ago. Trying to make silk purses out of the sows ears of traditional accounting numbers is an exercise in futility and is likely to be of only passing interest.

The way forward lies in the construction and presentation of more useful data, though whether such data should be incorporated within published accounts will remain a highly contentious issue for many years to come. But with the value of intellectual assets likely to increasingly dominate shareholder value, how long can accountants remain silent on this difficult issue? When pressed, the accounting profession falls back on its basic principles, which traditionally lie with prudence, consistency, and accuracy. Accountants distance themselves from any value judgments that might be required to report on performance issues that are not underpinned by auditable numbers. This approach is entirely understandable given the litigious tendencies of many Western companies, but it leaves users woefully short of what they need to know.

Perhaps a better way forward, at least in the short term, is for firms to take the necessary steps within their management accounting systems and provide much more information about intellectual assets *voluntarily.* Some are already moving down this path. One is Skandia AFS, which provides investors with structured information on its intellectual assets. While notions of valuation will always be difficult, managers can make considerable progress by adopting an internal measurement framework that monitors *improvement,* which should itself lead to increased value, whatever that value might be. The potential of scoring systems looks particularly useful.

Monitoring and valuing intellectual assets is a key challenge for today's organizations. The adoption of such measures will surely encourage the accumulation and better use of intellectual assets, and conversely (and just as importantly) discourage their destruction and misuse. As the third wave continues to unfold, will the chief information officer or the chief knowledge officer rise to rank alongside the chief financial officer? The importance of these developments is becoming too great to ignore.

Issue 9

Productivity

*Encourage and
Reward
Value-Creating
Work*

Achieving competitive success through people involves
fundamentally altering how
we think about the work-
force and the employment
relationship. It means achieving success by working *with*
people, not by replacing
them or limiting the scope of
their activities. It entails seeing the workforce as a
source of competitive advantage, not just as a cost to be
minimized or avoided.[1]

Jeffrey Pfeffer

ACCORDING TO AMERICAN ECONOMIST PAUL
Krugman, "Depression, runaway inflation, or
civil war can make a country poor, but only productivity growth can make it rich."[2] Productivity is
the engine of economic growth both for a country
and for an individual organization. Its improvement
is usually measured by comparing the output or
added value from a given set of inputs (e.g., people,
technology, materials) over a particular period.
However, economists have typically measured
manufacturing productivity, where inputs and outputs are relatively straightforward. They have been
less comfortable measuring the 70–80 percent of
economic added value now accounted for by the
non-manufacturing sector. (In national productivity
terms, a percentage point gain in service productivity is now worth about three and a half times as
much as an equal gain in manufacturing).[3] In other
words, traditional approaches to productivity have
little to contribute in the field of knowledge and
service work. What is certain, however, is that the
orientation of any new measures will be less concerned with the *volume of output* (such as the

191

number of orders processed) and more concerned with the *value-adding content of work* (whether orders are processed correctly the first time and without delay).

We have stressed throughout this book that second wave managers have been raised on the principle that productivity can best be increased by minimizing unit labor costs through higher throughput, by using better technology, or by work-based incentives. But this model of productivity improvement is now under serious question. In other words, the biggest improvements in productivity do not come from machines, technology, or incentives, but from *how well managers use technology to improve the organization and quality of the workforce, and whether such improvements meet strategic objectives.* The right management practices, good work organization, and clearly understood strategic targets make the difference. What other explanation can there be for foreign (primarily Japanese) manufacturing companies in Britain achieving productivity levels 45 percent higher than their British counterparts?[4] Nissan, for example, employs thousands of workers in the northeast of England, a black spot in the provision of education and training for sixteen-year-olds. So we cannot assume that Nissan has access to a better-than-average workforce. The only sustainable argument is its superior ability to manage the workforce.

So, what is it that leading-edge companies do so well, yet other companies find so difficult to understand? Issue 9 will review the second wave approach to productivity improvement, and look at the factors that we believe will have a significant impact on third wave productivity.

The Second Wave Model—In Pursuit of the Lowest Unit Cost

The second wave productivity mentality can perhaps best be captured not by the actions of managers but by those of shareholders. Just consider this comment from a newspaper report in 1996:

> Both the stock market and corporate layoffs are soaring. Indeed, they are two sides of the same coin. When AT&T fired 40,000 employees, its share price rose. Worse still, when the government announced that more than 700,000 new jobs had been created in February [1996], the stock market crashed.... Layoffs drive up share prices; higher share prices increase the value of stock options and raise executive compensation; therefore, the road to riches for a chief executive officer is to lay off as many workers as he can.[5]

FIGURE 9.1

Eight Steps to the Lowest Unit Cost Approach

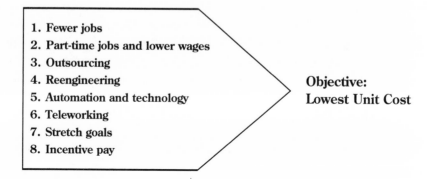

1. Fewer jobs
2. Part-time jobs and lower wages
3. Outsourcing
4. Reengineering
5. Automation and technology
6. Teleworking
7. Stretch goals
8. Incentive pay

Objective:
Lowest Unit Cost

Clearly, if this reaction is any guide, shareholders associate competitive success with fewer workers rather than with the ability of managers to increase the value produced by those workers. What more evidence do we need that the second wave mentality is still alive and well? What, then, are its characteristics and, what are the principal policies pursued by the second wave manager to improve productivity? We show eight possibilities in Figure 9.1.

1. Fewer Jobs

Productivity measures have a numerator (normally represented by output) and a denominator (the number of people it takes to produce the output). It follows that there are three ways to improve the ratio: increase the output, reduce the input, or effect a combination of both. In recent years productivity ratios have started to feature in corporate reports and newspaper headlines, thus making executives highly conscious of their impact on shareholders. The quoted news report concerning AT&T is a prime example.

Most managers know that it is far harder to increase the numerator (higher output) than it is to reduce the denominator (fewer jobs). According to Hamel and Pralahad,

> The United States and Britain have produced an entire generation of denominator managers. They can downsize, declutter, delayer, and divest better than any managers in the world. Even before the current wave of downsizing, U.S. and British companies had, on average, the highest asset productivity ratios of any companies in the world. Denominator management is an accountant's shortcut to asset productivity.[6]

Many second wave managers have butchered their workforces in the name of productivity, but with the loss of so many key supervisors and knowledge workers, how much damage have they inflicted on their future capabilities and how much ground have they ceded to their competitors? Though restructuring costs hit the profit-and-loss account usually in the form of "exceptional" or "extraordinary" items, the real damage does not surface until later when accounting reports begin to show declining *operating* results. Nor does it appear that the recent wave of downsizing has had any sustainable impact on productivity. Stephen Roach, chief economist at Morgan Stanley, recently recanting his former view, noted, "The surge of downsizing and other forms of cost cutting may have little or nothing to do with sustained enhancements in productivity. In fact, not one shred of theoretical or empirical evidence supports the interpretation of the recent wave of downsizing as a necessary step in a process of reviving productivity."[7]

Downsizing may have brought some temporary relief, but most studies show that further action is soon needed. A recent study by the American Management Association,[8] for example, concluded that fewer than half the firms that have downsized in the past five years have subsequently increased their profits, and that only a third have reported higher profitability. Clearly, these companies have not addressed the fundamental problem—poor management.

2. Part-Time Jobs and Lower Wages

Another common way to improve the productivity denominator is to reduce the number of permanent staff and lower the costs of employment. Part-time employees, for example, rarely qualify for such benefits as paid holidays, health insurance, pensions, and redundancy pay. In fact, this approach represents the most mechanistic price-driven view of employment economics. There is, of course, a role for part-time employment—particularly in casual, low-skilled work—and many employees prefer it. Indeed, there are a number of exceptional companies (usually fast-food chains and hotels) who manage their part-time workers well, but there are many more who employ them just to drive down costs, with little thought for the impact on customer service.

Sears Roebuck found to its cost in the 1980s that changing from full-time to part-time workers was the ultimate in false economy, resulting in falling service levels and disappearing customers, whereas rival Wal-Mart adopted more stable employment policies and took many of Sears's customers. As one Hewlett-Packard executive commented about temporary workers, "They don't tend to be dedicated to the corporate ideal.... They're here to make money, not to fulfill the corporate vision."[9]

The costs of temporary employees and the attendant high levels of employee turnover can be huge and are often hidden by traditional accounting statements. For example, during the Reagan administration's drive to cut the size of government, the Department of Energy went from 21,208 employees in 1980 to 16,103 in 1989.[10] But outside contracts increased 56 percent just between 1986 and 1990, and a study by the General Accounting Office found that "most of the department's $522 million in support contracts in the fiscal year 1990 were...signed because the agency lacked sufficient resources to properly perform the activities."

3. Outsourcing

Few companies have managed outsourcing in a strategically effective way. This is not surprising, given that all the evidence shows most firms outsource to save on cost rather than for strategic reasons.[11] In a wide-ranging study of the outsourcing of IT functions across industry, Paul Strassmann concluded that corporations that outsourced heavily were "economic losers" at the time they adopted the outsourcing practice: "They were shedding IT along with other functions because they were in financial trouble. I could not find any corporation with a consistently large economic value-added and rising employment which outsourced, despite all the claims about "synergy" or "advantages of getting rid of commodity work."[12] Moreover, cost-driven outsourcing policies typically result in patches of overcapacity scattered at random throughout the company's operations, which in turn leads to inefficient internal departments and large numbers of subcontractors that are extremely costly to manage.

There are other more insidious traps awaiting the outsourcer. For example, outsourcing contracts are invariably negotiated on the basis of the budgeted costs of the department under consideration, but it is usually difficult to determine whether these budgeted costs cover all the *problem-fixing work* undertaken by a department. In other words, as many activity-based studies have proved, much of the work undertaken by one department stems from inefficiencies and problems caused by other "upstream" departments. So, in this situation, who will take on this (often unseen) workload after the department has been outsourced? The answer is that the remaining staff must work even harder, or the outsourcing contractor will return to negotiate more favorable terms.

4. Reengineering

Reengineering initiatives have had a marked effect on employment and productivity levels in recent years. Productivity increases of ten-fold or higher have been claimed by its proponents. However laudable its objectives, the success of such initiatives has been minimal. Most reengineering programs (like comparable outsourcing initiatives) have been carried out in the name of cost reduction and are seen by employees as yet another top-down management tool that inexorably leads to fewer jobs.

A recent article explaining the common failure of reengineering projects noted:[13]

> Managers often underestimate the difficulty of breaking the functional mind-set. During the reengineering process, they spend enormous amounts of money defining which tasks the process-centered units should perform and which people should be assigned to those units.... They also give little thought to their own jobs. Many managers do away with functions but fail to change their own positions. They continue to act like functional chiefs even though the functions no longer formally exist.

The lesson is clear. Reengineering cannot work without an associated change in culture and reward systems—and to achieve these needs much more thought, planning, and effort than most second wave managers have so far demonstrated.

5. Automation and Technology

Many companies have sought to crack the productivity problem with a large dose of technology and, to the extent that such technology replaces repetitive and monotonous work, this has paid dividends. But in many other respects automation has not, on its own, produced the goods. The introduction of technology can be counterproductive when managers mistakenly believe that it supports employee empowerment and leads to greater customer satisfaction. But after conducting extensive research in this area, Schlesinger and Heskett noted:

> The growing body of data we have collected thus far suggests that customer satisfaction is rooted in employee satisfaction and retention more than in anything else, including clever technology (especially clever technology, since competitors can so easily replicate it). To go one step further, if the technology restricts employee latitude and perhaps even customer choice, as is the case in some of the businesses we have observed, it can actually create a constraint on strategic alternatives and long-term performance.[14]

Technology can help reduce time spent on a particular task, but it doesn't necessarily improve the quality or service content. This particularly applies at the point of contact with the customer, where it is the attention to service that counts. The customer neither knows nor cares how sophisticated is the technology behind the service. A pleasant smile still goes a long way. One cynic, noting the impact of artificial intelligence in the automation of factory processes, said, "It is rather ironic that the application of artificial intelligence to manufacturing is becoming a popular topic. If intelligence is so helpful to manufacturing in its artificial form, then why have the benefits of the real intelligence been overlooked so far."[15]

After spending billions on technology in the 1980s, some GE managers now believe that redesigning work is the real long-term solution to productivity problems. "We've taken automation out of the factories," says Gary Reiner, GE's vice-president for business development. "We found that in many cases technology impedes productivity." Instead, GE's big breakthrough has been in giving workers flexibility and unprecedented authority to decide how to do their work. "All of the good ideas—all of them—come from the hourly paid workers," says Reiner.[16]

A joint study conducted by McKinsey, Stanford University, and the University of Augsburg of more than one hundred global electronics companies reminds us again that it is managerial ability rather than technology that leads to superior performance. The authors tell us why:

> The logic is clear and consistent: delegation reduced delays in getting management approval; dedicated assignments limit distractions; small team size minimizes time spent on coordination; and higher skill levels support the judgment needed for flexibility on schedule and late design changes. Building such capability, however, does not depend on substituting information technology and automation for people. In fact, the successful companies in our sample spend about 25 percent less on information technology and over 50 percent less on automation. Simpler business processes reduce companies' need for IT and automation. The key issue—for both leaders and laggards—is the development of the whole work force through enabling the delegation of responsibility, *not* the size of the investment in information technology.[17]

6. Teleworking

Increasing numbers of workers are located away from the office or, more commonly, work from home. A *Wall Street Journal* article[18] reported that the number of company employees working from home increased in 1992 to 7.6 million, and a U.K. report noted that of responding firms, 60 percent expected to be using teleworkers by 1996.[19] Teleworking saves office space (and overheads) and in some cases improves customer response times. But a recent survey in the United Kingdom pointed to productivity as the primary driver of teleworking.[20] Laptop PCs, modems, mobile phones, and the Internet are all improving mobile communications and making it easier for these workers to operate, but this type of work places greater burdens on managers and in many cases on the teleworkers themselves.

Charles Handy believes that many firms underestimate these problems. In his view the manager's dilemma is that to manage people who work outside of the local sphere of control you have to *trust them*, but he sees an inevitable clash between trust and the control philosophy that most firms still employ. Managing increasing numbers of remote workers, no matter how good the technology, will present managers with a whole new set of problems, and while at first sight the productivity improvements might appear attractive, they may well rebound unless Handy's warnings are heeded.

7. Stretch Goals

"Stretch targets" are a popular way to demand superior performance from workers, but more often than not they don't have the necessary resources to meet them. So workers use the only resource they have— their own time—and the result is overwork, stress, and ultimately declining performance. Steve Kerr, chief learning officer at GE, offers the following advice for setting stretch targets:

> It's necessary that the stretch target is seen as achievable…. It's not the number per se, especially because it's a made-up number. It's rather the process you're trying to stimulate. You're trying to get people to think of fundamentally better ways of performing their work, to cut out unnecessary work. So in a way, you need to sell people on the notion that we use only a small percentage of our creative energy, that we have an infinite capacity to improve things. Once you do that, you don't need to waste time justifying every stretch target by proving that someone else, either in the company or elsewhere, has proven it can be done.[21]

Kerr also notes that not everyone should be given stretch goals. You can end up hurting your best people. In his view, "the golden rule of every work system is: Don't hurt the high performers. The folks in your best-performing business units may already be stretching themselves to the limit."

8. Incentive Pay

Second wave managers believe strongly in rewarding individuals for their output and thus are willing to fund extra compensation from higher productivity. To these managers, the simple appeal to the basic instincts of people hungry for extra wages is enough. Indeed, in the second wave manufacturing environment piecework was based simply on the amount of product produced in a given time. It was a win-win situation; employees gained more wages, and employers gained more (profitable) output. And despite the compelling research of a number of prominent human-relations academics who demonstrated that people were motivated more by status, working conditions, and achievement than by higher wages, second wave managers (at least as adjudged by their actions) remained unconvinced.

Alfie Kohn is one writer who believes that not only do incentive schemes not work, they typically undermine the very processes they are intended to enhance. Notes Kohn:

> Research suggests that, by and large, rewards succeed at securing one thing only: temporary compliance. When it comes to producing lasting change in attitudes and behavior, however, rewards, like punishment, are strikingly ineffective.... They do not create an enduring commitment to any value or action, rather incentives merely—and temporarily—change what we do.... As for productivity, at least two dozen studies over the last three decades have conclusively shown that people who expect to receive a reward for completing a task or for doing that task successfully simply do not perform as well as those who expect no reward at all.[22]

In Kohn's view, rewards buy temporary compliance, so they appear to work. But it's harder to spot the other problems they create. For example, rewards can be manipulated, people feel controlled, and this can cause a rupturing of relationships. Many studies have shown that employees care more about training, the workplace environment, and satisfied customers than about pay and rewards. So maybe the way forward is to reduce rewards over time and increase investment in training, make the work environment more appealing, and improve customer satisfaction. Other studies[23] have shown that profit participation (particularly through shareholding) is the way to build a strong, loyal, and committed workforce.

The Third Wave Model—In Pursuit of Value-Adding Work

The subject of productivity, pay, motivation, empowerment, and rewards has attracted more discussion and debate than just about any other management topic. But as with most key management issues, there is no one "magic formula" that can be adopted. All we can do is look into the crystal ball of the third wave and see how well some of the tried and tested principles of enlightened authors fit into the picture.

The world has finally caught up with the views of McGregor, Maslow, Argyris, and Herzberg. Most human resource managers would agree that

FIGURE 9.2

Eight Steps to the Highest Value-Adding Work

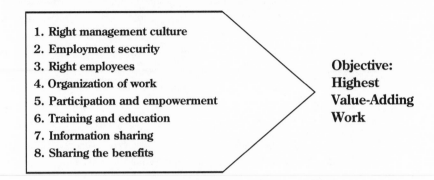

1. Right management culture
2. Employment security
3. Right employees
4. Organization of work
5. Participation and empowerment
6. Training and education
7. Information sharing
8. Sharing the benefits

Objective:
Highest
Value-Adding
Work

McGregor's *Theory Y* (people produce better results through more responsibility and higher job satisfaction) is more in line with reality than *Theory X* (people need to be told what to do), and that Herzberg's *motivator factors* or *satisfiers* (achievement, recognition, and responsibility) have gained preeminence over his *hygiene factors* or *dissatisfiers* (company policy, working conditions, pay, status, and security). Moreover, Herzberg's most telling point is not always remembered. He argued that the opposite of a dissatisfier is *not* a satisfier and vice versa. In other words, if an employee is unhappy because of problems with pay, status, or working conditions, he will not suddenly be motivated to greater effort and productivity by removing these problems. Motivation is a function of achievement, and no amount of pay on its own will drive a person to higher achievement. In Figure 9.2 we list eight key issues that will, in our view, have the greatest impact on third wave productivity.

1. The Right Management Culture

Productivity measurement is, of course, influenced by the organization's own history, values, and culture. However, Frederick Taylor's principles of scientific management, published in 1911, have had more influence than most. The following brief extracts serve to illustrate this view:

> The managers assume...the burden of gathering together all the traditional knowledge which in the past has been processed by the workmen and then...reducing this knowledge to rules, laws, and formulae.... All possible brain work should be removed from the shop and centered in the planning...department.... The work of every workman is fully planned out by the management...and each man receives... complete...

instructions, describing in detail the task which he is to accomplish, as well as the means to be used in doing the work.[24]

But Taylor has received bad press and, according to Peter Drucker, has been much maligned and misunderstood. Notes Drucker:

> Taylor's motivation was not efficiency. It was not the creation of profits for the owners. To his very death he maintained that the major beneficiary of the fruits of productivity had to be the worker and not the owner. His main motivation was the creation of a society in which owners and workers, capitalists and proletarians had a common interest in productivity and could build a relationship of harmony on the application of knowledge to work.[25]

Taylor's ideas, in other words, were *right for the time*. In a world where machines drove production, productivity and profitability were determined by the maximum possible output at the lowest possible cost. The impact of these ideas on standards of living over the next fifty years was dramatic, but with the increasing importance of knowledge work, such ideas have proved a liability. Bartlett and Ghoshal note the problem:

> Although a fifties-based culture was ideal in the postwar era when a company's opportunities exceeded its ability to fund them, in an environment in which innovation, responsiveness, flexibility, and learning had become vital sources of competitive advantage, a management context driven by compliance, control, contract, and constraint became more a liability than an asset.[26]

Those Japanese manufacturers who rose to dominate many world markets after the second world war did not of course have these liabilities. In a recent statement, the founder of Matsushita Electric, one of the largest and most successful companies in the world, had this to say:

> We will win and you will lose. You cannot do anything about it because your failure is an internal disease. Your companies are based on Taylor's principles. Worse, your heads are Taylorised, too. You firmly believe that sound management means executives on one side and workers on the other, on one side men who think and on the other side men who can only work. For you, management is the art of smoothly transferring the executives' ideas to the workers' hands...We have passed the Taylor stage.... For us, management is the entire workforce's intellectual commitment at the services of the company.[27]

McGregor et al. would have agreed entirely with these sentiments. Indeed, they were at pains to point out that the right managerial philosophy not only *matters*, it matters greatly. Though many firms pay lip service to this question and produce glossy brochures containing well-meaning mission statements, they often miss the point. It is the outcome of managerial *actions* that matters. In other words, employees only take note of what managers and supervisors do, not what they say.

Values and trust go hand in hand. Whereas second wave command and control organizations could (and often did) operate without the need for this type of trust, third wave networked organizations and process teams cannot. Their success depends on trust. Decisions are, more often than not, taken locally, and people no longer work within earshot of one another. As we have noted, they often work from home, within project groups, or as part of cross-functional teams. Thus it is crucial that managers do as they say and give workers *facts* rather than fluffy talk about values and mission statements.

Consider what underpinned the success of the GM-Toyota joint venture (NUMMI), which became one of the most productive auto plants in America. From 1989 to 1994 a team of researchers from UCLA spent considerable time at the company trying to understand the nature of the changes. The recipe for NUMMI's success, they suggested, was largely the establishment of a new culture, one that would not have happened without Japanese involvement. Its four principal attributes were the following:

- Both management and labor recognized that their futures were interdependent, committing them to become contributors.
- Employees felt secure and trusted assurances that they would be treated fairly, enabling them to become contributors.
- The production system formed interdependent relationships throughout the plant, helping to create a healthy work environment.
- The production system was managed to transform the stress and conflict of everyday life into trust and mutual respect.[28]

2. Employment Security

There is little doubt that both reengineering and downsizing have had a negative impact on current perceptions of job security. As one writer recently noted, "The most accurate description of business process reengineering is sacking two-thirds of the middle-management workforce and insisting that each manager who remains does the work that used to be done by three people."[29] Cutting jobs, reducing wage levels, and introducing automation is not the fast track to higher productivity. Henry Ford put it this way: "Cutting wages does not reduce costs—it increases them. The only way to get a low-cost product is to pay a high price for a high grade of human service...."[30]

It is difficult to see how any company can build long-term success without a loyal and secure workforce. There is overwhelming evidence that employees become more productive the longer they remain with the company. Wolfgang Schmitt, CEO of Rubbermaid,[31] was perfectly aware of this issue when, during the announcement of a poor set of third-quarter profits he noted, "Sure, we could take out a lot of our people. But we'd give up our future. One, we'd demotivate the ones who remained. Two, if there were any good people left, they wouldn't be here long. They'd be looking around. And uncertainty reduces risk taking." Schmitt's plan was to increase productivity rather than reduce people.

Much of the Japanese success has been put down to their lifetime employment policies. Indeed, in the NUMMI joint venture job security was an integral part of the initial union-based contract with the workforce. A recent company survey showed that 80 percent of the team members agreed that job security was the most important aspect of working at NUMMI. The policy also fostered the workers' belief that they were valued as assets rather than as costs to be trimmed during downturns and equally reinforced managers' respect for their employees.[32]

However, much of this evidence flies in the face of the chosen employment policies of both U.S. and U.K. governments, which have extolled the virtues of "flexibility" as the path toward higher employment. Flexibility, of course, has two sides: a "hire" and a "fire." Its proponents argue that firms are more likely to hire people if they have limited commitments (and costs) thereafter. In other words, they can easily divest themselves of recently hired workers if demand falters. While such flexibility might encourage more employment in bars, shops, restaurants, and hotels, it also creates insecurity that can lead to lower productivity. This is exactly what the workers at NUMMI wanted to avoid. Their memories of the old GM plant at Fremont were of strikes, disruptions, and the hire-and-fire attitudes of managers.

3. The Right Employees

The fastest-growing businesses in both America and Britain over the past few years have been "temp" agencies. Many companies find it easy and convenient to hire temporary workers and thus avoid the commitments of longer-term employment. As one would expect, temporary workers have little interest in learning about corporate values or in building customer satisfaction. They expect to be treated poorly and they are invariably not disappointed.

Recruiting the right people is a crucial aspect of building a knowledge-based company. This can become a virtuous circle. Innovative companies attract the best talent, and the best talent is attracted to innovative companies. At Microsoft, which receives 10,000 résumés a month, a large number of key employees are involved in the selection process. According to David Pritchard,[33] director of recruiting, "the best thing we can do for our competitors is to recruit poorly. If I hire a bunch of bozos, it will hurt us, because it takes time to get rid of them. They start infiltrating the organization and then they themselves start hiring people of lower quality. At Microsoft, we are always looking to hire people who are better than we are." Microsoft is looking for creative people, not those who can answer the right multiple-choice questions in written tests.

Companies must look for people who fit well with their values and culture. Allied Signal CEO Lawrence Bossidy put it this way:[34] "At the end of the day you bet on people, not on strategies. Strategies are intellectually simple, their execution is not. Your strategies will not make you a better company." Attitudes and ideas are in many ways just as important as certificates and track record. And the best firms involve employees—and sometimes even customers—in the recruitment process. Effort spent in finding the right employees clearly pays long-term dividends.

Reichheld has noted that those companies that place employee loyalty at the center of their strategy have managed to achieve exceptional levels of productivity, and it is superior productivity that has sustained their ability to grow employee compensation, customer value, and profits. Not surprisingly, these companies take an unconventional approach to productivity issues. USAA, for example, has invested heavily in technology; it is currently investing at a rate of 7 percent of revenues. But instead of replacing people with machines, the company's consistent goal has been to enrich each job and improve every employee's ability to serve the customer effectively.[35] USAA invests heavily in staff training (around 3 percent of revenues) and keeps its staff for a very long time (the average tenure is now 16 years). This means that when customers call in for service, they deal with experienced employees who know the business, know the company, and know how to make maximum use of the technology. It means that sales and service reps resolve 90 percent of customer requests and problems on the first try. There is no follow-up required. That means one of the highest productivity levels in the industry.

Indeed Reichheld builds a powerful argument for the positive effects of employee loyalty.[36] It starts with the early investment in the hiring and training of employees and results in the finding and keeping of *loyal customers*. Reichheld also notes that most firms grossly underestimate the costs of employee turnover. For example, by analyzing the economic penalties of excessive employee churn at a trucking company, researchers found that the client could increase profits by 50 percent by cutting driver turnover in half. And in a stock brokerage firm it was found that a ten-percentage-point improvement in broker retention (from 80 percent to 90 percent) would increase a broker's profits by 155 percent.[37]

Managers at Taco Bell, the fast food subsidiary of Pepsico,[38] discovered that when they examined employee turnover records for individual stores, the 20 percent of stores with the lowest turnover rates were also the highest performers in terms of sales and profits. Sales were double and profits were 55 percent higher than in those stores with the highest employee turnover rate. Taco Bell has now implemented employee satisfaction programs that involve better selection procedures, improved skill building, increased latitude for on-the-job decision making, further automation of unpleasant backroom tasks, and greater promotional opportunities.

Only when service and knowledge workers see that their efforts are properly recognized and rewarded will they continue to strive to offer better service and more creative output. Studies by Bain & Co. have demonstrated that the longer employees stay with a firm, the more their productivity rises. This applies equally to stockbrokers, insurance agents, and truck drivers.[39] Notes Reichheld:

> In many service-driven companies—including some manufacturers—the relevant driver of learning potential is not a company's worldwide market share or cumulative production volume. Rather it is how long individual employees have interacted with specific customers, vendors, and fellow employees in their specific niches in the company's business system. Companies don't learn; individuals do, and their learning takes time.[40]

Banks and insurance companies across America and Britain have failed to heed these warnings. Paying low wages to tellers and administrators looks like the obvious solution to the productivity problem until the learning and productivity penalties for a high rate of turnover among bank and insurance staff *and customers* are measured.

4. The Organization of Work

One of the major initiatives taken in recent years has been the move to horizontal team-based processes. Meyer notes that "every result a business achieves is the output of a process. In order to change substantially the timelines, cost, or quality of any output, one must change the process that creates it. Simply increasing the speed of an existing process will usually cause damage to quality or cost."[41] By reorganizing around key processes and activities, we focus attention on how work is performed. As a general rule, the fewer the steps involved in a process, the more efficient it is. Well-managed processes generally require fewer people to carry out activities. Horizontal, team-based structures mean lower costs.

Management levels are reduced, and the multitudes of auditors, controllers, chasers, and complaints departments are less in evidence. Teams are clearly focused on value-creating activities, directly responsible to the customer, and therefore more in tune with the customer's requirements. Teams have a powerful bonding influence on performance, as one employee at NUMMI noted:

> Once you start working as a real team, you're not just work acquaintances any more. When you really have confidence in your co-workers, you trust them, you're proud of what you can do together, then you become loyal to them. That's what keeps the absenteeism rate so low here. When I wake up in the morning, I know there's no one out there to replace me if I'm feeling sick or hung over or whatever....At NUMMI, I know my team needs me.[42]

However, managers cannot simply reorganize work into horizontal processes without changing the culture of how work is done, recognized, and rewarded. Majchrzak and Wang,[43] after studying the change to a process structure in a range of U.S. electronics companies, looked at the impact on cycle times (and thus productivity) of these changes. To their surprise, process-complete departments did *not* necessarily have faster cycle times than functional departments. In fact, the only ones to show faster times were those with managers who had taken steps to cultivate a collective sense of responsibility among workers that went beyond merely changing the organization's structure. They found that such collective responsibility could be fostered in a variety of ways: by structuring jobs with overlapping responsibilities, basing rewards on group performance, laying out the work area so that members could see one another's work, and designing procedures so that employees with different jobs were better able to collaborate.

In the same way that manufacturing firms are reorganizing around a number of core processes, so some service firms are using "case managers" to coordinate work for customers. Healthcare firms, insurance companies, and banks are among a number of service industries now using this approach, often increasing productivity by factors of ten. Mutual Benefit Life transformed its process for underwriting and issuing insurance policies. Before the case management approach was adopted, the process took an average of twenty-two days to complete (it involved eighty jobs). Now the process takes one person with two assistants two to six days. The reduction in costs of processing is 40 percent.[44]

When the Shenandoah Life Insurance Company spent some $2 million to computerize its processing and claims operations in the early 1980s, it realized almost nothing from the expenditure—handling a policy conversion still required twenty-seven working days and thirty-two clerks in three departments. Only after the company changed the organization of its workforce—relying on semiautonomous teams of five to seven people, upgrading training and skills, and paying more for workers with greater responsibility and higher skills—did case-handling time drop and service complaints virtually disappear. By 1986, Shenandoah was processing 50 percent more applications and queries with 10 percent fewer employees than in 1980.[45] Davenport and Nohria[46] have observed four components of a successful case manager's role. He or she (1) completes or manages a "closed loop" work process to deliver an entire product or service to the customer; (2) is located where the customer and various other functions intersect; (3) has an expanded role to make decisions and address customer issues; and (4) easily accesses available information from around the organization.

However, the key element of success is the use of the right information technology. The case management approach depends on the manager being able to "see" across functional boundaries via various information windows. The implications for the design of IT systems has caused major problems. Multiple windows into disparate systems is not ideal, yet redesigning systems from scratch can be prohibitively expensive.

5. Participation and Empowerment

When asked about empowerment at Eastern Airlines in the mid-1980s, chairman Frank Borman,[47] is reported to have said, "I'm not going to have the monkeys running the zoo." This casual Theory X comment, however, seems to capture the hidden attitudes of many managers who have been driven toward instituting policies of participation and empowerment, but who have not allowed them to succeed. Empowerment does not simply happen by decree. It needs the tools, training, and resources to succeed.

Many companies are realizing that the best ideas and solutions come not from the top management, but from the workforce itself. This comment about Hewlett-Packard is typical: "At one HP factory a decade ago, 4 out of every 1000 soldered connections were defective. Not bad for those days, but engineers were called in—and they cut the defect rate in half by modifying the process. Then HP turned to its workers. They practically rebuilt the operation—and slashed defects a thousandfold, to under 2 per million."[48]

In recent years many firms have sought ways to empower their service workers so that they can deal with customers' problems "on the spot." Some companies have told service workers who have regular interaction with the customer that in such dealings they have "all the authority of the chairman." The objectives of such policies are well recognized.

They seek to delight customers by exceeding their expectations, make fast recoveries from service failures, and turn problems into opportunities. But many empowerment programs fail because service workers, while notionally given the authority, lack the means to carry it out effectively. More specifically, they lack the training to act as "businessmen" and though they may make quick decisions based on good judgment, they lack the information, knowledge, and reward systems to support their new role. Bowen and Lawler[49] suggest that the empowerment equation is multiplicative—that is, if either power, information, knowledge, or rewards are not functioning properly, then the results will be zero. But when firms do get the empowerment equation right, the results can be spectacular.

A recent study provides clear evidence.[50] The Center for Effective Organizations at the University of Southern California surveyed *Fortune* 1000 companies in 1987, 1990, and 1993 to determine the degree and the effectiveness of implementing these policies. Respondents reported that empowerment improves worker satisfaction and quality of work life. Quality, service, and productivity are reportedly improved as a result of employee involvement efforts in about two-thirds of companies. And approximately one-half of companies also report that competitiveness and profitability have improved.

6. Training and Education

Effective training is essential for superior productivity but because accounting systems treat training as a period expense, there is often an incentive to minimize its cost. Some managers take the view that training is a wasted investment. Improving skill levels raises the worth of employees and thus makes them more vulnerable to poaching by competitors.

But the workplace is increasingly being organized around knowledge workers and their computer networks. It is fast becoming a workplace of *specialists*. Researchers, software engineers, accountants, doctors, teachers, and managers are some of the knowledge workers of the third wave. But in many cases, their productivity is *declining* because they are performing additional work far removed from their specialist capability. The productivity of knowledge workers must be measured in terms of the time devoted to their specialist task, but today's teachers spend much of their time on supervision, administration, completing regulatory forms, and security questions. And the same goes for doctors, accountants, and engineers. The problem becomes acute when knowledge workers are highly paid for work that could be done by less-qualified people, only to be told by superiors that they cost too much and are not as productive as they should be!

Though most managers know there is a clear link between education and productivity, such a link has recently been confirmed. Robert Zemsky, professor of education at the University of Pennsylvania and codirector of the National Center on the Educational Quality of the Workforce (EQW) has studied the relationship between education and productivity at more than three thousand U.S. workplaces. In May 1995, EQW reported that on average a 10 percent increase in workforce education level led to an 8.6 percent gain in total factor productivity, while a 10 percent rise in the value of capital equipment increased productivity only 3.4 percent. Schooling isn't a magic bullet, Zemsky cautions: "The two sets of investments [education and equipment] are complementary. You can't do one without the other."[51]

7. Information Sharing

We noted earlier that in knowledge-based companies such as NovaCare, Chaparral Steel, and the top-flight consultancies, shared information is essential to success. Solving problems and creating opportunities depends on shared knowledge and the building of effective databases containing documented case histories. Moreover, information sharing is a prerequisite of *trust*.

Trust is most easily recognized in transparent, open management processes. At the Japanese company Kao, for example, employees' access to information and decision making is particularly striking, reflecting Chairman Yoshio Maruta's belief in equality and commitment to continuous learning. Computer terminals throughout the company allow any employee access to the company's massive information system. Maruta is convinced that the increased creativity and informed decision making stimulated by such access far outweighs the risk of confidentiality leaks.[52]

Drucker notes the need for a new approach: "In making and moving things, partnership with a responsible worker is the *best* way. But Taylor's telling them worked too, and quite well after all. In knowledge and service work, however, partnership with the responsible worker is the *only* way to improve productivity. Nothing else works at all."[53] Many firms are recognizing that researchers, designers, and software experts must be encouraged to share their knowledge and be rewarded for so doing; but as we have argued, budgeting and reward systems act as a powerful counterforce by emphasizing good housekeeping and cost control. The result is that ingenuity, creativity, and innovation are stifled and dispersed in small islands of jealously protected knowledge. In many companies, knowledge is power—often the only insurance policy available to workers against losing their jobs—and therefore such knowledge is carefully concealed.

8. Sharing the Benefits

Nothing encapsulates the clash of second and third wave management cultures like the pay-for-performance debate. Its origins go back to the very beginnings of the industrial revolution when prominent British cotton manufacturer Robert Peel argued, "It is impossible for a mill at any distance to be managed, unless it is under the direction of a partner or superintendent who has an interest in the success of the business."[54]

Third wave service companies will recognize that the only way to reach and sustain superior productivity is to share its benefits. Indeed, those organizations where the workforce has a vested interest in success through share ownership, have often performed exceptionally well over long periods. U.K. retailer The John Lewis Partnership is the world's largest employee-owned company, with 35,000 employees. All profits, after deducting preference dividends and retained earnings, are paid out to current employees in proportion to their basic pay.[55] In 1995, bonuses equaled eight weeks' pay and in 1996 it was expected to rise to ten weeks.[56] The company's productivity has consistently exceeded that of its principal U.K. competitors, including Marks & Spencer, Sainsbury, and Tesco.

Third wave incentive measures are becoming more strategic and more closely linked to value-added performance. For example, a number of companies are using variations of economic value-added to measure management performance. Eli Lilly has adopted EVA throughout the organization. According to CEO Randall Tobias:

> Basically, Lilly's bonus plan now requires managers to achieve continuous, year-to-year improvements in EVA....If the targets are met or exceeded, there's a bonus, based on a proprietary formula. Last year, for example, the company did very well. Many managers got bonuses worth close to 50 percent of their total compensation. The bottom line is: As you're making decisions, you've got to think about aligning them with EVA. It's easy to see EVA as a very sophisticated financial tool, and indeed it is, but I think it's important to understand that it is really a tool to change behavior too. Linking bonuses to EVA is meant to change the whole culture.[57]

Though ideally teams should be the focus of reward systems, each employee must know where he or she stands. This usually involves some form of performance appraisal from which position, salary, and incentive-based targets result. But a hot debate has raged for decades regarding the value of such exercises. This is what studies at GE found in the early 1960s:[58]

- Appraisal interviews attempt to accomplish the two objectives of providing a written justification for salary action; [and]...motivating the employee to improve his work performance.

- The two purposes are in conflict, with the result that the traditional appraisal system essentially becomes a salary discussion in which the manager justifies the action taken.

- The appraisal discussion has little influence on future job performance.

- Appreciable improvement is realized only when specific goals and deadlines are mutually established and agreed on by the subordinate and his manager in an interview split away from the appraisal interview.

In today's knowledge-based companies, managers are looking for more initiative from their employees. Andy Grove, CEO of Intel, has three key questions for any person wishing to pursue a successful career in his company:[59]

- Continually ask: Am I adding real value or merely passing information along? How do you add more value? By continually looking for new ways to make things better in your organization. In principle, every hour of your day should be spent increasing the output or the value of the output of the people for whom you're responsible.

- Continually ask: Am I plugged into what's happening around me? Inside the company? The industry? Are you a node connected to a network of plugged-in people or are you floating by yourself?

- Are you trying new ideas, new techniques, and new technologies?— and I mean personally. Don't just read about them.

Third wave companies will gravitate toward some form of personal scorecard that will relate work to strategic objectives. Achieving agreed-on milestones and maximizing value-adding work will be the primary objectives. In the same way that we asked questions of processes and activities in Issue 6, we can ask similar questions of managers and workers. What proportion of their work relates to value-adding activities? Can this work ratio be improved? Are the best and most productive workers supporting winning products and customers, or are they propping up yesterday's fallen hopes? If the latter, can they be moved to more strategic processes, products, and markets? Is the quality of their work high enough, or can it be improved by reducing delays, removing bottlenecks and changing authority levels?

The Measurement Problem

The second wave approach to measuring productivity derives directly from the economic model that has underpinned business thinking throughout this century. Such thinking is reinforced by accounting systems that record people as costs rather than as assets. As Eli Goldratt noted, "Accounting is the number-one enemy of productivity."[60] Just how right he was can be seen when you consider the way accountants handle the costs of employment. The costs of hiring, training, and developing people are written off as an expense of the period in which they happen to occur. What sort of behavior does this encourage when the firm is under pressure and managers are struggling to meet quarterly profit targets? The answer is obvious. Managers will look to minimize the costs of education, training, and development, thus causing damage to the very processes that ultimately define their competitiveness.

For accounting systems to come to terms with these problems, they need to find new ways of measuring value-added work. Trying to measure the number of transactions a person handles, for example, tells a manager little about how the work was done, whether it was done right the first time, and whether it provided value for the customer. Identifying and eliminating non-value-adding work will occupy the minds of accountants and IT specialists in the third wave. But how will they approach the task? The way forward, as we discussed in Issue 6, lies with activity analysis. The breakthrough in manufacturing productivity can be traced back to Taylor's analysis of the activities of the production worker. By measuring the work content of each task and devising ways of cutting time and cost, Taylor's approach worked wonders. The same lateral thinking needs to be concentrated on service and knowledge work.

We have suggested that accountants develop systems that can track costs by the relevance and quality of each activity. Only then will the real contribution of both knowledge and service workers be seen in its true light. For work to be valued, it must add value either to customers or the knowledge base; otherwise it is simply a cost. Unless productivity measurers grasp these points, they will flounder in the third wave.

But the final measure of managing the workforce effectively is to examine the long-term success of the business. Indeed, Jeffrey Pfeffer offers powerful evidence that those companies that have made long-term commitments to the workforce, and placed employees at the center of their strategy have been most successful over the long term. For example, he notes that the five top-performing American companies by *stock market growth* over a twenty-year period (1972–1992) are (in order): Southwest Airlines, Wal-Mart, Tyson Foods, Circuit City, and Plenum Publishing. Moreover, he notes that none of these companies has any

distinctive competitive advantage such as product differentiation, economies of scale, high-technology products, or protective patents. The only
common thread in their competitive strategies (mostly based on operational excellence) is the similar way in which they all manage their
workforces.[61]

Issue 10

Transformation

*Adopt the
Third Wave
Model*

JOHN KOTTER'S VIEWS CAPTURE WELL THE problems facing second wave organizations. They need to adopt a new business model that encourages and rewards creativity, high-quality service, and value-adding work and places knowledge at the center of their strategic planning. Such changes will not come easily. As Bartlett and Ghoshal suggested, we are on the verge of a new managerial theory of the firm—one based on federal networks where local managers operate as entrepeneurs; where authority lies with those who have the knowledge; and where senior managers act as coaches and mentors who facilitate cross border cooperation. Some firms have already taken several strides in this direction, but most have a long way to go.

Before embarking on this journey, however, managers must first take a long hard look at their underlying values, structures, and measures, many of which are little changed from the theories of the early economists such as Adam Smith, David Ricardo, and Alfred Marshall. In this model the overarching objective of the firm is to maximize the shareholder's wealth, and most managerial actions (both short-term and long-term) are taken with this in mind. It is a model in which individuals are assumed to be self-interested, rational decision makers driven by (short-term) economic goals, and economic relationships (with employees, suppliers, customers, and external partners) are governed by binding contracts. But above all, it is a mechanistic model subject to mathematical formulae where costs, volumes, and profits can be optimized according to market conditions.

The continuance of such a model, however, will be a severe handicap in the third wave, where organizational success will be based on long-term relationships and the dynamics of human behavior. The third wave model recognizes that organizational learning, knowledge sharing, the continuous improvement of processes, working in teams with team-based rewards, employee empowerment, high levels of customer service and satisfaction, and the formation of business partnerships both across the firm and with external associates, will be the key ingredients of success. Such a model cannot be tied to an economic framework, nor can it be optimized. It can only be managed. The glue that holds it all together is empathy, trust, learning, and loyalty.

How does an organization steeped in second wave practices make the necessary changes? Of the many traps and barriers that lie in the way, some are more obvious than others. Changing organizational structures, investing in knowledge-based networks, and recalibrating measures and rewards are all essential steps, but winning the hearts and minds of the key influencers within cultural layers and communities of practice is one of the keys to success. So is management education. But communicating the right educational messages will also be a major challenge. Many internal training departments and external business schools have been slow to adopt a third wave curriculum, leaving managers to deal with the educational problem.

Issue 10 considers the problems of migrating from a second to a third wave organization and examines the role of management education in this process.

From Second to Third Wave— The Migration Problem

In confronting the process of change, many organizations will first consider their current competitive weaknesses and take action to improve them. Employee empowerment, activity-based management, decentralization, knowledge-based networks—these improvement programs are all on offer from the consultant's toolbox. But managers cannot simply cherry-pick items from the third wave menu and put them into their existing second wave mixing bowl. Successful change involves much more than this. To understand how two firms that appear to have the same set of third wave ingredients do not necessarily have similar performance characteristics, we can learn much from the process of biological evolution.

Celebrated British biologist Richard Dawkins,[2] uses the analogy of baking a cake to compare the "blueprint theory" and the "recipe theory" of human development. The blueprint theory holds that the DNA in a fertilized egg is equivalent to a blueprint of the adult body. There is a one-to-one relationship between each element of the blueprint and the whole body. A recipe in a cookbook, on the other hand, is in no sense a blueprint for the cake that will finally emerge from the oven. A recipe is not a scale model, not a description of a finished cake, not in any sense a point-for-point representation. It is a set of instructions that, if obeyed in the right order, will result in a cake. Dawkins believes that genes are much more like a recipe than like a blueprint. There is no one-to-one mapping between words of a recipe and crumbs of a cake, but the *whole recipe maps onto the whole cake.*

Each cake has its own unique recipe, so if we want to bake a different kind of cake, we must change the recipe, for example, by paying particular attention to the type of baking powder we use. Tinkering around with the existing recipe will only result in a tasteless cake or one that fails to rise. If we think of businesses as having their own DNA, and think of this DNA in terms of such ingredients of the business recipe as culture, management style, employee attitudes, organizational structures, financial and reward systems, performance measures and so forth, we can begin to see how introducing change programs such as reengineering, quality, or empowerment might upset the existing recipe and ruin the cake. To arrive at a *different* (third wave) "business cake," we must ensure that the *whole recipe maps onto the whole new business model*, paying particular attention to its key ingredients such as *philosophy* or *culture*; otherwise the new business model will not develop with the desired characteristics.

Most firms fail to consider the whole when they attempt to introduce and implement new management ideas. Still imbued with a mechanistic approach to business performance, they expect to make a change here and a change there, assuming that all other aspects of the working machine will adapt to these "foreign bodies" and that improvements will quickly flow. British economist Paul Ormerod notes how economists see this interplay:

> Economists see the world as a machine. A very complicated one perhaps, but nevertheless a machine, whose workings can be understood by putting together carefully and meticulously its component parts. The

behavior of the system as a whole can be deduced from a simple aggregation of these components. A lever pulled in a certain part of the machine with a certain strength will have regular and predictable outcomes elsewhere in the machine.[3]

Common sense and whole rafts of recent evidence, however, tell us otherwise. Major business changes will not work unless the culture also changes. Countless numbers of restructuring, reengineering, quality, and empowerment initiatives have failed because this lesson has not been learned.

Culture, according to John Kotter, refers to *norms of behavior and shared values* among a group of people. Norms of behavior are common or pervasive ways of acting found within a group. They persist because group members tend to behave in ways that teach these practices to new members, rewarding those who fit in and sanctioning those who do not. Shared values are important. Concerns and goals shared by most people in a group tend to shape group behavior and often persist over time even when group membership changes.[4] "In the final analysis," Kotter notes, "change sticks only when it becomes 'the way we do things around here,' when it seeps into the very bloodstream of the work unit or corporate body. Until new behaviors are rooted in social norms and shared values, they are always subject to degradation as soon as the pressures associated with a change effort are removed."[5]

In his book *Leading Change,* Kotter notes eight primary reasons why major change efforts fail (see Figure 10.1).

1. Allowing too much complacency
2. Failing to create a sufficiently powerful guiding coalition
3. Underestimating the power of vision
4. Undercommunicating the vision by a factor of ten
5. Permitting obstacles to block the new vision
6. Failing to create short-term wins
7. Declaring victory too soon
8. Neglecting to anchor changes firmly in the corporate culture.

The order is important. Thus anchoring changes in the culture comes last, not first.[6] This is a perceptive point. Kotter explains why: "Culture is not something that you manipulate easily. Attempts to grab it and twist it into a new shape never work because you can't grab it. Culture changes only after you have successfully altered people's actions, after the new behavior produces some group benefit for a period of time, and after people see the connection between the new actions and the performance improvement."[7]

In Issue 3 we noted how recent research in organizational learning

FIGURE 10.1
Kotter's Eight Barriers to Change

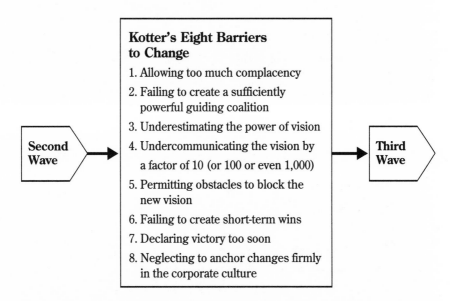

Kotter's Eight Barriers to Change

1. Allowing too much complacency
2. Failing to create a sufficiently powerful guiding coalition
3. Underestimating the power of vision
4. Undercommunicating the vision by a factor of 10 (or 100 or even 1,000)
5. Permitting obstacles to block the new vision
6. Failing to create short-term wins
7. Declaring victory too soon
8. Neglecting to anchor changes firmly in the corporate culture

Second Wave → Third Wave

SOURCE: Adapted from John P. Kotter, *Leading Change* (Harvard Business School Press, 1996), 16. Reprinted by permission of Harvard Business School Press.

has identified various cultural layers within the firm and how the mindsets of people varied among them. We also noted in Issue 6 that the imposition of some new initiative such as activity-based costing might be seen by executives and finance people as a better system for identifying profitable products and customers, whereas team leaders and operators might see it as just another imposed set of top-down accounting controls. The result? A low level of acceptance and likely failure.

Looking up the list of Kotter's seven other barriers to change, we would highlight number 5, Permitting obstacles to block the new vision. Such obstacles are often hidden within performance measures, budgeting systems, and incentive schemes, and go unrecognized when postmortems are conducted on the failure of change programs. In our view no amount of managerial hectoring will make one jot of difference if attention is not paid to the way managers are measured and if such rewards are not aligned with strategic objectives. And this brings us back full circle to the agonizing dichotomy between management *control* and performance *improvement*. Accounting systems, measures, and rewards are firmly rooted in the orthodoxy of financial systems, and their accounting masters are more often than not extremely reluctant to submit them to serious change. Thus many companies attempt to navigate their way around them—a crucial and often fatal mistake.

Another acute dilemma facing managers wishing to adopt the full third wave agenda concerns the reaction of shareholders. Managers need to sell influential shareholders on the long-term view of the third wave model and explain that this might involve periods of steady rather than spectacular growth. There are many role models to use as the basis of their presentations. Cummins Engine did just this in 1990 when its management team concluded a deal that resulted in 40 percent of the company's stock being in the hands of patient investors, including three of its important business partners, company employees, and the founding Miller family.[8]

Another Problem—Second Wave Education

Not only do managers have to cope with the practical problems of implementing change within the business, but their efforts at inculcating such ideas and attitudes receive little support from the education establishment. This inadequate preparation applies at all levels, from high school through further education courses and into management education itself. In other words, teachers and their curricula are still preaching second wave values and prescribing second wave solutions for second wave problems. So what's new? This is what Adam Smith said in 1778: "The greater part of what is taught in schools and universities does not seem to be the most proper preparation for that which is to employ them the rest of their days."[9]

Business leaders and politicians (usually those in opposition) frequently blame lack of competitiveness on the education system. The following quotes are enough to provoke most average Americans or Britons into worrying about their pensions. Here's one from Lord Hanson on the position in Britain:

> In 1994–95 we spent more than £35 billion of public money on education. About 5.2% of GDP—more than either Germany (4.1%) or Japan (3.6%).... In Germany, the lower half of the ability range is two years ahead of the same group here.... After commenting on the difficulty of obtaining reliable data (the National Commission on Education report on Literacy and Numeracy Standards) reported that it could find "little change" in reading standards since 1945.... In what other industry would absence of improvement since 1945 lead to anything but bankruptcy? In what other industry would there be such a dearth of hard data, particularly if that industry was—as we are constantly told of education—continually assessing its products?.... Despite the urgency of the problem

there have been no studies of what teachers need to know to teach our children successfully. Besides, how can we be told about the underlying reasons for our failing system by those who refuse to believe there is a problem?[10]

From the American perspective, the situation is equally grim. Try these snippets compiled by Jeffrey Pfeffer.[11]

> The New York Telephone Company reported that "it tested 57,000 job applications in 1987 and found that 54,900, or 96.3% lacked basic skills in math, reading, and reasoning."... A human resource planning document prepared at the Bank of America in 1990 reported that "Chemical Bank in New York must interview 40 applicants to find one who can be successfully trained as a teller."... "At Pacific Bell in Los Angeles, 95% of the 3,500 people who recently took a competency test for entry-level jobs not requiring a high school education failed."... and "at Motorola, 80% of its applicants cannot pass a simple 7th grade English comprehension or 5th grade math test."

The problem is not so much ill-prepared children and poorly educated workers as ill-prepared teachers and poorly educated managers. How is it, for example, that Nissan in Britain and NUMMI in America can achieve such outstanding productivity results and associated high skill levels with the same human raw material as their competitors? Moreover, take into consideration that Nissan is located in one of the most run-down areas of Britain and that NUMMI's workforce comprised 80 percent of the old (unionized) GM workers (more than 50 percent from ethnic minorities), whose employment record was a model of adversarial industrial relations. The difference in both cases is a combination of cultural change and management capability. However, this is not to suggest that British or American workers had to sing company songs or do morning exercises— they simply had to *relearn basic attitudes toward work*—for example, *learn to look for quality problems and suggest improvements*, and *learn to operate in teams*. The NUMMI management successfully demonstrated to its workforce that by converting waste to value-adding activity through continuous improvement, market share and resulting employment will grow.[12]

It is not as though these important issues have not been recognized. They are enshrined in America's quality award structure. The U.S. Baldrige Award competition, for example, has this to say about Human Resource Utilization:[13]

> Meeting the company's quality objectives requires a fully committed, well-trained work force that is encouraged to participate in the company's continuous improvement activities. Reward and recognition systems

need to reinforce participation and emphasize achievement of quality objectives.... Employees need to receive training in basic quality skills related to performing their work and to understanding and solving quality-related problems.

Quality guru W. Edwards Deming believed in the "intrinsic motivation" of humankind and that it is management's policies that often serve to demotivate employees. Instead of helping workers develop their potential, he argued, management often prevents them from making a meaningful contribution to the improvement of their jobs, robs them of the self-esteem they need to foster motivation, and blames them for systemic problems beyond their control.[14] Of course this takes us back to McGregor, Maslow, and Herzberg, the only difference being that Deming was driving the quality and empowerment movement from inside industry rather than from within academia.

The problem may be that because these so-called soft measures of human achievement and performance cannot easily be plugged into an economic model, they cannot be subjected to the type of academic research that attracts government or university funding. The most researchers can do is to analyze a number of companies that use one set of management policies and compare them with others that use a different set. This type of field research is indeed starting to happen, but the essential point is that universities and business schools have ignored the problems of *real businesses* for decades, being content instead to play around with simplified economic models filled with arcane mathematical formulae that fill academic journals but are of little practical relevance to managers who have to survive in the real world.

With the exception of a few top-flight business schools, most educational establishments are still operating in the depths of the second wave. While they may talk about quality and knowledge and have suitably titled course options, the main thrust of their written material remains the hierarchical, production-driven model where the priorities are volume and scale, the managerial mentality is one of contract and control, and the way to compete is to lower unit costs by all means possible. Johnson writes:

> Professors in American business schools...tend on the whole, to focus on issues and phenomena that have no bearing on what business people must know to run a competitive and profitable organization in the global economy.... Since the early 1960s, virtually all business school teaching and research in the United States have been firmly grounded in principles of "remote-control" management. Graduate schools train aspiring business PhDs to espouse the "hard" quantitative-analytical principles of top-down control, and to spurn the "soft" verbal-inductive principles of bottom-up empowerment.[15]

Kaplan is also concerned about the level of teaching and research that pervades business schools, particularly the fact that they appear to have completely overlooked the quality revolution. He notes that research conducted in 1991 showed that barely *one or two percent* of business schools in America have been truly affected by the TQM revolution. He points out that business school professors are still wondering whether quality improvement creates value for organizations, whether research on quality is a legitimate topic, and whether they will get recognition and be rewarded for performing such research. Moreover, he believes this is also true of the information-based management revolution.[16] Thus we can see the problems of misaligning strategy and rewards in the one place that should know better. Perhaps most business schools do not see business as their customer. They see themselves as serving academic masters and certification institutes, the curricula of which are geared more for job protection and fund-raising purposes than for producing well-informed students fit for third wave business clients.

Universities and business schools are, with few exceptions, functionally structured organizations with each department responsible for its own courses. There is little encouragement for cross-functional teaching or research. Earlier in this book, for example, we noted how the meeting of marketers and accountants will be indispensable as customer profitability becomes a major issue in companies. But how will such an important issue be handled within a business school? Will marketing or accounting deal with it, or will it fall between the cracks? Certainly there is little evidence that such a crucial topic is yet appearing in management accounting textbooks, nor can we see much on the behavioral implications of accounting and control systems or value-adding performance measures. Indeed, in what its front cover describes as "Europe's best selling management accounting textbook" (1994 edition) covering over 800 pages, there is no evidence that any of the key messages appearing through this book are covered in any depth whatsoever. Issues such as the recognition and valuation of intellectual assets; how accounting needs to adapt to process- and network-based structures; the clash between quality, service, and accounting measures; the linkage between strategy, processes, customers, and managerial reward systems; and the identification and elimination of non-value-adding work—all are completely ignored.

Third Wave Education

Unlike the times when employees received most of their education prior to joining the labor force, education in the third wave economy will be continuous. This will mean a greater emphasis on education within the workplace than at schools, universities, or even within centrally organized human resource departments. According to author and former Harvard professor, Stan Davis, "When the half-life of knowledge is so short and therefore mechanisms for upgrading it on a continual basis become ever more important, then training should cease to be a centralized function. It should become ubiquitous and intrinsic. As long as training is positioned as a separate function and one that is housed within the human resources department at that, it will be undervalued and underdeveloped."[17]

According to a recent article in *Training* magazine, American corporations spend more than $50 billion a year on formal training and *as much as half this gargantuan expenditure is being utterly wasted*—squandered on training that's unnecessary, training that's aimed at nontraining problems, and training that's doomed to fail by its poor design. Corporate training is failing to deal with the individual needs of its students. Classroom training delivers either too much or too little, too early or too late, and is too expensive.[18]

New technology has the potential to link third wave management experts directly with those students and organizations who know exactly what they want. Moreover, such education can be delivered "just-in-time" rather than "just-in-case." Multimedia, highly focused cable and satellite television channels, and—most significant of all—the explosion of the Internet all possess the inherent capability to drive through these changes. The implications for head-in-the-sand business schools are obvious. Moreover, many large companies are developing their own in-house educational facilities, some of which have a greater depth and scope than most business schools. And they are marketing their courses to other businesses fed up with the sterile and unimaginative approach from traditional establishments. Davis and Botkin see the threat to business schools in the following way:

> Business, more than government, is instituting the changes in education that are required for the emerging knowledge-based economy. School systems, public and private, are lagging behind the transformation in learning that is evolving outside them, in the private sector at both work and play, with people of all ages. Over the next few decades, the private sector will eclipse the public sector as our predominant educational institution.[19]

Motorola, GE, Disney, and McDonald's have had their own universities for many years, and Japanese companies have always opted for in-house education. Motorola University uses personal, computer-based virtual reality technology to teach employees to run assembly lines.[20] Cable operators and telecommunications companies are setting up virtual classrooms, and companies such as Bankers Trust are changing the learning environment through collaborative technologies such as Lotus Notes.[21] Apple Computer has achieved significant benefits from a performance support system known as ARPLE (the Apple Reference, Performance, and Learning Expert). The system—a client-server network that continuously sends information to remote servers worldwide—enables the company to distribute globally an array of multimedia resources including business presentations, technical documents, sales tools, and educational courseware. ARPLE services, also available on CD-ROM, are used by 25,000 people. According to Apple's Lucy Carter, "the closer you move the learning to its application, the more solid the experience." By cutting sales training from twenty-one hours to ten hours per month and thereby cutting lost field time, the performance systems group calculates that ARPLE saved the company $40 million in 1994. Classroom training has almost been abolished, and more than 80 percent of the company's training is now supplied electronically.[22]

Andersen Consulting, which annually spends $200 million on employee development, is another leading force in learning technology, especially the imaginative use of multimedia courseware. The organization reckons to have reduced learning time by 40 percent through its desktop alternative to classrooms, enabling annual payroll savings of $2 million and courseware savings of $8 million. In designing and implementing its systems, Andersen placed heavy reliance on the views of the director of the Institute of Learning Sciences at Northwestern University, Roger Schank. Schank's views on learning are worth noting. He offers three crucial rules:

- There has to be a goal toward which the learner can strive. Learning, in other words, comes through accomplishment.
- There has to be an opportunity to fail, that is, we learn best through mistakes.
- Instruction should come in the form of stories, not facts. It is within the frame of a story that our ability to find connections and meaning is most pronounced.[23]

The potential of the Internet as an educational provider is enormous. As video conferencing becomes more accessible and global research and teaching networks start to develop, business and students will be able to pick and choose their education requirements. Most of them will settle for nothing but the best. Many business schools are already venturing into distance learning, but once the market begins to settle it will undoubtedly be the major brand names that will have the greatest opportunity. Some predict that education on demand to homes, schools, and workplaces will be a vastly bigger business than entertainment on demand. There are some early indicators of the power and reach of this technology. For example, in the summer of 1994, a student at the University of Alabama offered a course on the workings of the Internet to Internet subscribers. Each day for six weeks, 62,000 students in seventy-seven countries received a short roadmap lecture or tutorial and assignments.[24] At Los Alamos National Laboratory, a physicist maintains a database of working papers for scientists in high-energy physics and related fields. Each day, his system automatically fulfills 20,000 requests for reprints.[25]

Within the next few years, executives will be able to gain access to on-line databases and find the latest research or academic paper on any related subject. They will be able to tailor management courses to their own corporate requirements, including videos and multimedia programs made by their own managers. Moreover, managers themselves will spend time teaching and coaching rather than attending operational meetings. Certification from established business schools will become less important than certification from leading-edge companies.

Third wave companies will not only need better education for their people, they will require it. All employees must understand the common purpose and learn how to *find problems* as well as solve them. Equally, specialists must be given more time to pursue and improve their specialties. And CEOs can link with their peers around the world in a sort of open forum of strategic thinking that can only benefit the future of their organizations.

The principles of good (third wave) management are teachable and cannot begin too soon. If previous generations had been told that they were working for customers who paid their wages rather than bosses who held their contracts of employment, and that their compensation depended on the quality of their work, who knows what the economic consequences might have been? Imagine the benefits that would flow if young people were entering the workplace with these disciplines already deeply ingrained. Alas, the education system is not even at first base.

Educators could do worse than start to employ the language of the third wave. For example, instead of conversing in the language of contracts, organization charts, budgetary control, breakeven and cost-volume-profit analysis, functions, departments, scale, volume, and variance, how about using customer, quality, service, value-added, teams, processes, competencies, knowledge, learning, trust, empathy, activity, and loyalty? These are not words associated with particular management fads, nor are they "flavors of the month." They are the staple language of third wave management. If educators continue to teach second wave lessons they will produce second wave managers. Aspiring third wave managers will know better and demand more.

Notes

The Challenge

[1] Peter F. Drucker, *Post-Capitalist Society* (Oxford: Butterworth-Heinemann, 1993), 1.

[2] Ibid., 5.

[3] Ibid., 7

[4] Alvin Toffler, *The Third Wave* (London: Pan Books, 1980).

[5] James Brian Quinn, *Intelligent Enterprise* (New York: The Free Press, 1992), 30.

[6] Stephen S. Roach, "The Hollow Ring of the Productivity Revival," *Harvard Business Review*, November–December 1996, 85.

[7] Quinn, *Intelligent Enterprise,* 7–10.

[8] A report by the Bank Credit Analyst team of Montreal, quoted in Peter Martin, "A Tale of Two Economies," *Financial Times,* March 10, 1997, 30.

[9] Eryn Brown, "Why Dell Computers Could Be America's Very Best PC Market," *Fortune,* April 14, 1997, 15.

[10] Klaus Schwab and Claude Smadja, "Power and Policy: The New Economic World Order, *Harvard Business Review,* November–December 1994, 42.

[11] John Moore, "British Privatization—Taking Capitalism to the People," *Harvard Business Review,* January–February 1992, 118.

[12] W. Brian Arthur, "Increasing Returns and the New World of Business," *Harvard Business Review,* July–August 1996, 100–101.

[13] Jeremy Rifkin, *The End of Work* (New York: GP Putnam's Sons, 1995), 94.

[14] Victor Keegan, "Hard Work, If You Can Get It," *The Guardian,* January 19, 1996.

[15] Rifkin, *The End of Work,* 9.

[16] Ibid., 103.

[17] Ibid., 144.

[18] Stephen S. Roach, "Productivity Revival," *Harvard Business Review,* November–December 1996, 82.

[19] Charles Handy, *Beyond Certainty* (London: Hutchinson, 1995), 24.

[20] Drucker, *Post Capitalist Society,* 176.

[21] Alan M. Webber, "What's So New About the New Economy?" *Harvard Busines Review,* January–February 1993, 27.

[22] Frederick F. Reichheld, *The Loyalty Effect* (Boston: Harvard Business School Press, 1996), 2.

Issue 1

[1] Michael E. Porter, "What Is Strategy?" *Harvard Business Review,* November–December 1996, 65.

[2] Ibid., 62.

[3] Gary Hamel and C.K. Prahalad, *Competing for the Future* (Boston: Harvard Business School Press, 1994), 16.

[4] Ian C. MacMillan and Rita Gunther McGrath, "What Is Strategy?" Letters to the Editor, *Harvard Business Review,* January–February, 154–156.

[5]   William Taylor, "Message and Muscle: An Interview with Swatch Titan Nicolas Hayek," *Harvard Business Review,* March–April 1993, 99–110.

[6]   John A. Byre, "Strategic Planning," *Business Week,* August 26, 1996.

[7]   Gary Hamel, "Strategy As Revolution," *Harvard Business Review,* July–August 1996, 70.

[8]   Jeffrey F. Rayport and John J. Sviokla, "Exploiting the Virtual Value Chain," *Harvard Business Review,* November–December 1995, 76–77.

[9]   Paul Ham and Matthew Lynn, "Direct Assault," *London Sunday Times,* November 17, 1996.

[10]   W. Chan Kim and Renee Mauborgne, "Value Innovation: The Strategic Logic of High Growth," *Harvard Business Review,* January–February 1997, 103–112.

[11]   Christopher A. Bartlett and Sumantra Ghoshal, "Rebuilding Behavioral Context: Turn Process Reengineering into People Rejuvenation," *Sloan Management Review,* Fall 1995, 11–23.

[12]   Ibid., 26.

[13]   H. Thomas Johnson, *Relevance Regained* (New York: The Free Press, 1992), 36.

[14]   See Tracy Goss, Richard Pascale, and Anthony Athos, "The Reinvention Rollercoaster: Risking the Present for a Powerful Future," *Harvard Business Review,* November–December 1993, 97–108.

[15]   Ibid.

[16]   Taken from Claire Gooding, "A Caress for the Customer," *Financial Times,* February 24, 1994, 19.

[17]   Quoted in Dorothy Leonard-Barton, *Wellsprings of Knowledge* (Boston: Harvard Business School Press, 1995), 31.

[18]   Ronald Henkoff, "A Whole New Set of Glitches for Digital's Robert Palmer," *Fortune,* August 29, 1996.

[19]   Quoted in Leonard-Barton, *Wellsprings of Knowledge,* 29.

[20]   John Jay, "Battle Stations," *London Sunday Times,* March 2, 1997.

[21]   Caroline Ellis, "Making Strategic Alliances Succeed," *Harvard Business Review,* July–August 1996, 8–9.

[22]   John Hagel III, "Are 'Webs' a New Strategy for the Information Age?" *McKinsey Quarterly,* 1996, no. 1, 6.

[23]   W. Brian Arthur, "Increasing Returns and the New World of Business," *Harvard Business Review,* July–August 1996, 105.

[24]   Hagel, "Are 'Webs' a New Strategy?" 10.

[25]   Byrne, "Strategic Planning."

[26]   Hagel, "Are 'Webs' a New Strategy?" 15.

[27]   Arthur, "Increasing Returns," 100–109.

[28]   Hagel, "Are 'Webs' a New Strategy?" 6.

[29]   Arie de Geus, "The Living Company," *Harvard Business Review,* March–April 1997, 51–59.

[30]   Theodore Levitt, "Marketing Myopia," reprinted in the *Harvard Business Review,* September–October 1975.

[31]   Peter F. Drucker, "The Theory of Business," *Harvard Business Review,* September–October 1994, 102.

Issue 2

[1]   Theodore Levitt, "Marketing Myopia," reprinted in the *Harvard Business Review,* September–October 1975.

[2]   Michael Treacy and Fred Wiersema, *The Discipline of Market Leaders* (London: HarperCollins, 1995), 19.

3   Ibid., 19–20.
4   John K. Shank and Vijay Govindarajan, *Strategic Cost Management* (New York: The Free Press, 1993), 231.
5   Michael E. Porter, "What Is Strategy?" *Harvard Business Review,* November–December 1996, 62.
6   Christopher Meyer, *Fast Cycle Time* (New York: The Free Press, 1993), 9.
7   Noel Capon, John U. Farley, Donald R. Lehmann, and James M. Hulbert, "Profiles of Innovators among Large U.S. Manufacturers," *Management Science* 38 (February 1992), 157–169. Quoted in Willard I. Zangwill, *Lightning Strategies for Innovation* (New York: Lexington Books, 1993), 2.
8   Robin Cooper, *When Lean Enterprises Collide* (Boston: Harvard Business School Press, 1995), 56.
9   From research by Albert Page of the University of Illinois. Quoted in Willard Zangwill, *Lightning Strategies for Innovation* (New York: Lexington Books, 1993), 135.
10 Willard I. Zangwill, *Lightning Strategies for Innovation* (New York: Lexington Books, 1993), 237.
11 Ibid., 237–238.
12 Robin Cooper, "The Changing Practice of Management Accounting," *Management Accounting* (U.K.), March 1996, 26.
13 Zachary Schiller, Greg Burns, and Karen Lowry Miller, "Make It Simple," *Business Week,* September 9, 1996.
14 The material on Chrysler in this section derives from Jeffrey H. Dyer, "How Chrysler Created an American Keiretsu," *Harvard Business Review,* July–August 1996, 42–56.
15 Jeffrey Rayport and John J. Sviokla, "Exploiting the Virtual Value Chain," *Harvard Business Review,* November–December 1995, 78.
16 David M. Upton and Andrew McAfee, "The Real Virtual Factory," *Harvard Business Review,* July–August 1996, 123–133.
17 Michael Treacy and Fred Wiersema, "Customer Intimacy and Other Value Disciplines," *Harvard Business Review,* January–February 1993, 86–87.
18 Donald V. Fines, "Make Your Dealers Your Partners," *Harvard Business Review,* March–April 1996, 84–95.
19 C. Fornell, "A National Customer Satisfaction Barometer: The Swedish Experience," *Journal of Marketing* 56 (1992), 6–21. Quoted in Abbie Griffin, Greg Gleason, Rick Preiss, and Dave Shevenaugh, "Best Practice for Customer Satisfaction," *Sloan Management Review,* Winter 1995, 88.
20 Abbie Griffin, Greg Gleason, Rick Preiss, and Dave Shevenaugh, "Best Practice for Customer Satisfaction," *Sloan Management Review,* Winter 1995, 88.
21 Frederick F. Reichheld, *The Loyalty Effect* (Boston: Harvard Business School Press, 1996), 15.
22 Frederick F. Riechheld, "Loyalty-Based Management," *Harvard Business Review,* March–April 1993, 65.
23 Justin Martin, "Are You As Good as You Think You Are?" *Fortune,* September 30, 1996, 86.
24 Gary Hamel, "Strategy as Revolution," *Harvard Business Review,* July–August 1996, 73.
25 Susan Moffat, "Japan's New Personalized Production," *Fortune,* October 22, 1991, 132–135.
26 Martin, "Are You as Good?" 82–87.
27 Reichheld, "Loyalty-Based Management," 64–73.

[28] Jeffrey Rayport and John J. Sviokla, "Exploiting the Virtual Value Chain," *Harvard Business Review,* November–December 1995, 80–81.

[29] Ronald Henkoff, "Growing Your Company: Five Ways to Do It Right," *Fortune,* November 25, 1996, 35.

[30] Leonard A. Schlesinger and James L. Heskett, "The Service-Driven Service Company," *Harvard Business Review,* September–October 1991, 77.

[31] Steven E. Prokesch, "Competing on Customer Service: An Interview with British Airways' Sir Colin Marshall, *Harvard Business Review,* November–December 1995, 101–116.

[32] Karen Bemowski, "Something Old, Something New," *Quality Progress,* October 1996, 31.

[33] Sumantra Ghoshal and Christopher Bartlett, "Changing the Role of Top Management: Beyond Structure to Process," *Harvard Business Review,* January–February 1995, 95.

Issue 3

[1] Christopher A. Bartlett and Sumantra Ghoshal, "Changing the Role of Top Management: From Systems to People," *Harvard Business Review,* May–June 1995, 141.

[2] Peter F. Drucker, *Managing in a Time of Great Change* (Oxford: Butterworth-Heinemann, 1995), 12.

[3] Thomas H. Davenport, "Some Principles of Knowledge Management," http://knowman.bus.utexas.edu/pubs/kmprin.htm

[4] Dr. Cyril Brookes, "Gaining Competitive Advantage through Knowledge Management," http://www.gvt.com/kmpap2us.htm

[5] Thomas A. Stewart, "Your Company's Most Valuable Asset: Intellectual Capital," *Fortune,* October 3, 1994.

[6] David A. Garvin, "Building a Learning Organization," *Harvard Business Review,* July–August 1993, 80.

[7] James Brian Quinn, Philip Anderson, and Sydney Finkelstein, "Managing Professional Intellect: Making the Most of the Best," *Harvard Business Review,* March–April 1996, 71–80.

[8] James Brian Quinn, *The Intelligent Enterprise* (New York: The Free Press, 1992).

[9] Stewart, "Your Company's Most Valuable Asset," 32.

[10] Ibid.

[11] Thomas H. Davenport, Sirkka L. Jarvenpaa, and Michael C. Beers, "Improving Knowledge Work Processes," *Sloan Management Review,* Summer 1996, 54.

[12] Sumantra Ghoshal and Christopher A. Bartlett, "A New Moral Contract," in *The World in 1996,* 115. A publication of the *Economist.*

[13] Alan M. Webber, "What's So New About the New Economy?" *Harvard Business Review,* January–February 1993, 25.

[14] Dorothy Leonard-Barton, *Wellsprings of Knowledge* (Boston: Harvard Business School Press, 1995), 8.

[15] Garvin, "Building a Learning Organization," 86.

[16] Nancy A. Nichols, "Scientific Management at Merck," *Harvard Business Review,* January–February 1994, 98.

[17] Stan Davis and Jim Botkin, "The Coming of Knowledge-Based Business," *Harvard Business Review,* September–October 1994, 170.

[18] Quinn, Anderson, and Finkelstein, "Managing Professional Intellect," 75.

[19] Stratford Sherman, "Hot Products from Hot Tubs, or How Middle Managers Innovate," *Fortune,* April 29, 1996.

[20] Keith Cerny, Making Local Knowledge Global," *Harvard Business Review,* May–June 1996, 22–38.

[21] Quinn, Anderson, and Finkelstein, "Managing Professional Intellect," 78.

[22] Ibid., 76.

[23] Thomas A. Stewart, "Getting Real About Brainpower," *Fortune,* November 27, 1995, 97.

[24] Davenport, "Some Principles of Knowledge Management."

[25] Alan M. Webber, "What's So New About the New Economy?" *Harvard Business Review,* January–February 1993, 28.

[26] Philippe Baumard, "From Info War to Knowledge Warfare: Preparing for the Paradigm Shift," http://www.indigo-nat.com/annexes/289/baumard.htm

[27] See Edgar H. Schein, "Organizational Learning: What Is New?" MIT School of Management, http://learning.mit.edu/res/wp/10012.html

[28] Thomas A. Stewart, "The Invisible Key to Success," *Fortune,* August 5, 1996, 125.

[29] See Schein, "Organizational Learning."

[30] John Seely Brown and Estee Solomon Gray, "The People Are the Company," http//www.com/fastco/issues/first/people.htm

[31] Britton Manasco, "Leading Lights: An Interview with Institute for Research on Learning's Susan Stucky," Knowledge Inc., http://www.webcom/quantera/stucky.html

[32] Robert Paterson, Senior Vice President, Policy Development and Strategic Management, Human Relations, CIBC," Exploring New Values and Measurements for the Knowledge Era" (1994), http://www.cica.ca/new/pa/explore.htm

[33] Stewart, "Getting Real About Brainpower," 98.

[34] Leonard-Barton, *Wellsprings of Knowledge,* 5–16.

[35] Quinn, Anderson, and Finkelstein, "Managing Professional Intellect," 76.

[36] C. Argyris, "Good Communication that Blocks Learning," *Harvard Business Review,* July–August 1994, 77.

[37] Webber, "What's So New?" 24.

Issue 4

[1] Thomas H. Davenport, "The Fad that People Forgot," http://fastcompany.com/fastco/Issues/First/Reengin.html

[2] Quoted in Sumantra Ghoshal and Christopher A. Bartlett, "Changing the Role of Top Management: Beyond Structure to Processes," *Harvard Business Review,* January–February 1995, 88.

[3] Charles Handy, *Beyond Certainty* (London: Random House, 1995), 34–35.

[4] The ABB case is based on a paper by Christopher A. Bartlett and Sumantra Ghoshal, "Beyond the M-Form: Toward a Managerial Theory of the Firm," http//www.gsia.cmu.deu/bosch/bart.html

[5] Robin Cooper, *When Lean Enterprises Collide* (Boston: Harvard Business School Press, 1995), 303.

[6] Ibid., 303–327.

[7] L.D. DeSimone in "How Can Big Companies Keep the Entrepreneurial Spirit Alive?" *Harvard Business Review,* November–December 1995, 184.

[8] George N. Hatsopoulos, CEO, Thermo Electron Corporation, in "How Can Big Companies Keep the Entrepreneurial Spirit Alive?" *Harvard Business Review,* November–December 1995, 185–186.

9   Karen Bemowski, "Something Old, Something New," *Quality Progress,* October 1994, 34.

10 Ann Majchrzak and Qianqei Wang, "Breaking the Functional Mind-Set in Process Organizations," *Harvard Business Review,* September–October 1996, 99.

11 Quoted in Thomas Davenport, Sirkka L. Jarvenpaa, and Michael C. Beers, "Improving Knowledge Work Processes," *Sloan Management Review,* Summer 1996, 54.

12 James P. Womack and Daniel T. Jones, "From Lean Production to the Lean Enterprise," *Harvard Business Review,* March–April 1994, 93–103.

13 Thomas A. Stewart, "Getting Real About Brainpower," *Fortune,* November 27, 1995, 99.

14 David A. Garvin, "Leveraging Processes for Strategic Advantage: A Roundtable with Xerox's Allaire, USAA's Herres, SmithKline Beecham's Leschly, and Pepsi's Weatherup," *Harvard Business Review,* September–October 1995. Reprinted in James Champy and Nitin Nohria (Eds.), *Fast Forward* (Boston: Harvard Business School Press, 1996), 158.

15 Ibid., 160.

16 Ibid., 174.

17 Majchrzak and Wang, "Breaking the Functional Mind-Set," 94–95.

18 Christopher Meyer, "How the Right Measures Help Teams Excel," *Harvard Business Review,* May–June 1994, 101.

19 Philippe Baumard, "From Info War to Knowledge Warfare: Preparing for the Paradigm Shift," http://www.indigo-nat.com/annexes/289/baumard.html

20 Henry W. Chesbrough and David J. Teece, "When Is Virtual Virtuous? Organizing for Innovation," *Harvard Business Review,* January–February 1996, 65–73.

21 Randeep Ramesh, "BA Strips Down to Be 'Virtual Airline,'" *London Sunday Times,* September 22, 1996, 2–8.

22 Quoted in *Sloan Management Review,* Summer 1994, 52.

23 Randy Barrett, "Outsourcing Success Means Making the Right Moves," http//www.reengineering.com/articles/jul96/InfoManagement.html

24 Michael Hammer and James Champy, *Reengineering the Corporation* (London: Nicholas Brealey, 1993).

25 Thomas H. Davenport, "The Fad That People Forgot," http://fastcompany.com/fastco/Issues/First/Reengin.html

26 Ibid.

27 John Seely Brown and Estee Solomon Gray, "The People Are the Company," http://www.fastcompany.com/fastco/issues/first/people.htm

28 Ibid.

29 Bill Vlasic, "The New Workplace," *Business Week,* April 29, 1996.

30 Ibid.

31 Ibid.

32 Charles Handy, "Trust and the Virtual Organization," *Harvard Business Review,* May–June 1995, 41.

33 Brown and Gray," The People Are the Company."

34 T.J. Larkin and Sandar Larkin, "Reaching and Changing Frontline Employees," *Harvard Business Review,* May–June 1996, 95–104.

35 Christopher A. Bartlett and Sumantra Ghoshal, "Beyond the M-Form: Toward a Managerial Theory of the Firm," http://www.gsia.cmu.edu/bosch/bart.html

36 A.D. Chandler, *Strategy and Structure* (Cambridge: MIT Press, 1962).

[37] R.M. Cyert and J.G. March, *A Behavioral Theory of the Firm* (Englewood Cliffs, NJ: Prentice-Hall, 1963).

[38] The views of Chandler, Bower, and Cyert, and March were gleaned from Bartlett and Ghoshal, "Beyond the M-Form." The referance to Bower's work is J.L. Bower, *Managing the Resource Allocation Process* (Boston: Harvard University Division of Research, Graduate School of Business Administration, 1970).

[39] Bartlett and Ghoshal, "Beyond the M-Form."

Issue 5

[1] Steven E. Prokesch, "Competing on Customer Service: An Interview with British Airways' Sir Colin Marshall," *Harvard Business Review,* November–December 1995, 105.

[2] Frederick F. Reichheld and W. Earl Sasser, Jr., "Zero Defections: Quality Comes to Services," *Harvard Business Review,* September–October 1990, 105–111.

[3] Frederick F. Reichheld, *The Loyalty Effect* (Boston: Harvard Business School Press, 1996),76–78.

[4] Ibid., 81.

[5] George Foster and Mahendra Gupta, "Marketing, Cost Management and Management Accounting," *Journal of Management Accounting Research,* Fall 1994, 65.

[6] Cathy Anterasian, John L. Graham, and R. Bruce Money, "Are U.S. Managers Superstitious about Market Share?" *Sloan Management Review,* Summer 1996, 67–77.

[7] Reichheld, *The Loyalty Effect,* 35.

[8] Robin Bellis-Jones, "Customer Profitability Analysis," *Management Accounting,* February 1989, 26–28.

[9] Foster and Gupta, "Marketing, Cost Management and Management Accounting," 46.

[10] Robin Cooper and Robert S. Kaplan, *The Design of Cost Management Systems* (Englewood Cliffs, NJ: Prentice-Hall, 1991), 472.

[11] Tom Peters, *Thriving on Chaos* (London: Macmillan, 1987), 98.

[12] Reichheld, *The Loyalty Effect,* 23.

[13] John O. Whitney, "Strategic Renewal for Business Units," *Harvard Business Review,* July–August 1996, 84–98.

[14] Adapted from the Strategic-Renewal Matrix: Customers in Whitney, "Strategic Renewal," 91.

[15] Reichheld, *The Loyalty Effect,* 14.

[16] Thomas O. Jones and W. Earl Sasser, Jr., "Why Satisfied Customers Defect," *Harvard Business Review,* November–December 1995, 88–99.

[17] Rahul Jacob, "The Struggle to Create an Organization for the 21st Century," *Fortune,* April 3, 1995, 62.

[18] Jones and Sasser, "Why Satisfied Customers Defect," 99.

Issue 6

[1] Quoted in Robin Cooper, "The Changing Practice of Management Accounting," *Management Accounting* (U.K.), March 1996, 32.

[2] Joseph A. Ness and Thomas G. Cucuzza, "Tapping the Full Potential of ABC," *Harvard Business Review,* July–August 1995, 133.

3   Gary Siegel and C.S. Kulesza, "The Practice Analysis of Management
     Accounting," *Management Accounting,* April 1996, 20–28.
4   Quoted in Theodore Levitt, *Marketing Myopia.* Reprinted in *Harvard Business
     Review,* September–October, 1975.
5   H. Thomas Johnson, *Relevance Regained* (New York: The Free Press, 1992), 51.
6   James P. Womack, Daniel T. Jones, and Daniel Roos, *The Machine that
     Changed the World* (New York: Rawson Associates, 1990), 29.
7   Johnson, *Relevance Regained,* 44.
8   Ibid., 50.
9   Peter F. Drucker, "Managing for Business Effectiveness," *Harvard Business
     Review,* May–June 1963.
10   See Tony and Jeremy Hope, *Transforming the Bottom Line* (London: Nicholas
     Brealey, 1995), Chapter 3.
11   Terence P. Pare, "A New Tool for Managing Costs," *Fortune,* June 14, 1993, 125.
12   Robin Cooper and Robert S. Kaplan, "Profit Priorities of Activity-Based
     Costing," *Harvard Business Review,* May–June 1991, 130–135.
13   Robert S. Kaplan, "Management Accounting (1984–1994): Development of
     New Practice and Theory," *Management Accounting Research* 5 (1994),
     247–260.
14   Robin Cooper and Robert S. Kaplan, "Activity-Based Systems: Measuring the
     Costs of Resource Usage," *Accounting Horizons,* September 1992, 1–8.
15   Ness and Cucuzza, "Tapping the Full Potential," 130.
16   Ibid.
17   Robin Cooper, *When Lean Enterprises Collide* (Boston: Harvard Business
     School Press, 1995), 135.
18   Taken from Robin Cooper and W. Bruce Chew, "Control Tomorrow's Costs
     through Today's Designs," *Harvard Business Review,* January–February 1996,
     86–97.
19   Cooper, *When Lean Enterprises Collide,* 244.
20   Quoted in Janet Gray, "Quality Costs: A Report Card on Business," *Quality
     Progress,* April 1995, 51.
21   Ibid.
22   Hope and Hope, *Transforming the Bottom Line.*

Issue 7

1   *Fortune,* May 29, 1995.
2   H. Thomas Johnson, *Relevance Regained* (New York: The Free Press, 1992), 22.
3   Ibid.
4   Henry Mintzberg, "Musings on Management," *Harvard Business Review,*
     July–August 1996, 63.
5   Robert Simons, *Levers of Control* (Boston: Harvard Business School Press,
     1995), 61.
6   Ibid., 71.
7   Ibid.
8   Ibid., 79.
9   Ibid., 75.
10   Ibid., 83.
11   Robert M. Gerst, "Assessing Organizational Performance," *Quality Progress,*
     February 1995, 85–88.
12   Simons, *Levers of Control,* 87.

13 Alfie Kohn, "Why Incentive Plans Cannot Work," *Harvard Business Review,* September–October 1993, 54–63.

14 Quoted in James Ogilvy, "The Economics of Trust," *Harvard Business Review,* November–December 1995, 47.

15 From William Dawkins, "Vulnerable to Catastrophe," *Financial Times,* June 21, 1996, 17.

16 Michael Goold, "Strategic Control in the Decentralized Firm," *Sloan Management Review,* Winter 1991, 69.

17 *The Economist* 19 (11), 94.

18 Peter Bunce, Robin Fraser, and Lionel Woodcock, "Advanced Budgeting: A Journey to Advanced Management Systems, *Management Accounting Research* 6, 1995, 253–265.

19 H. Thomas Johnson, *Relevance Regained* (New York: The Free Press, 1992), 1.

20 Henry Mintzberg, "Crafting Strategy," *Harvard Business Review,* July–August 1987, 66–75.

21 See James Brian Quinn, *Strategies for Change* (Homewood, Illinois: Richard D. Irwin, 1980).

22 Simons, *Levers of Control.*

23 Robert Simons, "Control in an Age of Empowerment," *Harvard Business Review,* March–April 1995, 82.

24 Robert Bruce, "Uprooting the Corporate Orthodoxies," *Accountancy,* July 1995, 60.

25 Simons, "Control in an Age of Empowerment."

26 Charles Handy, "Trust and the Virtual Organization," *Harvard Business Review,* May–June 1995, 46.

27 Simons, *Levers of Control,* 98.

28 Ibid., 106.

29 Christopher Meyer, "How the Right Measures Help Teams Excel," *Harvard Business Review,* May–June 1994, 95–103.

30 Simons, *Levers of Control,* 101.

31 Christopoher A. Bartlett and Sumantra Ghoshal, "Changing the Role of Top Management: Beyond Systems to People," *Harvard Business Review,* May–June 1995, 139.

32 Simons, *Levers of Control,* 163.

33 Robert S. Kaplan and David P. Norton, "The Balanced Scorecard–Measures that Drive Performance," *Harvard Business Review,* January–February 1996, 71–79.

34 Robert S. Kaplan and David P. Norton, "Using the Balanced Scorecard as a Strategic Management System," *Harvard Business Review,* January–February 1996, 75–85.

35 Robert S. Kaplan, "Management Accounting (1984–1994): Development of a New Practice and Theory," *Management Accounting Research* 5, 1994, 247–260.

36 Kaplan and Norton, "Using the Balanced Scorecard as a Strategic Management System," 77.

37 Robert S. Kaplan and David P. Norton, *The Balanced Scorecard* (Boston: Harvard Business School Press, 1996), 17.

38 Goold, "Strategic Control," 71.

39 Ibid., 74.

40 Ibid., 76.

41 Ibid., 73.

[42] Ibid., 75.

[43] Christopher A. Bartlett and Sumantra Ghoshal, "Beyond the M-Form: Toward a Managerial Theory of the Firm," http://www.gsia.cmu.edu/bosch/bart.html

Issue 8

[1] James Brian Quinn, *Intelligent Enterprise* (New York: The Free Press, 1992), 36–37.

[2] Quoted in Thomas A. Stewart, "Trying to Grasp the Intangible," *Fortune,* October 2, 1995.

[3] Quoted in Betsy Morris, "The Brand's the Thing," http://www.magazine/specials/mostadmired/brand.html

[4] Terry Smith, "Grand Illusions," *Management Today,* 54.

[5] See Matthew Lynn, "Creating Wealth: the Best and the Worst," *London Sunday Times,* December 10, 1995.

[6] Ronald B. Lieber, "Who Are the Real Wealth Creators?" *Fortune,* December 9, 1996, 61–66.

[7] Brian Singleton-Green, "What Do Shareholders Want?" *Accountancy,* May 1995, 44.

[8] See Barr Rosenberg, "The Capital Asset Pricing Model and the Market Model," http://www.barra.com/ResearchPub/NonBarraPub/tcap-j.html

[9] Anne B. Fisher, "Creating Stockholder Wealth," *Fortune,* December 11, 1995.

[10] Shawn Tully, "The Real Key to Creating Wealth," *Fortune,* September 20, 1993, 26.

[11] Lynn, "Creating Wealth."

[12] Regina Fazio Maruca, "The Cost of Capital," Briefings from the Editor, *Harvard Business Review,* September–October 1996, 9–10.

[13] James L. Dodd and Shimin Chen, "EVA: A New Panacea?" http://research.badm.sc.edu/research/bereview/be42_4/eva.htm

[14] Paul Strassmann, "The Value of Computers, Information and Knowledge," http://www.strassman.com/pubs/cik-value.html

[15] Quoted in Lisa M. Wood, "Brands: The Asset Test," *Journal of Marketing* 11, 1995, 547–570.

[16] Ibid.

[17] Karl E. Svieby, "The Swedish Community of Practise" (Paper presented to the PEI conference in Stockholm, Sweden, October 25, 1996), http://www2.eis.net.au/~karlerick/CompaniestoLearnFrom/html

[18] Karl E. Svieby, "Celemi's Intangible Assets Monitor," http://www2.eis.net.au/~karlerick/IntangAss/CelemiMonitor.html

[19] Thomas A. Stewart, "Your Company's Most Valuable Asset: Intellectual Capital," *Fortune,* October 3, 1994, 31–32.

[20] Quoted in Annie Brooking, *Intellectual Capital* (London: Thomson Business Press, 1996), 27.

[21] Wood, "Brands."

[22] Kurt Badenhausen, "Blind Faith: How Did We Value the 364 Brands?" *Financial World,* http://www.financialworld.com/method.htm

[23] Ibid. http://www.financialworld.com/brannrank.htm (Try this address or that listed in note 22 above.)

[24] Paul Ormerod, *The Death of Economics* (London: Faber and Faber, 1994), 55.

[25] Paul Strassman, "Is Your Information Productive?" http://www.unisys.com/execmag/atwork/strassmann.html

[26] Strassmann, "The Value of Computers, Information and Knowledge."

Issue 9

1 Jeffrey Pfeffer, *Competitive Advantage through People* (Boston: Harvard Business School Press, 1994), 16.
2 Paul Krugman: *Peddling Prosperity* (New York: W.W. Norton, 1994), 56.
3 Ibid., 270.
4 David Smith, "UK's Foreign Legion Boosts Productivity," *London Sunday Times,* June 16, 1996.
5 Irwin Stelzer, "Capitalism Under Fire," *London Sunday Times,* March 17, 1996.
6 Gary Hamel and C.K. Prahalad, *Competing for the Future* (Boston: Harvard Business School Press, 1994), 9.
7 Stephen S. Roach, "The Hollow Ring of the Productivity Revival," *Harvard Business Review,* November–December 1996, 82.
8 Quoted in Frederick F. Reichheld, *The Loyalty Effect* (Boston: Harvard Business School Press, 1996), 95.
9 Quoted in Pfeffer, *Competitive Advantage through People,* 24.
10 Ibid., 23.
11 Quoted in *Sloan Management Review,* Summer 1994, 52.
12 Paul A. Strassmann, "Outsourcing: A Game for Losers," http://www.strassmann.com/pubs/outsource-losers.htm.
13 Ann Majchrzak and Qianwei Wang, "Breaking the Functional Mind-Set in Process Organizations," *Harvard Business Review,* September–October 1996, 95.
14 Leonard A Schlesinger and James L Heskett, "Customer Satisfaction Is Rooted in Employee Satisfaction," *Harvard Business Review,* November–December 1991, 148.
15 Pfeffer, *Competitive Advantage through People,* 9.
16 Howard Gleckman, John Carey, Russell Mitchell, Tim Smart, and Chris Roush, "The Technology Payoff," *Business Week,* June 14, 1993, 39.
17 Arthur P. Cimento and Russell J. Knister, "The High-Productivity Electronics Company," *The McKinsey Quarterly,* 1994, no. 1, 20–28.
18 S. Shellenbarger, "Some Thrive, but Many Wilt Working at Home," *The Wall Street Journal,* December 14, 1993, B1.
19 Quoted in David Birchall and Laurence Lyons, *Creating Tomorrow's Organization* (London: FT Pitman, 1995), 104.
20 Ibid., 107.
21 Strat Sherman, "Stretch Goals: The Dark Side of Asking for Miracles," *Fortune,* November 13, 1995.
22 Alfie Kohn, "Why Incentive Plans Cannot Work," *Harvard Business Review,* September–October 1993, 54–63.
23 See Pfeffer, *Competitive Advantage through People.*
24 Ibid., 126.
25 Peter F. Drucker, *Post-Capitalist Society* (Oxford: Butterworth-Heinemann, 1993), 31.
26 Christopher A. Bartlett and Sumantra Ghoshal, "Rebuilding Behavioral Context: Turn Process Reengineering into People Rejuvenation," *Sloan Management Review,* Fall 1995, 15.
27 From Pfeffer, *Competitive Advantage through People.*
28 Wellford W. Wilms, Alan J. Hardcastle, and Deone M. Zell "Cultural Transformation at NUMMI," *Sloan Management Review,* Fall 1994, 103.
29 Robert Bruce, "Dedicated Followers of Fashion," *Accountancy,* January 1995, 48.
30 Reichheld, *The Loyalty Effect,* 119.

31 Marshall Loeb, "How to Grow a New Product Every Day," *Fortune,* November 14, 1974, 270.

32 Wilms, Hardcaste, and Zell, "Cultural Transformation," 105.

33 Ron Leiber, "Wired for Hiring: Microsoft's Slick Recruiting Machine," *Fortune,* February 5, 1996.

34 Noel M. Tichy and Ram Charan, "The CEO As Coach: An Interview with Allied Signal's Lawrence A. Bossidy," *Harvard Business Review,* March–April 1995, 76.

35 Reichheld, *The Loyalty Effect,* 118.

36 Ibid., 100–102.

37 Ibid., 96.

38 James L. Heskett, Thomas O. Jones, Gary W. Loveman, W. Earl Sasser, Jr., and Leonard A. Schlesinger, "Putting the Service-Profit Chain to Work," *Harvard Business Review,* March–April 1994, 164–174.

39 Reichheld, *The Loyalty Effect,* 124.

40 Ibid., 122.

41 Christopher Meyer, *Fast Cycle Time* (New York: The Free Press, 1993), 161.

42 Paul S. Adler, "Time-and-Motion Regained," *Harvard Business Review,* January–February 1993, 100.

43 Majchrzak and Wang, "Breaking the Functional Mind-Set," 93–99.

44 Thomas H. Davenport and Nitin Nohria, "Case Management and the Integration of Labor," *Sloan Management Review,* Winter 1994, 12.

45 Pfeffer, *Competitive Advantage through People,* 9.

46 Davenport and Nohria, "Case Management," 13.

47 Quoted in Tom Peters, *Thriving on Chaos* (London: Macmillan, 1987), 285.

48 The Editors of Business Week with Cynthia Green, *A Business Week Guide: The Quality Imperative* (New York: McGraw-Hill, 1994), 11.

49 David E. Bowen and Edward E. Lawler III, "Empowering Service Employees," *Sloan Management Review,* Summer 1995, 74.

50 Ibid., 75.

51 Thomas A. Stewart, "How a Little Company Won Big By Betting on Brainpower," *Fortune,* September 4, 1995, 76.

52 Bartlett and Ghoshal, "Rebuilding Behavioral Context," 17.

53 Drucker, *Post Capitalist Society,* 83.

54 John F. Wilson, *British Business History, 1720–1994* (Manchester, England: Manchester University Press, 1995), 27.

55 Pfeffer, *Competitive Advantage through People,* 103.

56 Lisa Buckingham, "John Lewis Set for Record Bonuses," *The Guardian,* September 13, 1996, 19.

57 Justin Martin, "Eli Lilly Is Making Shareholders Rich. How? By Linking Pay to EVA," *Fortune,* September 9, 1996.

58 Herbert H. Meyer, Emanual Kay, and John R.P. French, Jr., "Split Roles in Performance Appraisal," *Harvard Business Review,* January–February 1965.

59 Andrew S. Grove, "A High-Tech CEO Updates His Views on Managing and Careers," *Fortune,* September 18, 1995.

60 "An Isreali Shakes Up US Factories" *Business Week,* September 5, 1983, 128.

61 Pfeffer, *Competitive Advantage through People.*

Issue 10

1   John P. Kotter, *Leading Change* (Boston: Harvard Business School Press, 1996), 161.

2 Richard Dawkins, *The Blind Watchmaker* (London: Penguin, 1986), 294–296.

3 Paul Ormerod, *The Death of Economics* (London: Faber and Faber, 1994), 36.

4 Kotter, *Leading Change,* 148.

5 Ibid., 14.

6 Ibid., 4–14.

7 Ibid., 156.

8 Michael E. Porter, "Capital Disadvantage: America's Failing Capital Investment System," *Harvard Business Review,* September–October 1992, 74.

9 Adam Smith, *The Wealth of Nations,* Vol. 2 (Everyman, 1910), 257.

10 James Hanson: "Why the Rot in Schools Is Industry's Ruin," *London Sunday Times,* November 12, 1995.

11 Jeffrey Pfeffer, *Competitive Advantage through People* (Boston: Harvard Business School Press, 1994), 17.

12 Wellford W. Wilms, Alan J. Hardcastle, and Deone M. Zell, "Cultural Transformation at NUMMI, *Sloan Management Review,* Fall 1994, 112.

13 Quoted in Pfeffer, *Competitive Advantage through People,* 208–209.

14 Ibid., 209–210.

15 H. Thomas Johnson, *Relevance Regained* (New York: The Free Press, 1992), 176.

16 Ibid., 176–177.

17 Britton Monasco, "Leading Lights: An Interview with Author and Consultant Stan Davis," http://www.webcom.com/quantera/davis.html.

18 Britton Monasco, "Enterprise-Wide Learning: Corporate Knowledge Networks and the New Learning Imperative," http://www.webcom/quantera/enterprise.html.

19 S. Davis and J. Botkin, "The Coming of Knowledge-Based Business," *Harvard Business Review,* September–October 1994, 170.

20 Blake Ives and Sirkka L. Jarvenpaa, "Will the Internet Revolutionize Business Education and Research?" *Sloan Management Review,* Spring 1996, 33.

21 Ibid.

22 Monasco, "Enterprise-Wide Learning."

23 Ibid.

24 Ives and Jarvenpaa, "Will the Internet Revolutionize?" 34.

25 Ibid.

Index

About the Authors

JEREMY HOPE is a consultant specializing in management training and education. He regularly gives presentations on the topics discussed in this book. He was the lead author of *Transforming the Bottom Line*, which has sold well in the United States and Europe and has been translated into Spanish and Italian. For several years he was a controller at 3i, the United Kingdom's largest venture capital business, where he handled a portfolio of investments and new business opportunities. Thereafter he became CFO of a distribution business based in London; joint founder and CEO of a computer services business; and, more recently, a consultant and an author. Mr. Hope is a chartered accountant and holds an M.A. degree in accounting and business finance from the University of Manchester.

TONY HOPE is an international consultant, lecturer, and speaker as well as a visiting professor of accounting at INSEAD. His speaking engagements and management consulting work have taken him to major companies worldwide, including Motorola, Hewlett-Packard, British Telecom, Nestlé, and Cadbury-Schweppes. In addition, he holds seminars on performance measurement at Management Centre Europe. He is the author or editor of five books and many research publications. Professor Hope has taught at the University of Manchester and, as a visiting professor, at the Tulane University of Louisiana, the University of Arizona, the State University of New York, the University of Edinburgh, the University of Bradford Management Center, IMI (Geneva), and the Euroforum (Madrid). A chartered accountant, he holds postgraduate degrees from Liverpool University and the London School of Economics. He is coauthor (with Jeremy) of *Transforming the Bottom Line*.